The Poker Club

Julian's Private Scrapbook

Book 2

The Poker Club

Special Edition

a summer frolic
by
Eldot

Kravitz & Sons
INNOVATORS IN PUBLISHING, MARKETING AND ADVERTISING

Kravitz and Sons LLC
204 E Arlington Blvd. Suite B
Greenville, NC 27858

Published by Kravitz and Sons LLC.

ISBN: 979-8-89639-432-7 (sc)
ISBN: 979-8-89639-431-0 (e)

Library of Congress Control Number: 2025920258

To RMH with gratitude for his example and support

—Eldot

The Poker Club: Julian's Private Scrapbook, Book 2

Eldot

Reviewed December, 2018

Second in Eldot's Julian's Private Scrapbook (a summer fantasy) series: *The Poker Club* details Julian's ongoing adventures during a two-week stay at Boy Scout Camp. Julian (like many teenage boys) lacks a father figure in his life, and has a mancrush on Mark, the scoutmaster who invites him to stay in his cabin at camp. Julian already knows Mark, they're neighbors back at home. Mark senses Julian's ache for the presence of a caring dad in his life, and is happy to provide that, as he can. Julian is an ingenue in the true sense of the word. He's guileless, gifted, sweet-natured, gung-ho and quick with a searching and curious mind. Like the older scouts, Mark feels very protective of Julian, and tries to acquaint him with the convivial (but sometimes risky) world of maleness, with its jovial mischief, code of behavior, and amped up libido that tortured us as adolescents. Mark tries to answer all Julian's questions about sex, with admirable frankness and discretion. Julian is somewhat overwhelmed by his feelings for Mark (it's all so much to process) but there's great warmth in their platonic connection.

Like the other scouts, Julian has his goals: learning new skills, earning merit badges, improving his swimming technique, depicting experiences in his artist's notebook. Julian's sophisticated technique is impressive and puts him much in demand. Other key characters include Danny, Tom, Nick, Geoff, Bruce and Sid. There are all kinds of activities to master. Archery, riflery, backpacking, planning skit night, to name a few. Lots of the boys enjoy swimming the cold, exhilarating lake, exploring underwater breathing, speed, rescue and distance. Like the YMCA and other all-male gatherings, they happily and casually swim naked, often without a second thought. This sets Julian's interests in motion, but no more so than other guys.

The Poker Game referenced in the title is a diversion for the older, more intrepid scouts (Tom, Geoff, Jack, Brian) where slyly introduced removal of clothing leads to avid sexual experimentation and fulfillment. This is 1962, and the world outside may not be quite so understanding of such behavior, so the guys must be discreet and careful. Eldot recognizes that teenage boys (consider *Spring Awakening, The Last Picture Show*) have an impetuous, profoundly intense need to actualize the rush of male hormones that runs through their veins. Not all the guys are headed for a life of same-gender coupling, but they want to express their manhood, and enjoy each other's company, in a zillion different ways. They are giddy, game and secretive, but never disrespectful or brutal. They are kind and gradual, never foisting themselves. Eldot imbues these passages with a kind of celebratory energy, while avoiding hyperbole. Julian gladly helps his friend Danny by rubbing lotion on his painful, sunburned "buns". What follows is spontaneous, friendly, and mutually pleasurable.

I struggle to explain the balancing act that Eldot manages in Julian's Private Scrapbook series. Eroticism between guys is a part of the tapestry, to be sure. But by creating a rich, layered context of male companionship and clustering, it takes on a different hue. Eldot confides the goofy, ridiculous, sweet, hilarious, imperative and earnest world of boy scout camp with its all-male milieu.

Julian's previous lack of closeness with other boys serves as a springboard for discovering what it means to connect and bond. Male Fart Culture, silly skits, learning to shoot, dive, cook for the other guys, it's all in there. There's a kind of spirited, military feel, with none of the negative implications that so often accompany that experience. Erotic enjoyment is described in plain, forthright, unflinching language that is neither inflated or suffused with salacious intent. What makes *The Poker Club* so effective is Eldot's mastery at evincing that sexuality is simply one aspect of a vast, full, contented life. He convincingly shares the rowdy, raucous joys of maleness, in all its boisterous and sometimes nuanced mystery.

QRS Highest recommendation

The Poker Club: Julian's Private Scrapbook, Part Two

Eldot

Publisher: Xlibris   Pages: 279   Price: (paperback) $15.99
ISBN: 9781477118344
Reviewed: March, 2014
Author Website: Visit »

This unusual novel is sure to cause controversy for its subject matter. The second in a projected five-novel series, the book takes place at a scout camp during the summer of 1962, and follows several groups of boys as they form friendships, learn new skills, and fall in love. Much of the book concerns their various sexual explorations; indeed, the "Poker Club" of the title refers to one group's method of beginning such activities – and the author is careful to note on the back cover that the book "is meant for mature readers."

In between the sex, several plotlines start to form. Julian, who has a crush on his scoutmaster Mark, learns more about life matters while interacting with his fellow scouts. Tom, an older boy who has been with many other boys, finds himself falling for Nick, one of his earlier conquests and now a friend. Geoff, a co-founder of the Poker Club, recruits other scouts to join in the fun, including Tom and Nick.

While the extensive explicit sex scenes can feel somewhat exploitative, generally they are handled well, combining experience with innocence in an endearing way. Julian in particular, while certainly experienced in some sexual matters, still has much to learn. His sweet, innocent looks make Mark and the other scouts want to protect him from such things, so that, for instance, while a remark about "choice buns" makes Julian curious about what that means, he doesn't learn the answer until nearly the end of the book.

The developing relationship between Tom and Nick is also fascinating; in the previous book, Tom hoped to seduce Julian but now only wants to be with Nick and feels guilty for his earlier pursuits.

The author includes a summary of the first novel along with maps of all locations. If readers are open to the subject matter, they will find intriguing insights into the complex world of boys in this unique novel.

Also available in hardcover and ebook.

Author's Current Residence

Portland, Oregon

Available to buy at:

Publisher's Note:

This book is written for a mature audience. Though LBGT romance fiction has become popular, the subject remains controversial and sensitive to many. It is not written to serve or encourage prurient interests; it contains no pornography or graphic language, but there are several intimate male/male passages. Readers who are offended by that should be prepared to skip over a few scenes. For the convenience of new readers, the prefatory note from the first book is included at the back of the book. It addresses the social rationale that underlies the series.

The placement of this story in a scout camp has not been made with permission. The story is not about any organization or its activities, goals, or personnel. It is about fictional characters and what is happening in their lives outside of the scouting domain. Presumably much of what the characters do would not be approved or condoned by any scout organization, and nowhere is such a thing suggested or inferred. But in the time and place that this story takes place, as in much of the developed world, the scouting enterprise was so universal and ubiquitous that scout camp was nearly generic. It is a logical setting in which to focus on these characters' lives. The scout organization in this story, entirely fictional as well, is depicted with respect and admiration whenever and vwherever it is mentioned.

Though its origin is a response to true-life experience, *Julian's Private Scrapbook* is a work of fiction. Similarities to actual persons and places have been modified to eliminate any basis for recognition. Some of the places exist, but are used fictitiously.

Table of Contents

First, a word from Eldot   x

Tuesday   1

1 Morning in the cabin 3
2 Breakfast surprises 13
3 Sunburn treatment 25
4 Recruiting Tom 35
5 The Poker Club 47
6 New faces at the lake 67

7 Free swimming continues 77
8 Afternoon developments 89
9 Mark gets a helping hand 97
10 Second troop campfire 107
11 Lumpy Louise 115
12 Tom and Nick, again 127

Wednesday   133

13 Gatekeepers 135
14 Poker meeting two 143
15 The Snorkel 153
16 Danny and Geoff 165

17 After Archery 175
18 Sid's cabin adventure 185
19 After the campfire 197
20 Late night 213

Thursday   222

21 Breakfast news 223
22 The platform office 231
23 Forestry discoveries 241

24 Jack and his basket 249
25 Musical fruit 261
26 Winding down 275

Maps and floor plans

Bar's Meadow Map xii, 117
Scoutmaster's Cabin 4
Second Floor, HQ 38
Camp Walker Map 48
Waterfront Map 68
Headquarters Building 90

Back of the book extras

Preview	284
A word about the style	285
First Preface	287
Synopsis of Part One	289
Site Descriptions	292
Glossary	294
Song Credits	297
Index of Names	302
Troop 9 Roster	307
Camp Walker Staff	308
A word about the author	310
Reviews	312

Key to Symbols

Symbol	Meaning
	Title page
	Non story segment end,
	Day teaser synopsis end
	Jump forward in time
	Chapter end
	Jump to concurrent event or perspective
	Flashback Segment
	Day end

first... a word from the author

Welcome—or welcome back—to the world of 1962 and to a very special summer camp in the Blue Mountains of North Carolina. It's a fictional camp of course, but pretending it's real is just as much fun, and it's nice to be free from fact checkers and the real world for a little while.

This book has its own story to tell—but as the second in a five book series, it is part of a longer, more complex tale. If you're new to this world you might want to check the synopsis of Book 1 before starting. It's located at the end of the final chapter.

Social change and technological advances have been dramatic and transformational in this decade, especially in the last five years, placing this story and its subject closer to the mainstream. It was always relevant, but now it's "allowed," and growing in demand. That's why it is being reissued in an updated and improved edition. The story and characters are the same—nothing has been changed, but the narrative has been polished in a few places. Reader and critical feedback was taken seriously, and this is the result.

Now that the public is paying attention, maybe the media will as well. This story is in part a response and an offset to an abuse they perpetrate from time to time: grabbing market share with sensationalism and scandal hype in the name of righteousness—without regard to the harm it does to real people.

But rather than engage in polemic, this series chooses to entertain, to see the human and the comical side—that is a pleasurable as well as informative way to look at an age old problem that often afflicts adolescents coming of age: falling in love with the "wrong" person. Like anything human, it can be funny, and looking at it can be fun too. That's what these books seek to achieve.

Honesty to the subject and the characters is a top priority; this allows the reader to explore and discover with them as they find their way. That means including explicit passages in places. Readers who don't care to know that much detail should be prepared to skip a page or two once in a while.

The Preface to the first edition is included in the supplementary materials at the back of the book.

Eldot

Fonts used in *The Poker Club:*

Times New Roman: all narrative and character content, all third person point of view is in standard Times, sentences are capitalized; all first person is in *italics*, sentences are not capitalized.

Optima: sound effects, noise, anything heard that isn't or can't be identified by quotation marks; these are placed between arrow brackets:

> > *squipp-squipp…* < < *and* > > *whack!* < <

Lucida Handwriting: is used to indicate a dream stream-of-consciousness; this is always first person point of view.

American Typewriter indicates quoting a handwritten word, phrase or sentence.

Chalkboard is used to convey information from the author about the setting and story.

Barr's Meadow

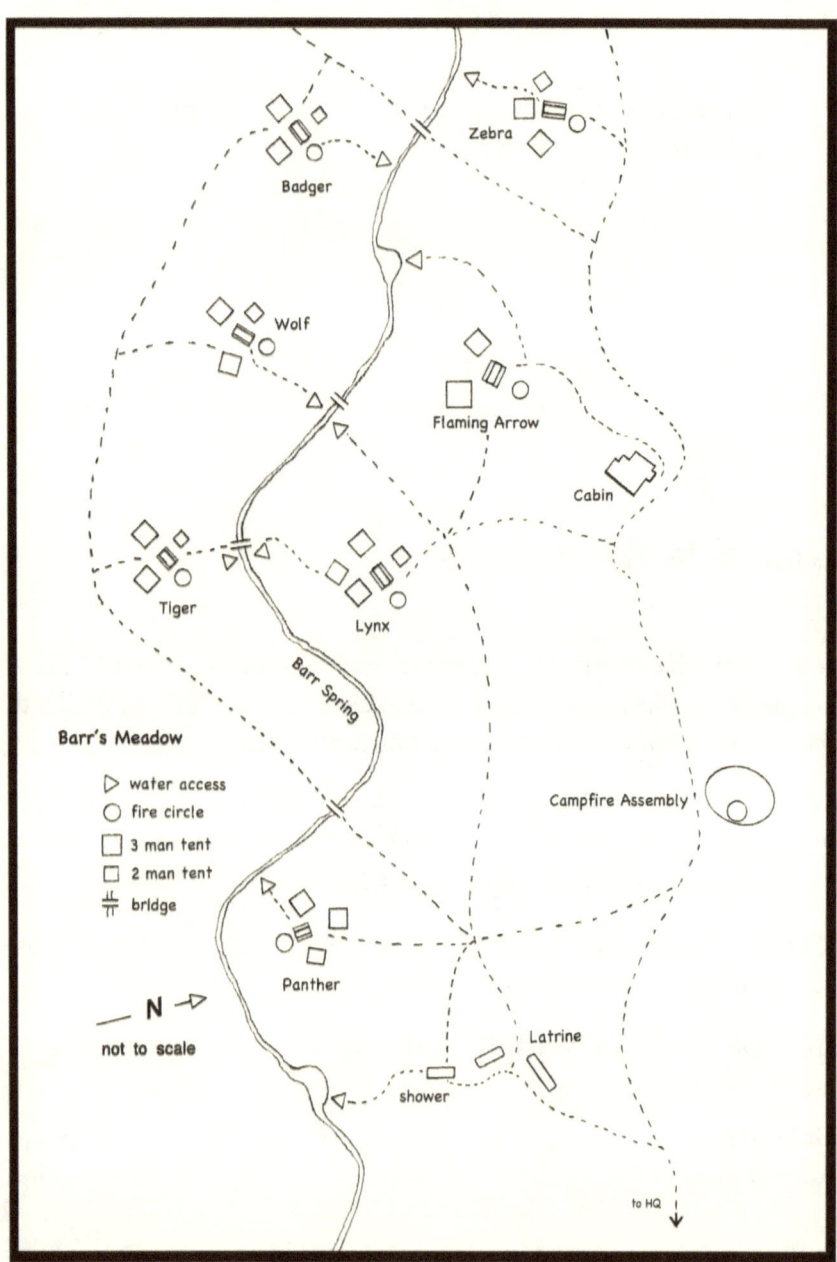

Zebra

Badger

Wolf

Flaming Arrow

Cabin

Tiger

Lynx

Barr Spring

Barr's Meadow

▷ water access
○ fire circle
□ 3 man tent
▫ 2 man tent
♯ bridge

Campfire Assembly

N →
not to scale

Panther

Latrine

shower

to HQ

Tuesday

Third Day

Summer 1962: the third day of the two-week scout camp begins. Last night **Julian** watched **Mark** shaving, fulfilling a wish he'd nursed for more than a year. The final event of Book 1 was the fulfillment of **Nick's** longstanding wish to do unto **Tom** as he did to others. It was a milestone in their relationship that neither expected. These two relationships in Troop 9 remain the central interest, but new characters and stories are woven into the narrative during the three days of Book 2.

Today we meet **Geoff** Staples, a transplant from the west coast. His British father and Cambodian mother have provided him with a unique heritage and background. He, **Jack** Haley and **Brian** Rogers are from the suburbs of Atlanta. They have a very special and exclusive club.

Introducing **Casey** Snyder and **Robin** Simmons from Troop 9. Like several others, they've had the dubious honor of being "broken in" by **Tom** Dawson. They are drawn into Tom's newly discovered club.

We meet **Bruce** Ruggles, the seriously overweight Second Class scout who was introduced briefly in Book 1, Barr's Meadow. He and Julian were volunteer victims for the Lifesaving Merit Badge test.

1 *morning in the cabin*

The finches and cardinals began their cheerful songs just before daylight arrived. They seemed to be coaxing the sun to hurry and peek over the horizon. Mark had been hearing their antiphonal chorus for a while, becoming conscious gradually. This was unusual. Normally, he awoke with a start, raring to go. *not used to this blasted mattress yet.* It had forced him to wake up at odd times during the night because he'd developed a sore spot someplace. The lumps were irregular and didn't move out of the way when he shifted around in his sleep. *I wonder if they have anything in the warehouse. worth checking: put that on your list, Mark.*

Resigned to the inevitable, he opened his eyes. A small circle of luminous numbers hovering in the darkness a few feet away answered his question: *it's early! an hour and a half before I have to be up and at 'em.* He wasn't inclined to go back to sleep—doing that usually made him sluggish the rest of the day.

whatever I do, I need to be quiet about it. no point in waking Julian early. boys need their winks. Mark smiled, recalling last night. *Just before lights out Julian asked if he could watch me shave. what a revelation... I'd been so worried that he might ask something inappropriate, I forgot the obvious.* All he wanted was what any adolescent boy wants; he's never had an adult male in his life. Months earlier Francine had confided that she had never shared anything about his father. It must have been an unpleasant divorce.

Julian's facial responses as he watched me shave were priceless. he's a few years away from needing to shave... but learning how wasn't why he needed to see it. he has a blank area in his life. I can't fill it, of course—but I can do my part. he was so entranced. well: the lesson to take home, Mark, is that you better stop making judgments and

3

assumptions. Julian's got more blank spaces to fill; you need to be on hand to help.

He could ignore the demands of his bladder no longer. He sat up and looked over to the cot... it was too dark to see for sure, but Julian must be asleep. He flipped back the covers and swung around. *floor isn't as cold this morning...* He walked to the bathroom.

He was skilled at being silent; closing the door helped. He shut his eyes before flipping the light switch. That enabled him to blunt the blast that came from the world's brightest overhead light. He proceeded with the daily routine. *easier today...* unlike most mornings, he had not awoken with an erection. After flushing, he waited for the water tank to fill before opening the door. The water pump kicked in, but it was nearly inaudible.

Quietly he left the bathroom and stepped over to the cot—*still sound asleep.* Mark smiled... he was a mix of feelings. It was comforting to see the boy there, safe and sound. *no need to disturb him...* the early hour provided an opportunity: *a good morning run is what I need*

Barr's Meadow Cabin

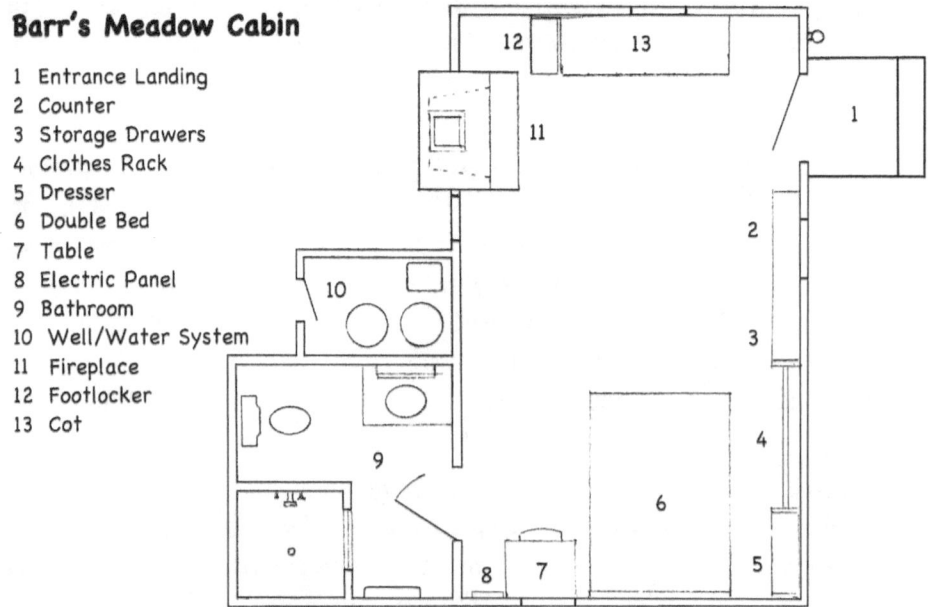

Barr's Meadow Cabin

1 Entrance Landing
2 Counter
3 Storage Drawers
4 Clothes Rack
5 Dresser
6 Double Bed
7 Table
8 Electric Panel
9 Bathroom
10 Well/Water System
11 Fireplace
12 Footlocker
13 Cot

His jogging sweats, shoes and socks were on the counter... he had assembled everything yesterday, but didn't get the opportunity to run. He stepped outside and closed the door quietly. Fortunately, the outside door didn't squeak either. One floorboard near the fireplace and the bureau drawers were the only noisemakers in the cabin. Still, dressing outside would ensure that silence was maintained inside. He dressed and set out down the main trail. *two or three miles will be good. other than swimming certification, yesterday was a bust for any exercise. I need this.*

Inside the cabin, Julian was sound asleep, snugly curled up in his army surplus sleeping bag on an army surplus cot. If one were to approach and look carefully, they would see that he was not as soundly asleep as it seemed: his eyes, though closed, moved slightly—irregularly... a dream was in progress. The tussled state of his wavy blond hair indicated that it had been an active dream night. The songbirds outside were about to penetrate; before long whatever he was watching, or experiencing, would pop like a giant bubble and slowly fade from his memory.

...walking down the path with Justin looking at different plants. how odd... Justin is nude, except for his kerchief. oh... look at his buns. they change shape as he walks. the dents in the sides are interesting. the archery range is ahead... look... a row of scouts, drawing their bows. they all have bare buns too. that's good, because I just noticed that I'm nude too. we're supposed to be nude only at swimming. nobody seems to mind... look at all the buns in a row. should I ask Justin if any of them are "Choice?" Justin disappeared. Danny's there instead, bending over to pick a flower. his dents disappear when he bends over, and come back when he stands up. Danny probably has Choice Buns. what if I step up and stroke them... what would they feel like if I was pressing my hand on them when the dents disappear? maybe I'll try that later. for now, I'll draw pictures of them

in my tablet. oh... somebody already drew a lot of buns. some of them look weird. did I draw these? flip to a blank page and start some new ones. pencil seems to be missing all of a sudden. where did I leave it? maybe it fell on the ground. better search... oo-ee... need to go to the bathroom now. it's a long way to the cabin. there's a tree... oh-oh. somebody else is there already. darn. where's another... they're all so far away. can't hold it much longer. what if I have to go right here in the path...

Julian awoke suddenly. *I'm about to wet the bed!* He sat up quickly... *where...?* It took a few seconds to remember where he was. *yow!* He threw open the sleeping bag and raced to the bathroom. He got there just in time, too. *oh gosh! I have to do a number two!* He closed the door quick.

When he had completed his task, he carefully came back into the room. Enough light peeked through the curtains over the table to reveal that Mark wasn't there—*what a lucky thing. I didn't even look on the way; I prob'ly would have woke him up.* He fanned the door back and forth, attempting to clear the air. There was no fan, and he wanted it to be okay by the time Mark came back. *hmm... where is he, anyway?* He stepped around the table to look at the clock... *still plenty early, about fifteen minutes before I have to go help Danny fix breakfast.* He walked back into the bathroom and whiffed the air. *better.* He fanned the door some more; *we need to get some Air Wick in here.*

air is kinda chilly; he rubbed his arms and scurried over to the door; *maybe Mark is out there.* He poked his head out and looked back and forth: *there he is, jogging up the trail!* Wearing a headband, his sleeves were pushed up to the elbows. His feet made a soft plopping sound. *man, he looks so cool.* A sudden breeze... *brrr!* he had turned into a solid goose bump! He shut the door and raced back to the cot.

He wrapped himself in the cover blanket and climbed onto the cot. He sat Indian style and rubbed his arms. It felt funny to sit on the cot this way. He scootched to get comfy and turned his head toward the door. *I want to watch him come in... that headband is new.*   The goose bumps were nearly gone.

Mark planned to shower before awakening Julian. He opened the door carefully... he peeked in, expecting to see the top of Julian's head poking out of the sleeping bag. Instead, he saw a grinning face. What a surprise! Julian's hair was comical; obviously he hadn't been awake for long. The golden rumples were evidence that he probably enjoyed a sound night's sleep. *enviable.* Mark closed the door and walked to the dresser. "Good morning. You're awake bright and early."

look at the sweat run down his temples! Julian had never seen Mark like this. Too marvelous for words. "I never knew you went running. How far did you go?"

"I'm not sure; probably three or four miles. Did I wake you up?"

"Nope." Seeing Mark like this was a revelation. Julian knew Mark only in his scoutmaster uniform or his business suit. *does he run at home every morning?*

> > scree—eep! < <

The fresh underwear drawer complained as usual.

"Look at your chest! You sweated a lot! And your armpits!" He had never seen a sweaty man close up before. He wanted to touch the wet fabric. *I sweat sometimes, but never like that.*

"Yep. I'd better take a shower." Mark grabbed fresh socks and underpants from the drawer. It just occurred to him to ask: "You don't need one this morning, do you?"

Julian was memorizing the view as well as he could, considering— the curtains were still drawn. "Oh... no I don't need one; 'sides, I'll go swimming with Danny after inspections." *why didn't you pull those curtains open, Julian?!*

"Great." Mark pulled off his sweatshirt and hung it on the end of the clothes rack to dry. The running shorts he draped over the clothes rack pipe. He grabbed the fresh underwear and headed for the bathroom. "I won't be in there long. But if you're under pressure, you can go ahead while I'm in the shower." He resisted the urge to give Julian's disheveled wavy locks a playful fluff as he passed by.

Julian was perfecting his appear-to-be-preoccupied-while-actually-studying-closely position. The dim light was his ally there... He loved every second of the show. He especially enjoyed studying Mark's backside as he walked into the bathroom. *now, those are choice buns.* The image of Mark stepping into the shower last night flashed to the front of his mind. His eyes wowed. *Choice... capital C.*

He just remembered what he was dreaming: *buns. why am I thinking about buns all of a sudden? that's right! yesterday at the lake! Nick said that! 'Julian, you don't have buns; you have **Choice Buns.'** Nick wouldn't explain what he meant for some reason. He was talking about Bruce, who'd just been "rescued" at the Lifesaving merit badge class. Bruce weighed a lot— *almost twice as much as me, probably.*

He tried to understand. *I don't know why, but I do like to look at Mark's; I've only seen them a little. they don't look nearly as sexy when he has pants on, though. choice... what does that mean? I need to look at myself back there; maybe I can see what... darn: there isn't a mirror around here, except for the one above the washbasin in the bathroom. I remember Danny's buns from yesterday—when he was carrying that big pot to the creek to get water, he balanced it on his head. he wagged his rear end on the way and lost his balance. I could see them, sort of, even though Danny had his shorts on. hmm. I know: at free swimming today, I'll pay attention to buns. before now I always paid attention to what's around front. what about Nick's buns? can't remember. Tom? him either. I bet Sid has odd ones because he's so skinny.* He chuckled, imagining Sid standing next to Bruce. *I bet most guys are in between those two.*

yeah! He grinned: he had just invented the Sid/Bruce scale; SB for short. *from now on, I'll rate all the buns I see on that scale. Sid will be the zero end, and Bruce the ten end. wait. I better make that a larger number. there are a lot of buns out there. twenty-five? silly boy, make it a hundred! yeah. so where would Choice be? fifty on the scale? this is the hard part.* He pondered... *I might have to get a second opinion on this. maybe I'll ask Nick about it—he seems to know about buns.*

Mark finished his shower promptly and toweled himself dry. *quiet out there... maybe he's gone back to sleep.* He looked out into the main room ... Julian was sitting up, still wrapped in the blanket. He looked like a blond Buddha, concentrating on a great matter. "Good morning, again." He stepped over to check the clock. Ten minutes. Not bad. He pushed in the alarm button. *let's get some light in here.* He opened the curtains above the table and pushed the window open full. He stepped over to the window by the fireplace.

Julian snapped out of his preoccupation. *I screwed up again!* He'd missed the re-appearance from the bathroom. He watched Mark open the curtains. *ooo.*

"You get to open the curtains on your wall, remember." Mark winked on his way to the last window, next to the clothes rack. It didn't look like Julian had moved a single muscle. *what's he so preoccupied about?*

Julian snapped out of it. He had been so fixed on studying what was walking by at eye level that he missed the wink entirely. "Oh! Yeah..." He flung the blanket to the side and stepped onto the floor. He grinned wide and looked over at Mark. "Good morning." He turned around and opened the drapes. With a firm push, the window swung open; *the track needs to be greased or something. wow... it's warmer today.* He looked up at the sky: no clouds; no breeze to speak of either. *oo: how long do I have?* He dashed over to the clock: "ten minutes!" *I gotta get going!* He stepped in to the bathroom. *first off, brush your teeth ... didn't get to do that last night.*

Mark watched, bemused. *what could he be thinking about? there are times when being able to read minds would be handy.* He chuckled and walked over to the table. *might as well get the morning agenda squared away.* He sat down at the table and opened his case.

Julian opened the medicine cabinet. He was after his toothbrush but stopped at the sight of the can of shaving foam. Wow... he picked it up gently, as if it were fragile. He looked at it closely, remembering last night... *how does it do that? it just foams up. magical.* He felt a rush— *I'm holding Mark's shaving foam.* The sound of the chair being pulled out from the table snapped him back to the real world. *Mark is sitting at the table, just like yesterday!* With a giggle he returned the shaving foam and grabbed the toothpaste off his shelf.

Mark rummaged in his case for the pocket firearms instructor's guide. He had a training job to do this morning. Refreshing his memory on things like that always paid off... *we're supposed to have some new rifles this year. aha! there you are... now then.* He pulled over his notepad. *first, make a list of safety basics.*

Julian brushed his teeth rapidly... he didn't want to be late. *what will we be fixing today? everybody liked my pancakes yesterday... I wonder if we do those every day.* He watched the ring around his mouth spread slightly. It reminded him of Mark shaving last night. *that was so cool. maybe Mark will let me practice that sometime.* He bent down to rinse. *too bad they don't have a glass or something... uggo uggo.*

When he was finished washing his hands and face, Julian stepped to the wall rack for a towel. He was assigned the one on the middle bar. As he pulled it free, he noticed Mark sitting at the table. *I forgot he was there!* He held the towel up and dried off his face vigorously with one end. The huge towel nearly touched the floor.

Mark glanced to his right and saw a wiggling wall of white terrycloth. Amused, he returned to his self assigned refresher course.

Julian's mind raced as he dried his hands... *be cool. that's all you have to do... he's busy. as long as you're cool, he won't know.* He folded the towel and returned it to the wall rack. He made certain it was straight and neat. Danny might want to inspect again today. He took a deep breath and headed toward the doorway. His eyes were pre aimed. Yesterday he saw the view from the other side. He expected today's glimpse to be better.

He was absolutely correct: the slit in Mark's briefs was loose, and open about a half inch wide at the center. It was wonderful and marvelous and better than he had hoped for. He had a new center picture for his mental file of Mark views. He hastened past Mark and went to his footlocker with a skip. He didn't want to get caught gawking. And he'd gotten a good peek—a very good peek. The tingle below was returning. *maybe it won't get too hard... it will go down on the trail.*

Julian pulled out the T-shirt he'd worn yesterday and held it up. *still looks good.* He slipped it over his head. He had to be careful about using up his clean clothes—he only had six sets for fourteen days. Unconsciously, he softly hummed fragments of a favorite melody while he dressed.

Mark's concentration was interrupted by an unexpected sound. *Julian is humming to himself! what a wonderful sound... the tune... I know that tune.* He blushed. *that was Erik's favorite. I was singing that last night in the shower! what a strange coincidence.* He shook his head and returned to the handbook. The very boring handbook.

Julian's pocket comb caught his attention as he tightened up the belt on his scout shorts. *there goes my new motto again: something will come along.* He'd been looking for an excuse to go back to the bathroom, and here it was. He pulled the comb out and walked across the room.

Mark was hunched down, writing something—no way to see anything. *oh well...* he went into the bathroom and combed his hair. He gave himself an approving wink. *oh!* He stood back and turned around to look at his backside. *hmm.* Only the top part was visible... *I need my green stool.* He ran his hand around, as if to measure the contour. He wasn't exactly sure what to look for. *hmm. how am I gonna find out what Nick is talking about? looks just like always, as far as I can tell.* He shrugged. *trouble is, there's no one else I can ask about this... hey! Danny. maybe he knows something about it.*

Mark caught the tail end of Julian's attempted self-assessment. He didn't pay any particular attention... *making sure his shirt is tucked in.* "Say, how about starting the coffee first thing today?"

that's right! "Yeah, I will for sure. Sorry about yesterday." Julian approached Mark's side. "What time is it, by the way?"

Mark reached over and turned the face of his Big Ben around. "You have exactly two minutes before you're late."

Julian was ready... Mark's twist to reach the clock opened the view nicely—but when he sat back... *mmm. I just love old saggies.* "Great!" He glanced at the tablet and handbook. "What are you studying?" He bounced on his toes happily. He had lots of time. Might as well enjoy the view a little longer.

"Just brushing up on firearms safety—I get rifle range duty today."

whoa... rifles. "I've never seen a rifle up close." He wasn't too sure he wanted to, actually. He'd seen a BB gun one time, is all. The kid was trying to shoot a robin. Julian didn't approve. *why would anybody want to hurt a robin?*

Mark sensed that Julian disapproved. *maybe that's a topic to go over, later.*

"I better scoot." Julian grinned and bounced away toward the door. He stopped halfway. "Oop! Tablets, dum-dum!" He raced back to the table.

"Umm. I need my tablets... I think they're behind your case." Last night he decided to do only sketches in the one that has no lines—*the regular one will be for the notes I have to write for Nick.*

Mark lowered the lid of his case and picked up the tablets. "There you are," he gave Julian the usual wink of approval. *this day has started off well.* He watched Julian dash to the door. He expected to see the Cheshire cat grin—sure enough. He waved and turned back to the table.

Julian skipped merrily up the path toward the Flaming Arrow camp. That wink and blue eyed look had its usual elevating effect. Julian was ready to meet the day.

2 *breakfast surprises*

ooo... careful, careful... Danny stirred—his back was cold and tender. *if I pull the sleeping bag closed, it hurts. if I don't, I get cold... I can't win.* He hadn't slept at all well... *the birds are having a town meeting or something. I have to take a leak anyway, might as well get up. it's plenty light enough; lucky the table is right there to block the sun when it comes over the edge.* He swung his legs around and sat facing his footlocker. He checked his watch. *Julian will be here in a little while to help with breakfast.*

man, I sure miscalculated on the suntan. I thought it would take a lot longer to get results. a real sunburn after only one day... what a dummy. I knew I should have taken my sun cream to the lake... just too lazy to go back for it. He stood—not having anything on felt strange. He'd taken off his skivvies last night because the waistband hurt so much. *Luckily, the others are asleep.* He put on his briefs... *ooo-ooo-ow... this is bad... no way am I going to put on a T-shirt today.* He put on his short pants with great care; he lifted his short-sleeved button up off the footlocker and put it on next, very loose. He put on his tennies: no sox. He took care to be quiet, just in case... he looked at the other cots. *good. Nick and Tom are zonked.* Careful not to brush against Nick, he edged out of the tent. He moved very slowly... *yow... my legs too! slow down, Danny... there.* That reduced the rub of the fabric. He headed toward the latrine. Built to handle six at a time, Danny was confident he wouldn't have to wait in line. *if I get there early, I won't have a problem.*

boy! just in time... I'm about to wet my pants. the two far stalls are occupied. one of the showers, too. good timing: having to wait in line in the morning is the worst thing about this camp. He only had to take a whiz after all, so he stepped over to the trough. He looked back at the shower. *who would take a cold shower before breakfast?* He shook his head… crazy. *although, if it would fix this sunburn, I'd have a go.*

Danny aimed his stream… *what about the day ahead?* The plan to romp with Julian was on the shelf now, of course. *I'll sure have him spread lotion on, though. if I get greased up every couple of hours or so, maybe I'll be back to normal tomorrow. oh! now I remember: it's the altitude! you're supposed to use more sun cream when you're up in the mountains, because you're closer to the sun or something—Camp Walker is up around four thousand feet! cripes. I'll probably spend the rest of the summer peeling. no burning down in front, thankfully… my butt, though… I'm in trouble there.* He finished up and headed back to the camp. He had to walk slowly… going uphill was a little easier than down.

As he came close to camp he could see Julian making the coffee. "Hey, Julian!"

"Hi Danny. I'm making the coffee first today; Mark wants a cup quick." He placed the pot on the burner, and fished on the shelf for a match. "What are we supposed to fix today?"

"Scrambled eggs, bacon and toast." Danny sat down on the bench for a sec.

Julian lit the match under the coffee— *those little flames are so cool.* He turned around— *something's wrong; Danny isn't his usual bubbly self.* "What's the matter?" He saw the scout shirt; *we're not supposed to wear that until lunch.*

"I've got a pretty bad sunburn. I laid out on the platform during both swim periods. Maybe you could help me put on some sun cream?" Danny grimaced.

"Wow, yeah! Where is it?"

"There's a bottle in my footlocker; it's the one behind, facing the back."

Julian double-checked the coffee; the burner was going full bore. He went over to the Flaming Arrow three-man tent, about twelve feet away from the table. Tom's head was the first thing that he saw as he approached—his cot is on the left side. Just like over at the Wolf Camp, three footlocker chests formed an island in the center, each one facing a cot— *Danny's is where mine was, facing the back cot.*

Tom's right knee projected outward, almost blocking his way. The sleeping bag had slipped off behind, and... *oh!* Julian's shadow had blocked the sun on his way in; now he was confronted by an extraordinary sight: Tom's enormous hard-on was thrusting upward, completely uncovered. *whoa... Tom isn't wearing anything... not even his undies!* Julian stopped to look. He checked Tom's face: asleep. Carefully, he scooted around the knee... he stared at it for a second. No longer in his shadow, the massive pole was bathed in the morning sun. *awesome! how could it be so big?!* His eyes bulged at the sight, and his own gave a tingle. *I saw a hint of that last night after supper—bulging in Tom's shorts. wow. I'd like to see that one fire off! I bet Tom could shoot clear across the camp!*

Julian tiptoed around to the footlocker and opened the lid—the bottle of cream was in the front right corner. He lifted it out it and carefully closed the top— *you don't want to wake these guys up, Julian.* He glanced at Nick on the other side... nothing to see other than the top of his head. He looked back over at Tom; it gently moved up and down as he breathed. His camera eye was in high gear, registering every detail. *look at all the hair he has, too... boy, if only I could sneak a touch.* He adjusted himself quickly. He walked out the other side, along Nick's cot. *wow. hard not to look back...* That was one thing he never ever expected to see.

"Where are you burned?"

"Everywhere. Mark put some on last night, but not near enough." Carefully, he took off his shirt and leaned forward on his elbows.

"Boy, Danny. You are really red!" He took the cap off and splashed a stream across Danny's back. *eew... this stuff is kind of runny.*

The cold blob of cream jolted Danny upright. "B-b-brr!"

"You gotta tell me if I'm doing it right, okay?" Julian had put some on his Mom's back once a long time ago, when the Bears went to the ocean. But she wasn't burned. She just wanted to stop from getting burned. He spread the lotion across Danny's back with light gentle swipes.

"Ohmmm. That's so good. It cools it down fast. Have you ever had a sunburn?"

"No. My mom always makes me grease up with sun cream. Come to think of it, I didn't use any yesterday. But I was in the water most of the time. My nose feels maybe a little like it got too much. What do you think?" Julian leaned close to Danny for an opinion.

Danny examined him closely. *ohh,* he wanted to cuddle with that face! He looked at Julian in the eyes and smiled. They both felt a connection. *nice.* "Looks okay to me. Maybe you should take something along with you today. Me, I'm gonna stay in the shade all day, if I can."

Julian was surprised at the effect Danny's look had on him. He was still tingly from seeing Tom, and this seemed to make it a little worse. *or better, actually... I like the feeling, to be honest. what's more boring than a limp one? you never know it's even there.* He smiled at his analytical ability, and finished up Danny's back. *'you go right ahead, Little J...'* he chuckled to himself. Danny had helped him to adopt that name yesterday. It was fun to use it.

"It's red right down to the belt, Danny; is your rear burned too?"

"It sure is… maybe you could help me with that after we do the dishes." He didn't mean it to sound like a proposition, but...

"Dee-lighted!" Slowly rubbing that very nice rear end he had seen yesterday was welcome— *perfect timing for my special study project. maybe I can tell whether or not Danny's buns are Choice.* Today they'll be rosy and tender. *let's see... my guess is between 40 and 60 on the S/B scale. I wouldn't mind another glance at the yummy item on the other side, either.*

Looking at Julian reminded Danny of his daring "experiment" in the supply tent yesterday before inspections. *oh-oh... I'm about to get a boner, in spite of the sunburn!* Julian had let him perform a massage in the supply tent. They had ended up jacking each other off. *boy, was that hot! maybe I can do something with Julian today after all.* He smiled, but Julian wasn't looking; he was putting the lid on the lotion.

Julian looked at his right hand— *ug. it's all goopy now.* "So, tell me what to do over here." He stepped over to the stove. "You can just issue orders if you want." *hmm... I don't want to stain my scout shorts...* He wiped his hand off on his left arm. *silly to go clear over to the Lynx camp to wash up—maybe when I take Mark his coffee.*

"Nah, I'm not crippled, just tender. Thanks. That cream helps a lot. I'll let you do that again." He stood—it felt strange to leave his shirt untucked, but it felt better. He stepped toward the cooler. "C'mon," he beckoned. *darn... back feels wet.* He took the carton of eggs and handed Julian the package of bacon. *man... it's sore behind my knees too.* He stepped over to the table. "You ever done scrambled eggs?"

Julian was slightly embarrassed. "I guess I've always watched."

"Okay. Get the mixing bowl and large spoon over at the chest. I'll get the pans." Danny took the frying pan and griddle out of the stove drawer. He turned the burner under the frying pan to a medium setting. "Get a butcher knife too, and a couple of platters."

Julian fetched with speed and efficiency. He watched Danny grab the cutting board that hung on the side of the stove. Danny's skill was impressive. *I'm lucky Mark assigned me to help... I want to learn how to do all this.*

"Everybody gets four slices of bacon; Tom will want extra, so I'll make him one more." He did his what-the-heck-anyway shrug. Tom had been quite clear about his portion sizes at the briefing on the first day. He counted the strips... *there's an extra. Might as well use the whole package; Mark can have the other extra.* "You chop each strip in half. They cook easier that way." He carried the cutting board over to the pan and placed the slices as close together as he could. "The secret is to cook them as evenly as you can on one side, then you turn them over and do the other side." He looked at Julian to see if he was following.

Julian nodded, then checked the coffee pot. It was making noise, but no bubbles.

"We're supposed to have two eggs each. But since they're scrambled, I'll use the whole dozen. You ever crack an egg?"

Julian shook his head no.

"Okay. The thing is, you don't want any pieces of shell to get in here."

Danny showed Julian how to break an egg and put it into the mixing bowl. Julian did several; Danny enjoyed seeing him succeed. "Next, you mix them together just enough to break the yolks." Suddenly, they heard the coffee start to percolate.

Julian ran over and turned the flame down. The bacon was spitting little drops of grease. *Mom always puts on a cover.*

Danny joined him at the stove. "See what the bacon looks like? Now we turn it over and cook the other side… I need a fork."

Julian ran for a fork. As he gave it to Danny, he looked at the coffee. "When is this done?" He didn't pay attention to that yesterday.

"It doesn't take long—maybe five or six or seven minutes. It takes a little longer up here in the mountains. You can't tell by looking at it; if it looks dark, you've ruined it. I always check my watch. I figure you have about three minutes left. Then you just turn the heat down until it stops bubbling."

Julian took Danny's wrist and looked at his watch. "I don't want to foul up like yesterday." Mark had to stagger into camp yesterday to get his first cup.

"Cripes! There's no grease bucket yet… I know: get me a small cereal bowl. Oh—see the paper towels? Bring those too."

Julian did as Danny asked, and soon the bacon was drained, the grease emptied, and the eggs started. He watched the eggs start to turn opaque… *oo! I almost forgot!*

Julian reached for a mug and filled it with coffee. "Be right back!" He took off for the cabin… *oop! careful!* He splashed a little out on the way. *I hafta learn how to do this…* He steadied the cup on the landing. He opened the door: "Coffee…" ?? *where's—oh. Mark's in the bathroom.* He entered and closed the door. *neato: I get to surprise him…* he took a position just in front of the bathroom door. He held the cup up high, next to his Cheshire grin.

Mark shook Roger and zipped up. He flushed and stepped over to open the door. He burst out laughing.

Julian handed the mug to Mark. "I remembered the cup today."

"Mmm. Thank you," Mark took a whiff and sighed. "Just right." He sipped gingerly. He confirmed his approval with a nod.

"I better get back. We're doing scrambled eggs and bacon." Julian enjoyed watching Mark pucker his lips to sip. He looked up at Mark's cheek… "Didn't you shave this morning?"

Mark shook his head. "I do that at bedtime now." He gave Julian a wink.

Julian blushed. *Mark is always so cool.* Watching Mark shave last night was such a treat.

"Breakfast about ready?"

Julian nodded. "Five minutes."

"I'll be right there!" He raised his cup and took a second sip.

Julian giggled and gave a little wave. He ran back to the door. *oh.. should I close it?* He looked back at Mark, but he was fussing at the table. Julian took a minute to watch. *there's a lot about him I don't know. I never thought about that before.* He looked at the doorknob... *leave it open. he said he was about to leave.* Julian ran back to the Flaming Arrow camp as fast as he could.

Danny had started the toast—the pancake skillet took four slices at once. His shirt pulled loose from the cream on his back when he turned. He heard Julian run up. "Does my shirt look all greasy in the back?"

"No... it looks fine." Julian watched Danny stir and flip the eggs. *they look so good.* Julian was impressed; he'd never been interested in cooking before.

Danny was efficient when he fixed breakfast; he put the eggs on a platter and placed it next to the bacon in the oven. He covered them both with a paper towel.

"How did you learn to do all this stuff?!"

Danny blushed at the praise. Nobody more important could have said that. His flush was only partly masked by the sunburn. "I just learned it as I went along, I guess. It's not hard, really." He looked at Julian: *boy, just as hot today as he was yesterday.*

"Okay, all we do now is set the table and pull out the trimmings." He beckoned Julian back over to the cooler. He squatted down with care so his shirt wouldn't pull across the sunburn. "Take these over," he handed up the milk and orange juice. He carried the jam and butter to the table himself.

Julian set out all the dishes and silverware while Danny turned the slices of toast. "Everything's done." Danny looked around— *no one else is up.*

"You get to announce!" He gestured to the tent where Nick and Tom were still in the sack. "I need to watch the toast."

Julian opened his eyes wide. *maybe I'll get another look at Tom!* He did a mock salute. "Yessir!" He stepped over to the tent and looked in. Tom's knee no longer poked out over the edge of the cot, but he was still uncovered. *does Tom always sleep in the nude? hmm. how long should I look?* He glanced back to see if Danny was watching him. *nope... good; putting the toast in the oven.* Julian looked as closely as he dared; it didn't seem as hard. It was quite beautiful... *if something this big could be called that.* He wondered if he would ever be able to stroke it. *probly not. oh well.*

aha! He'd figured out what to do. He stepped around the footlockers and bent down close to Nick's cot with his back to Tom. Gently, he shook Nick's shoulder.

"Hey, you guys: rise and shine! Breakfast is ready."

Nick opened his eyes. He looked at Julian. "Oh, hi. Man, did I sleep in?" He sat up and swung around. "You up, Tom?"

"Yah!" Tom swung around to sit on the edge of the cot. He rubbed his eyes and shook his head. He'd been aware of the cooking racket, but had tried to ignore it for as long as possible.

It worked; Julian didn't want Tom to know he'd seen his bare cock up close like that. He wasn't sure why—a secret he was enjoying. He turned around, "You want me to bring you a cup of coffee, Tom?"

"Nah. Just put one on the table. I'll be there in a sec. Thanks, Julian." He looked up at him. *hum.* Julian looked different today, somehow. He shook his head again. *groggy this morning...*

Julian nodded and left the tent. He didn't look back, even though he wanted to. *Tom must have the biggest one in the troop. should I ask Danny? he probly hasn't seen it up close like that.*

Nick looked at Tom. *that's a new look on his face.* He thought about last night... something told him he needed to tread very lightly, very carefully. He searched for his socks—his clothes were in a pile on the footlocker lid.

Tom held his hands over his face after a good eye rub. He looked at Nick through his fingers. Things began to fall in place. What magic had Nick done on him? In him? *he looks the same—or does he? maybe I haven't really looked at Nick before. my butt feels... this is a new feeling. huh.* Now it came back... *it felt like this last night too. He grabbed his scout shirt off the footlocker.* He was a little disoriented. He did not usually sleep in like this. *shorts. shorts are next. where are they, anyway?* He heard Mark's voice; *he's up from the cabin already. I have to get it together, here. yikes! where are my skivvies?!* He had forgotten that he had taken them off last night—he'd never done that before.

"Good Stuff!" Mark walked into camp briskly, holding his coffee mug. "I want seconds." As he sat down, Julian brought the pot over to the table. "You look a little too rosy, Danny." Mark winked a thank you for the refill.

"Yeah. I'll never be able to carry a pack with this, for sure." He planned to drop Backpacking anyway. He sat down carefully and poured himself a glass of OJ.

Nick and Tom emerged from their tent. Nick hurried over and poured a mug of coffee for Tom. He was a little concerned, considering what they did last night.

Mark noticed that Tom was a little slower than usual. *everyone has a slow morning once in a while.* He watched Julian bring the food platters from the oven. *what a superior day this has been already. scrambled eggs! perfect. lots of pepper.* He reached for the shaker.

Breakfast went down everyone's throat fast. They were very hungry and wasted no time on small talk. The compliments were generous and genuine.

"Danny did it all, today," Julian boasted. "He is a genius at this, that's all." He meant it too. He led them in giving applause.

Tom gave a nice deep belch, and nodded at Danny.

"Thank you." Danny was glowing because of Julian's rave review. He was sitting next to him, so he couldn't look him in the face.

Mark started the morning meeting, and they set out to plan the day. He kept it informal today, council style.

Tom had a little intestinal trouble all of a sudden. Lower intestinal. He burped again, softly. His butt hole was prickly, buzzy... it felt sort of good, in a way, but he was not used to this sensation. What Nick had told him last night was absolutely true. The good news, for him at least, was that it didn't hurt. But he was beginning to comprehend the concept of having to recover. His butt seemed to be happy, but wanting to rest up, or something. *hum... how long will this meeting last? I need to visit the latrine before going to the meeting at HQ.*

Mark was in mid sentence, describing his schedule. "I get rifle range duty today, which knocks me out of being available..."

>> burb-b-b-bl <<

It happened without warning. Tom farted audibly. It gurgled at the finish. Everyone was startled, then amused.

"That can't be very good..." Mark froze in place, resisting the urge to laugh; the situation was awkward... he had no prepared comment that fit here.

Danny and Julian laughed in spite of themselves, more at Mark's remark than anything. They didn't dare look at each other. They tried to stifle it without much success. If only someone would say something!

Tom was red faced. He had no idea how this had happened. He couldn't shrink out of sight like he wanted to. He started to laugh too. "Sorry," he muttered at last; he glanced at Nick—Nick was blushing instead of laughing.

Mark kept a straight face... it was difficult. Especially since he knew, from personal experience, what caused that kind of fart. He glanced at Nick and saw the remnants of his blush. Mark was truly amazed. This was a complete surprise. *I have to think about this.* For now, he needed to find a way to help Tom recover a semblance of dignity. *of course! I know a way.*

"Okay, boys, okay; let's get it back together here. We all know that could happen to any of us. But I have been neglectful, and I apologize." This calmed them, and they looked at him in surprise. The chuckles stopped at last. "So I'll make up for it. After we adjourn, I'll get what is needed set up. Beginning today, there will be an official Farting Post. I'll put it over there, since that's downwind most of the time. From now on, when anybody has a fart, they are to back up to the post and let fly. Okay?"

They all howled at this, Tom included. Mark got to laugh now, himself. Maybe this was the beginning of a tradition. His idea worked; Tom was being patted on the back and welcomed back. It was a blessing in disguise, really. *Tom could use a little humble pie; it's good to have it here rather than in the large group.*

The laughter died away at last. "Meeting adjourned. See you at suppertime." Mark made a tactful exit. The boys had to take it from here. *now I see why Tom was a little slow this morning. must have been some night.* He headed for the campfire wood supply pile—a likely source for what was needed.

Julian got up from the table and stepped over to the stove. He grabbed the big pot and headed for the creek. *time for KP.*

"Wait up!" Danny couldn't run because of his legs... but his back felt a little better. "Hey, Julian? Why don't we do them the way Nick and Tom did last night? You know, right on the table?"

"Yeah, that's a good idea." Working at the table was a lot better than squatting on the bank. *besides, we can heat the wash water that way too.* It was good to be moving around. Julian looked at Danny. *tight black curls are nice. the sunburn isn't too bad on his face. I'm gonna take my sun cream along today, for sure.* Julian giggled. *farting post. that Mark.*

—ɯɯ—

what luck! Nick watched Danny follow Julian to the creek. They were alone for a minute. He nudged Tom with his elbow. "You okay?"

Tom looked up, a little sheepish. "Yeah." He didn't know how to say this. "Man, Nick, it's weird. I see what you were talking about, now."

Nick's heart went out to him. "Does it hurt?"

"No!" he said too loudly.

They glanced toward the creek to see if he had been heard. Danny and Julian chattered away as they walked toward the creek. They didn't turn around.

"No. That's what's so weird. It feels sort of good. It's all prickly. I see what you mean about not knowing if it's closed or not. Is it always like this?"

Nick was relieved that Tom wasn't pissed off. "Yeah, pretty much. I looked with a mirror once. It's closed all right. And it wants to stay that way, too, for a while."

Tom wiggled his butt on the bench, testing. "Man, when I cut that fart, I thought I'd die. I thought maybe I was blowing bubbles, or something!"

They broke up laughing.

"I've done a couple of those after, you know. When you go to the latrine you better take along a fresh pair of skivvies. It sounded a tad wet." He felt bad for not warning Tom this could happen.

They laughed some more. They saw Mark approaching from down the trail. He was carrying a large tree branch from the campfire stash. He stopped about fifteen feet out, toward the cabin. He looked at them with a grin.

"How's this?" Mark called out, indicating that he would plant the new feature at this spot. It was about a foot off the path.

They broke up again and nodded their heads. Mark installed the Farting Post. He stood back and admired it. He brushed his hands off, waved, and headed to HQ. *I'll secure it with a shovel later. it's only four feet tall, but it will do.*

"Geez, we're lucky…" Tom shook his head. "Can you imagine any other scoutmaster doing that?"

"Nope." They watched Mark walk away. They'd do most anything for him.

Tom stood. "I think it sounded juicier than it was. I'll just check. He lowered his pants and underwear. They both looked. "Whaddaya know! Dry!" He looked at Nick with a wide grin.

"Better be careful for awhile, though. Another one might sneak up that won't be." *I've had a couple of brownies… not good.*

Tom froze. "Whoa! How long do I have to worry?" I don't want to have another slip-up, that's for sure.

"Not long; you'll be fine, especially after you take a dump. Just be careful when you cut one. Don't force one, that's for sure!" He hit Tom on the arm. "C'mon. I gotta go too. I want to see if my name is on the Lifesaving Badge list. They're supposed to post it at HQ this morning."

They tidied up their sleeping bags. Nick made certain all the necessaries from last night were put away. He fetched his tablet and joined Tom on the path to the latrine.

3   *sunburn treatment*

Danny and Julian worked at the large washing pan while the big pot of water heated. "How's the burn?"

"Getting better, I think." *it isn't, but I hate it when anybody is sorry for me;   besides, it's my own fault.*   Danny considered the prospect of spending three hours of merit badge sessions out in the sun. Canoeing meant being out in the open water. *not good. no way can I drop out of that too.*

"When we're done, I'll give you another coat of goop."

"Thanks." Danny helped Julian empty the pan out by the supply tent. "What are you doing today?"

"I have Forestry first; that's with Justin. Then I go to Archery with Cory. That's the hard one." *will my arm hold up today? I forgot to ask Mark about weights last night. I'll get a ten pound bow today. maybe that will solve it.*

"Why's it hard?"

"They have these huge bows, as tall as I am! Cory told me I should have picked a smaller one. I was sore for a long time afterwards yesterday." *I'll tough it out. I'm gonna try to double the number of arrows I loose today. I can probably do that with the small one. it's neat that they call it loosing.*

They carried the pot of hot water to the table and rinsed the soapy dishes; Danny rinsed each item and handed it off.

"You?" Julian arranged the dishes in a zig-zag line to maximize exposure to the air

"Canoeing and Backpacking. I'm gonna drop Backpacking though. I'll do it later. It would eat up all my time at camp."

They emptied the used rinse water. KP was all done! This was a much better system. Julian looked at Danny. "You want to get gooped now, or should we do inspections first?"

"Good idea! Let's do the inspections. That way, what you put on before will all be soaked in." Danny went to get his clipboard.

They were in a quandary about the inspections. Everybody was perfect today. Danny wondered what the point was. Julian suggested maybe they could give bonus points. There weren't any obvious extras to reward, either. At the next Flaming Arrow meeting maybe they could get Mark to cancel them. So they had an hour, maybe a little more, before free swimming. Both of them were thinking along the same line, but neither one really wanted to push anything. They returned to the Flaming Arrow camp and sat down to complete what few notes there were.

"So, are you ready for another dose of suntan lotion?" Julian remembered that the buns were still untreated, and he was concerned.

Danny wanted to play around again today, but his entire backside hurt, clear down to his feet. "I dunno. Look and see what you think." He took off his shirt. *still tender, all right.*

Julian looked at it up close. "All I put on before breakfast is gone. Did your shirt rub it off?" He touched Danny between the shoulder blades. "Does that hurt?"

"Well, not hurt, exactly. But it sure is tender. The top of the shoulders is where it's worst." He undid his waist button and slid down his pants. "Check my rear, will you?" Carefully, he pulled down his skivvies. "Is it red?"

Just what Julian had in mind, looking at this… *very red.* "Wow. The outline of the elastic is pressed into your skin!" *looks painful.* He touched the top of Danny's right cheek. "Hurt there?"

"Mmm, yeah. Maybe we should coat all of it. So far, nothing has been put on below the waist." He hesitated. "You don't mind, do you?"

"Heck no! Where did the bottle go, anyway?"

"I put it back in my locker. I can get it…"

"I'll go. You take your shorts all the way off and stand on the bench. That way I can reach everything better." He dashed into the tent to fetch the lotion.

Danny stood on the bench. He felt around his waist. *Julian's right… I can feel the imprint.* He poked his left cheek… *ai-yi-yi!* No doubt about needing lotion there. He looked down; at least the front side wasn't toasted too. *hum… standing high up like this without any pants on feels strange…* he could see the Badger camp just across the creek. He looked all around. *I'm on exhibit… this might not be too smart.* "Julian?"

"Yeah?" Seeing Danny on the bench with his pants down was funny… and sexy. *boy, is his butt ever red.*

"I was just thinking. I know the Meadow is sort of private, but what if somebody comes around? They restock the cooler every day… I don't know when. Maybe we should go into the tent." *besides, there might still be a Zebra in camp—they're a straight beeline shot. so are the Wolves.*

"Wow, I didn't think of that. You're right… Mark isn't here to okay things either." Julian thought about it. *the tent is too awkward.* "I know! We can go down to the cabin. There's a chair to stand on, and everything."

"Brilliant!" Danny climbed down and carefully worked his shorts back up. He followed Julian at a trot. He was right behind as they went in the door.

Julian went to the table; he pulled out the chair and turned the back around. The curtains above the table were open wide—the light was perfect.

Danny closed the door and took off his pants. He carried his clothes with him and stood on the chair. He plopped the clothes on the table and folded his arms. The Lynx camp was visible through the window… Panther's too. *nobody was there during inspections, so there's no problem.*

Julian began his ministrations instantly. He carefully ran along the imprinted waistline first. That looked very sore and puffy. Next, the buns: he paid full attention to the aesthetic qualities as well as the sensual. He was intent on treating the sunburn properly, but he was just as intent on studying these objects up close: how they feel, and how they look. *are these Choice? should I ask Nick?* He was determined to find out just

27

what Choice Buns were like. *these aren't like Mark's at all. smaller…* *but that isn't all. I didn't get that good a look.* He'd gotten a glimpse just as Mark stepped into the shower… the curtain was pulled closed too fast. *maybe I can get a better look tonight. I have to figure a way to be at the table when Mark takes off his skivvies. tricky.* He made a second pass through the dents… cool. *feel nice—a little goopy though.*

"Am I rubbing too hard, or anything?"

"N-nno," Danny had lost focus for a minute. The fact that Julian, of all the people in the world, was massaging his buns was nigh on to a miracle. It felt double good. The lotion helped the burn without question. The touch was giving him a wonderful erection. He assumed Julian would see it before long; that was just fine too.

"Put a little extra on the top, where it goes up to the back. That's where it's *really* sore." *that's worse than my shoulder tops.*

"Okay. I'll do the back of your legs too… they look very pink." He smoothed lotion on the back of Danny's legs. *I like doing this… feeling the form helps me understand how it looks, somehow…* Elements of a drawing began to form in his mind. *I can add this to the bun page maybe. ooo… it's stimulating Little J, too… that's not exactly surprising.* Little J had tried to come alive a couple of times today already. "There. You are solid lotion from the butt down."

"I sure appreciate this, Julian." *for sure. behind my knees really hurts… even so, I hope Julian will do the front side… I'm getting horny as the…* Just as he was thinking that, Julian took hold of his legs and turned him around.

"I better do both sides, just like the bacon," Julian chuckled. He saw the hard-on. "Wow, Danny. Lookee what you have!" *I like Danny's cock.* "Say, you're not burned there too, are you?"

Danny shook his head no.

"Boy, that's good. That would be **awful**." Julian remembered yesterday's special "rest" session in the supply tent. *Danny wanted to give me a massage.* Until this morning, Danny's cock was the only one besides his own that he had ever looked at up close. *Tom's is about twice this size!*

Danny thought for a minute... "I did get sunned a lot, though, on this side." He wouldn't mention that he had turned onto his tummy when he got hard out there on the platform. He was lucky nobody saw that.

"Hmm. Better play it safe, I guess." It wouldn't do at all for Danny's Little D to have a sunburn! He took Danny's hard-on in his right hand and carefully gave it a coat of lotion. *ooo! that feels nice, all slippery like that.* He leaned close and watched it pulse and respond. *handy, with Danny on the chair... makes looking at it real easy. looks odd, all shiny and slicked up.*

"Mmm," Danny's knees nearly caved in. "Wow, Julian," he exhaled forcefully. "That feels fantastic!" *I want more of that.*

well, now... this could be interesting. Julian stroked it deliberately; with each pull upward, Danny's knees nearly failed to hold.

This was intense; after a couple more Danny had to make him stop. "Julian, Julian! You have no idea! I can't keep my balance up here. I need to sit down, or something." He looked at Julian with a big grin.

Julian could tell that Danny wanted him to do a lot more of this. He wanted to, as a matter of fact.

"You're all gooped up, is the problem. A butt print on the table might not look so good... I know!" He went to his cot and pulled off the blanket. He spread it out on the floor. He stood back and gestured an invitation to Danny to join him there.

"Much better idea." Danny climbed down and walked over to Julian. He sat down on his heels. "Ow!" *that won't work. behind the knees says no.* He raised upright, still on his knees—*I can do that. I just can't sit back on my heels.*

Julian looked at this. Nothing on the front side had been coated, except the wagging shiny stick in the center. "You want me to coat your chest first?" *it doesn't look pink, but...*

"I don't think so. It feels okay." He felt no burn on the front. "Do more of what you were before!"

"Okay." Julian took up the stroke again. Except for the greasy feeling in his hand, he enjoyed doing this. It made the cock feel different.

The floor was a bit hard; his knees were not too happy. "Is your back okay?

"Mmm-hm." Danny focused on what Julian's hand was doing. "Wow... you should try this, Julian." After a dozen or so pulls, he got this great idea! He put his hand on Julian's. "Wait... I'm so dumb sometimes..."

Julian looked up. "What do you mean?"

Danny thought about how to phrase this... after what they did in the supply tent yesterday, it made perfect sense—this would be the ideal second step.

"You should take off your pants and let me rub you at the same time. It's really something with this cream, Julian."

oh... "Okay." Julian could tell that Danny really liked it this way. He was curious to see if it was that good... he stepped out of his shorts and skivvies. He sat back down across from Danny. *I was about to get a stiffy, anyway.*

"Hand me the lotion." Danny poured some into his right palm. "You have to sit up too, so I can reach." When Julian was across from him, he reached out.

"Ooo! It's cold!" Little J didn't like that.

"It'll warm up quick. Sorry, I forgot to mention that." He spread the cream all over Julian's cock. He squeezed it and jacked up and down a few times. "See?"

Julian did indeed. "Boy!" He reached across for Danny's cock and resumed what he had been doing.

They kneeled facing each other trying out this new pleasure. It was very nice.

Danny knew something about this method, and took over. *sun cream is just as good a lubricant as any.* He held Julian's balls in his other hand and made his skin more taut, if that was possible. Julian did the same, it intensified everything.

They eased into a nice mutual rhythm.

This was exquisite. Danny opened his eyes. *he's so cute with his tongue poking out of the corner of his mouth.* He couldn't resist: he leaned forward... closed his eyes and kissed.

Julian responded at once. He loved the feeling of Danny's lips. He wasn't far from shooting... "Mmm..." *I can't stop.* He pumped in time with Danny's hand movement. When Danny's hand tightened, Julian shot. "Mmm!" He inhaled deep. He felt Danny squeeze tighter. *oh!* "Uhm!" He shot again.

Danny was in heaven... Julian seemed to know exactly where to hold, where to squeeze. When Julian moaned it turned him on so fast that he knew he would come any second. Danny started to pump too. He dripped some pre-cum, and it made the feeling so much better. He wanted to let Julian finish first, but after the first shot he couldn't hold it. Off he went, too. "Aahh!" He kissed harder. He shot twice more... he squeezed his buns tight for one last shot.

Julian held Danny tight until he finished shooting. He let go and sat back on his heels to rest. *that was something! I've never felt anything like that. it went so fast!*

Danny looked at Julian's face. *wow. yes, I could fall in love with Julian... I don't want to tell him yet, though. I don't want to scare him away.* He looked down: *what am I going to do with this goopy hand? we didn't bring a towel.*

Julian was transported. He had gone beyond his objective of checking on Danny's buns. Were they choice? Probably. The question had gotten put aside... *I'll save that for later. what is it about Danny? I felt this yesterday too.* The kiss had an odd effect. He liked that a lot more that he had thought. It was completely unexpected. His reaction had been sort of automatic. He remembered what Danny said yesterday about wanting for a long time to kiss him. This kiss made more sense now...

"Julian?" Danny wanted him to return from wherever his mind had taken him. "Can we clean up in the bathroom?"

Julian opened his eyes. "Oh! Yeah, sure." *anything else would be stupid;* he stood up and led the way. "Why did that feel so much better than yesterday?"

Danny had not thought about that question before. *hmm.* "Maybe the lubrication makes it better."

"Lubrication? What's that?"

"Using something slippery. Haven't you ever done that before? Like saliva?"

"Saliva? I don't get it."

Danny was surprised all over again. He had forgotten what he had figured out yesterday: this kid was completely inexperienced. The lotion was a happy accident. "Some time when you're jacking off, lick and spit into your palm and stroke with it wet. Like we just did, only with your saliva. It feels a lot more intense than dry stroking."

"Huh! I never thought of that."

"Some guys use Vaseline. It's real slippery."

Julian felt stupid. He didn't know what Vaseline was. *should I ask? well, yeah. how else can you find out? you probably can't ask just anyone.* "Danny, I don't know what that is."

"What?! Doesn't your mom ever use it? It comes in a jar, kind of like jelly. My mom uses it sometimes for first aid stuff."

Julian's mind whirred; he reviewed his mother's medicine chest in his mind. *she has a lot of creams and things in jars. she's always smearing things on herself. must be one of those.*

"It's kinda yellowish, but mostly clear. It kind of smells, but not too bad."

It still didn't ring a bell. "Danny?" Julian hung his towel back on the rack.

"Yeah?"

"After camp, when we get home, some time can you show me some? I don't think we have any."

it just keeps getting better. "Sure. You can count on it." He had a few other ideas about what he could show Julian when they got home. *maybe even before we leave camp, a few other things could be tried out. Julian's on the small side, but that might make a good suck that much easier. sunburn, get cured quick, please.*

Julian thought again about that kiss. It made him uncomfortable, the more he thought about it. *is this going to become a problem?* Something deep inside was warning him. He didn't know what about, exactly. He knew that he could not talk to Danny about his feelings toward Mark. He had no idea how he could talk to Mark about Danny. He sensed that he needed to be careful. *it's different from the way I feel about Mark... but maybe it isn't, completely.* He couldn't say that he loved Danny. *I can say that I love Mark. I have think about this until I know what to do.* He had decided that maybe kissing Danny should be avoided.

Julian checked the clock as he reentered the big room. "Free swimming is just about to start. What are you gonna do?"

"Stay out of the sun."

Julian wanted to work on his diving some, and he especially didn't want Tom's help; he had planned to swim with Danny. hmm... if Tom came up to him, he had to figure out a way to put him off and not make him mad or anything—*I don't want Tom to do any more of those underwater squeezes.* Yesterday, Tom's help in diving was terrific... *but at the end he made that strange comment about showing me how to do other things. then he squeezed Little J before swimming away. I don't want Tom to show me how to do anything with Little J for some reason. especially now that I've seen Tom's... Little T? no... Big T. Very Big T... I think I'd like someone else do the showing-how-tos for now, thanks. Danny's doing just fine there.*

He went back to dress and put the blanket onto his cot. oop some telltale spots, right in the center. He scratched his head... *maybe they'll disappear when they dry out. maybe Mark won't notice.*

Danny saw no point in going to the lake. "I think I'll go to HQ and see about changing from Backpacking. I can see if there's something else open. Come to think of it, that's a good idea. There are two or three other guys who want to drop Backpacking too; maybe I can help find a slot for everybody."

"Okay. I better do a touch up on your back," Julian chuckled. "Maybe some other spots too."

"Good idea." Danny leaned on the back of the chair.

Julian gently applied lotion to Danny's back from the neck down. He spent particular attention to Danny's buns. He noticed that the dents in the side were more visible. *It depends how you stand. right now they really look choice. Choice... I'm starting to like that word. hmm. I bet Mark's are better, actually.* Julian didn't forget about asking Danny's opinion about buns—but he figured that maybe it would be better to wait.

oh-oh... now my hand is all goopy again.

4   *recruiting Tom*

Tom and Nick jogged from the latrine over to the main path. HQ was less than fifteen minutes away at this pace—one of the advantages of having the Barr's Meadow Camp. Most of the troop camps were a good thirty or forty minutes out. The Outlook camp was over an hour. When they approached the building, forty or fifty scouts were milling around in front.

"What are all these guys doing here?" The long overnights weren't until next week. Nick checked on that yesterday.

"No idea." *must be more than one meeting today.* "Too early for the climbers and hikers." *darn it!* Tom was disgusted with himself. *I forgot my sunglasses.*

"There's Mark!" Nick pointed; Mark was leading a group of counselors carrying long cases. "That's right! He said he was doing rifle range duty." *probably having a training session.*

They entered the lobby. Two scouts were waiting on the bench at the First Aid Station. A dozen were clustered around the bulletin board. Nick gave a short wave to Tom and went to make sure he had made the Lifesaving list. Tom followed the red arrow to the left that said conference.

It took a minute, but Nick got up to the board at last. *yes! my name is right there. Jay's too! Qualified. uh-oh... a star next to my name.* A notice with a big star was off to the side. He read the paragraph under it. ... *report to a meeting in the dining hall at nine thirty.* His watch said he had ten minutes. *might as well go on in now ... not enough time to do much else.*

Tom went up the stairway. The small conference room was back toward the center of the building, just above the main entrance. A few Junior Assistants were there already. A sign up clipboard was on a table at the side. He signed in... his name was there, along with fourteen others. *I didn't realize—that's right! Mark said there were that many troops here this year. no wonder it was crowded at the lake.* He didn't know anybody here; he'd seen a couple of these guys around, probably in the mess hall. He grabbed one of the folding chairs and sat down. The guy in the next chair stuck out his hand.

"Chuck Thompson, Troop 118."

"Hey, Chuck. Tom Dawson, Troop 9."

Chuck raised his eyebrows. *that's the top dog troop, the one to beat.* "So, you're an Eagle, then?" He had just made Eagle two weeks ago, himself.

"Yeah. I'm working on my Gold Palm. When I finish Aviation I'll be there. It's a tough one, too."

"Wow." Chuck was impressed. "Where do you work on that?"

"GP airstrip. It's just out of Lexington. Our scoutmaster knows the manager there real well... made it pretty easy to get started." Tom's biggest trouble was getting the money to pay for the flight time. "I should have it licked before Christmas."

The others were arriving fast. He and Chuck had to scoot and make room. Tom's butt told him to go easy, please. *don't scoot sideways—not for a while, at least.* He discovered that he had to sit sort of forward, his legs slightly apart. Otherwise the prickling was more pronounced. He tested a few other positions; legs stretched out in front with ankles crossed was good... *takes up a lot of room, though. I seem to be okay...* He felt stable; no more surprises were going to happen.

The Camp Director arrived with an assistant. He picked up the clipboard and faced the room. "John Jorgensen, gentlemen; this is our Recreational Director, Mr. Bradley. Thanks for coming in this morning. I know you all have other things to do, so I'll be as brief as possible. First, is there anyone who was not here last year?"

Six raised a hand.

"That will help a lot. Last year, as you know, as most of you know, the closing program had a few problems."

There was a big laugh at the understatement. Two acts had tried to come onstage from different sides. It took forever to sort it out. Later on, Troop 47 wasn't ready for their entrance and everyone had to wait again.

"So, what we're going to do is make sure that doesn't happen this year. You are going to be the organizing committee that will run it, and you will coordinate everything. The goal is to get everyone in, seated, entertained and dismissed in no more than two and a half hours."

Everyone was behind that idea. A few talked briefly among themselves. Tom noticed that one of the JA's opposite seemed to be watching him. He looked half Oriental... maybe Philippine? He came into the room with a couple of other guys—this one had elbowed the guy next to him. Tom got the impression that they were talking about him. *hmm... don't remember ever seeing them before.*

Jorgensen gave pencils to a couple of scouts. "Mr. Bradley will be overall event director," Jorgensen continued, "and you will be his assistants. You'll help plan, organize, and run it. Now, I know that your troops will be competing. So we have to plan it in such a way that everyone has the same chance. We had a couple of troops complain that they were at a real disadvantage for one reason or other."

Bradley passed out a piece of paper to each JA. "One thing you'll be able to do on this committee is make sure your troop gets a fair shake."

Jorgensen stepped to the far end of the room. "I want you to put your name and troop at the top. Then list any special talents or experience that might be useful in what we will be doing."

Tom started to jot down his information. All he had to write on was his bare knee. *no good... wait until the director is through talking.* He sensed that he was being looked at. He glanced up, and sure enough. *am I being checked out? how do I find out without him knowing I'm checking...* Tom activated his peripheral view... *I'll look over when his head turns.*

"There will be four main functions," Jorgensen continued. "I'll describe them so that you can list what you'd like to do. If we can, we'll let you have what you want. We'll need four of you for logistics. That means setting up beforehand, lining up any special equipment, such as lights, microphones, or a record player. Two will be needed to operate sound and lights during the program. Those will spend more time than the others because they may have to attend rehearsals; they will also gain extra points. These two committees alone will fix most of the problems we had last year."

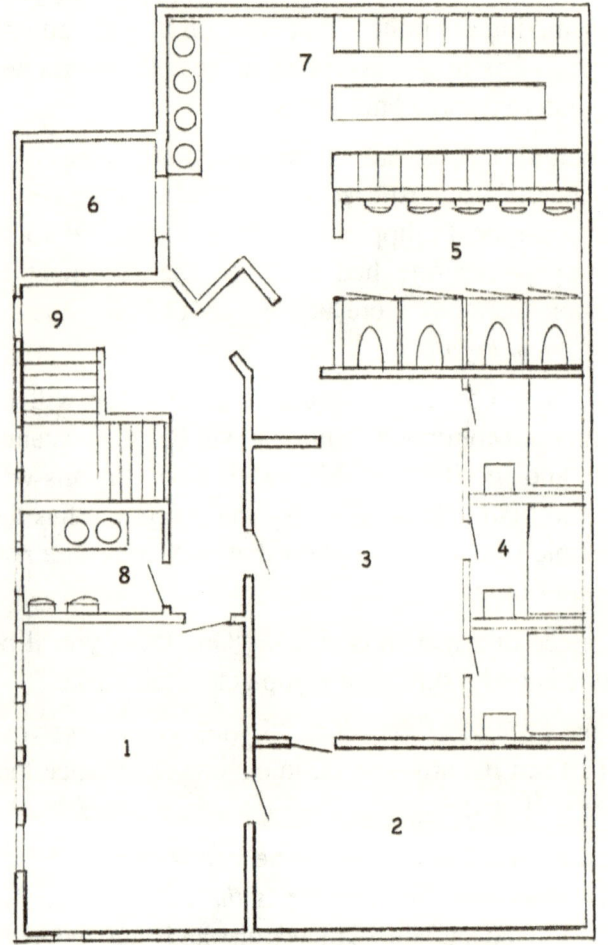

Second Floor

1 Conference Room
2 Storage
3 Staff/Counselor Lounge
4 Rest/Nap Room
5 Rest Room
6 Showers
7 Lockers
8 Lavatory
9 Stairway Down

Tom glanced back across the room. All three seemed to be giving him the eye. *what the devil is going on? the center one is cute, too—is he part Japanese, maybe?*

"Four will serve as a crew during the show—both in the audience and back stage. Four will organize and lead the cleanup and closing of the facility. They will get to stay late. Finally, two will be my assistants, and will be assigned a variety of things, including last minute problems." He looked back and forth. "Any questions, so far?"

"Sir, when will we know our assignments?" Brian was one of the three who were eyeing Tom.

Tom took advantage of the opportunity… *looks like a wrestler.*

Bradley gestured to Jorgensen.

"Excellent question. We plan to work that out today; we'll tell your scoutmasters either at lunch, or after the free period this afternoon. No later than that, I promise."

Chuck raised his hand. "How many meetings do you think we'll have?"

"Another excellent question." He gestured to Bradley.

"As few as possible." They laughed politely. "Really, that is a good question. We can probably get it organized in two or three. Tell you what: on your papers, put down the times when you're most available from your other duties. I'll try to pick a time that's good for everyone. I want us all to meet though, so that everyone knows what's going on. Keep your eye out for announcements on the bulletin board."

Jorgensen looked around. There didn't seem to be any more questions. "All right, that's it for today; turn in your paper before you leave. Take as long as you need. Hand it to Mr. Bradley, or me... I'll be in the office downstairs, just to the left. Thanks for helping to make this year's camp the best yet." Jorgensen left for his office.

Someone mumbled, "Thanks for having us write out this stuff without a table." A small ripple of laughter came from a few who had heard the comment.

Tom got down on his hands and knees and wrote on the floor. *hmm. this is sort of a nice position.* His rear end liked it fine. He smiled to himself. *what these guys don't know.* The prickles made him remember a few choice moments from last night. He was still amazed by it.

His idea caught on. Most everyone else was writing on the floor too. He filled out the paper, pointing out that on the spur lifeguard duty could cause a conflict. He put down stage crew as first choice, and cleanup as last choice; he figured the cleanup guys would end up having to make their troop last to leave camp.

Tom paused—*what should I add? I don't know what the Troop 9 skit will be yet, so... what the—??* The Chinese guy just kneeled down opposite; *he's reading what I wrote down.* Tom looked across at his sheet. *hmm... I never could read upside down. it does look interesting—lots of loops and flourishes.* Tom looked up at the guy's face, and their eyes met. He felt a slight buzz and looked away. He was afraid he might be blushing.

He sat down on his heels. *hoo! now that felt good.* It fascinated him that his butt was keeping him such good company today.

He stood—Mr. Bradley was busy talking to a guy on the other end of the room, so he headed for the doorway. He didn't want to hang around, especially. After he turned in his paper, he wanted to check the board to see if Nick had made it. When he rounded the corner at the foot of the stairs, the Camp Director was just going into the office. Tom followed close behind. "Sir?"

Jorgensen was halfway to his desk. He turned around to see who had called.

Tom stopped and gave a salute. "Tom Dawson, Troop 9. Here's my sheet. This is a really good idea, sir."

Jorgensen was impressed. *well, Troop 9.* It figured that Mark's JA would be in top form. "Thanks, Tom." He returned the salute at last, realizing that Tom was waiting. He'd forgotten about Mark's boys—they always saluted.

Tom turned to exit. He headed back out and—"Oop! 'Scuse. Sorry…" He almost bumped into the… *what is he? Korean?* Tom had never met any Orientals, whole or part. *he's cute, whatever he is. and he's a JA too.* He stepped to the side to let him pass, then continued down the short hallway. As he turned toward the bulletin board, he saw the guy hand his sheet to one of his friends.

"Hey, Tom! Wait up a minute."

Tom turned and looked at him directly. He hadn't seen him before today. *up close, he's hot… dangerous eyes.* Tom tilted his head as if he was about to ask a question. *doesn't sound much different—not foreign anyway.*

"Hi. Uhh, you probably don't know who I am…"

"That's real easy to fix." Tom paused. "How do you know my name?"

"I read it on your paper. Naughty me, I know." He took a deep breath. "Hi. I'm Geoff Staley, Troop 419." He gestured to the other two who had scooted up. "This is Brian Rogers, Troop 227, and Jack Haley, Troop 152."

They shook hands all around. This felt strange. Scouts didn't usually shake hands like this. These guys had something in mind. *might as well see what it is.* They looked like they were worth his attention. *especially Geoff. intriguing, for sure—a slight accent—hard to identify.* Jack reminded him a little of Danny... without the curls. Brian would probably become the Incredible Hulk someday. Tom looked at them, expectedly. There was a brief, awkward pause. "What's up?"

"We're from just outside Atlanta," Jack gestured to the others.

"Oh. That explains the big troop numbers. How many troops are there in Atlanta, anyway?" *I went to Atlanta once. too big.*

"Who knows? Geoff shrugged. "They let us in here because the Atlanta Area Council camps were full this month."

"Ah." Tom sensed that Geoff was a little nervous... *doesn't seem to know what to do with his hands. I still can't figure what they're up to.*

"You got a minute?" Geoff raised his eyebrows.

"Yeah, sure. You want to stay in the hallway, or walk outside?" *I'll find out about Nick later... this looks interesting.*

The three from Atlanta shrugged. The hallway had too much traffic; Tom nodded toward the door. They stepped outside.

"We saw you yesterday at the lake... that is, I saw you, and I thought..." Geoff looked to Brian for help—*I don't want to foul this up. sometimes I come on too strong. Brian's brawn might be a plus in this situation.*

"How long you been an Eagle?" Brian didn't want to do any waltzing around. He saw the Bronze and Silver Palm patches on Tom's shirt. They looked real fine.

"Couple of years, almost... I'm close to my Gold Palm. I'm on the last badge; everything else is done. You?"

"A year. I've got three to go for my Bronze. Jack is two away. I don't know about Geoff." *man... a gold palm. must be a gung-ho type.*

Geoff held up a zero. He was a year away from his Eagle, at least, because of his Community Project. He puffed out his chest so they could all see his Life Patch. He was delighted to have his cohorts take the lead in these discussions. He wanted to study this "specimen" more closely.

"You a poker player, Tom?" Brian figured he was.

poker! That was out of the blue. "Well, I've played poker some, yeah. Sometimes it's a good way to pass the time if we're caught in the rain on a campout." He saw three smiles. *what's up, here?*

Jack piped up quickly. "Y'see, Tom, we have this club. It's a special poker club. We were sort of hoping we could recruit you to join in a game."

How odd. Why the mystery? *I wouldn't mind, though I have enough to keep me busy. oh...* it dawned on him. He looked at them and feigned innocence. *I don't want to be wrong about this. if I'm right, I sure would join the game. I've played that a couple of times... it's terrific.* He looked at Jack a second time. *nice butt, that's darn sure. Brian's a yawn. Geoff. now that would be worth the trip. yes, sir.*

"Sounds interesting. So who all is a member of this club?"

"Well," Jack pointed to the others, "there's us three, and Lester."

"Who's Lester?"

"He's a friend from my troop," Brian shrugged. "He couldn't make it to camp this year." *too bad, too; Lester is an outstanding player.*

It became clear to Tom: he would be a fill in. *what a good idea. I can stay if I want, probably, or just be temporary. looks like a good deal all around. I'll play coy just a little longer. these big city types are funny sometimes.*

"Yeah, why not? Only I don't like to gamble for money. They'd bust us double hard if they found out." Tom figured that money wasn't the object of this game anyway. *might as well play stupid.*

"Oh no no no!" Geoff held up his hands. "What we do is start out with an equal number of chips. We just hand them out to start with."

"All right!" Tom continued his little subterfuge. *I'll play sweet and stupid... right up to the last stitch.* "We usually use wooden matchsticks. Same difference."

He watched the three city slickers congratulate themselves. *this is fun. they're so easy to figure out.* "There's only two questions, I guess."

Jack suspected that Tom might be trying to find a loophole. "What are they?" The other two were concerned as well.

"Well, when and where? I don't know about you guys, but I have a lot to do around here." *let's just see how smart these guys are.*

"**Where** we got covered, no sweat. We can show you." Brian was in a hurry to get this going. "I guess what we have to do is see when we all have some open time—y'know, an hour or two. It beats sittin' around, y'know."

Tom didn't want them to know how much time he had on his hands. It wasn't a huge amount, but he did have the luxury of being able to jockey some of it around. Not having to work on a badge or advancement put him at a real advantage. *after they give out their open times, I'll pick the one I want.*

"Let's go over to that table and figure it out." Tom knew how to manage this. *I'll do what Nick would most likely do... both Geoff and Jack have notebooks. darn...* he squinted as they stepped into the sun. *sunglasses. how could I forget those? I always have my sunglasses. now I have to be careful; not cool to get caught looking... you don't want 'em to know what you're checking.*

One of the camp picnic style tables was off to the side, near the southwest corner of the building. They sat on the benches, Jack and Brian on one side, Tom and Geoff on the other. Purposely, Geoff sat where he could steal peeks… the hard part was waiting. He had already made a deal with Brian to be first in line.

Tom observed Geoff's deft move… a very good sign. *butt seems happy on this bench, too.* In fact, his rear end seemed to have settled down quite a lot since breakfast. He squirmed gratefully.

"Hand me your tablet, Jack." Tom had his own pen. He opened to a blank page and turned the tablet sideways. He drew a simple grid. On the left he wrote down everyone's name in a list. Across the page he created ten columns, and labeled them Tuesday, Wednesday, and every day through to the end of camp.

"Okay. Today is first. Brian? What do you have open—or… wait, you guys. Would it be easier to put down when we can't get together?" He wasn't sure about that himself. *Nick is better at figuring this stuff.*

Brian didn't care one way or the other… he glanced over at Jack. Had he seen Tom's bulge? *looks like Geoff was right about that. I got a good idea on the way over to the table.* Tom's pants in motion left little doubt about what was being held captive. *the sooner we get to it the better.*

"I think it would be easier to put down openings." Jack was delighted by Tom's initiative. It meant the game was on. "I have a lot of different things. In fact, free swim periods are the only ones I can say for sure are open."

They agreed with this. Brian had the free swim periods today, and he had mornings on Thursday and Saturday. Probably next Tuesday, too.

Jack had already said free swimming periods. Off the top of his head he couldn't commit to anything else. Geoff also had the swim periods. He might have one of the merit badge periods open. He was considering dropping out of Backpacking. That was from two to about three thirty or four, every day.

Tom's grid was simple; he was the only one who didn't have any merit badges to work on. "Gents, it looks like our swimming is going to suffer some." He paused for effect. He saw them each mentally licking their chops. *this is fun.* "I have to do lifeguard duty during some of the free swimming periods." He paused for even more effect. "What about..." he looked around to be sure there were no unwanted ears. "What about after lights out?"

It was as if he had dropped a bomb. None of them had thought it through that far. They were scared at first... but the idea was sure attractive. Their location was pretty good for that—it was isolated enough to be secure. The problem might be using some of the trails at night.

"Cool!" Geoff was the first to speak. "I like that idea! I never even **thought** of that." He looked at his friends and raised his eyebrows; it was a roaring hot idea.

Brian looked at Geoff, annoyed. *easy enough for him, he's right there already. I'd have to hike for over half an hour to get there.* "I don't like the idea, to be honest. If they caught us, we'd get it pretty bad, y'know."

Jack was on the fence. "Brian could be right. But I'll go along with whatever you guys decide." Jack smiled to himself; *Brian would agree to about anything, actually. well, he's seen the bulge. Geoff was right about that. Brian likes big ones... his legs are practically running in place under the table.*

"Awful risky. We'd have to be sure that we wouldn't be missed. Tell you what: let's keep that an open possibility. If anyone thinks they are certain it's okay on some night, he can contact the rest of us and we'll meet and decide on the spot. No way can we plan that one ahead." Tom doubted that they would ever risk it.

They all nodded agreement.

Tom looked at the tablet. He looked at the trio. "So where is this place? Can you show me now?" Tom played all pure and innocent. His butt had just given him limited permission, if it was needed. Sitting next to Geoff for the last five minutes had been a very pleasant experience; he had enjoyed the attention. Tom had caught him looking at his crotch at least three times; he had worked his legs a few times as a surprise treat. He glanced at the schedule in his hand... they had over two hours before anyone would give a rip about where they were. *how horny can I make them before the threads start to fall?*

"It's at Geoff's camp," Jack nudged Brian with his leg... *the game is on!* "The Hawk. It's perfect."

"True. It is great." Brian had to make sure he allowed for enough travel time. "The only problem I have is the trail to my camp. I'm at the Wolverine. It's a little brushy, and it's probably an extra mile or more."

Tom stood and looked at Geoff right in the eyes: *those eyes are as dark as any I have ever looked at....* They gave him a bit of a buzz down in front. *I thought I'd need more time, after last night. maybe I recover fast or something. the Big Boy in front is sending all the usual signals.* "Lead the way!"

5   *the Poker Club*

The trailhead to Geoff's camp was close to the Barr's Meadow fork, but it branched off going north northwest. A sign read "To Bird and Animal Clusters." Tom had not been up to any of the animal camps, but Troop 9 had been at the Owl camp one year, so he knew this trail. The grade was considerably steeper.

"How far up is it?"

"About a mile. I wish my camp was this close in." Jack was at the Falcon, farther up the same trail.

Tom didn't mention that the Meadow was half that. *ah... now then.* He studied the view as he went up the trail... he had the savvy to fall in right behind Geoff. *a mile of this view should prime me nicely.*

After a quarter mile they came to the fork in the trail. A signpost pointing right said "Animals." They went left. That sign said "Birds." Tom had not been up here for a long time; he had visited a few of the Tribal camps over to the east, the year Troop Nine was in the Choctaw camp. *at least we're not over there any more. the trail is steeper and it's super dry up there... no creek at all.*

Tom had forgotten how much steeper this trail was compared to the Barr's Meadow trail. For some distance, maybe another quarter mile, they had to work a little. The grade lessened gradually, and was nearly level when they turned left at the sign that said Hawk Camp. He remembered seeing that. He'd never gone into the Hawk camp though. The grade dropped off slightly as it neared the campsite. *so, the camp is very close to the main trail... nice.* The troop flag greeted them, gently waving atop a pole near one of the mini camps, the one with an oversize Adirondak log shelter. *that looks very classy. why don't we have a fancy flag like that?*

"How many patrols do you have?"

"Five."

Tom saw three camps; the others were up side trails. "Where does your Scoutmaster stay?"

Camp Walker

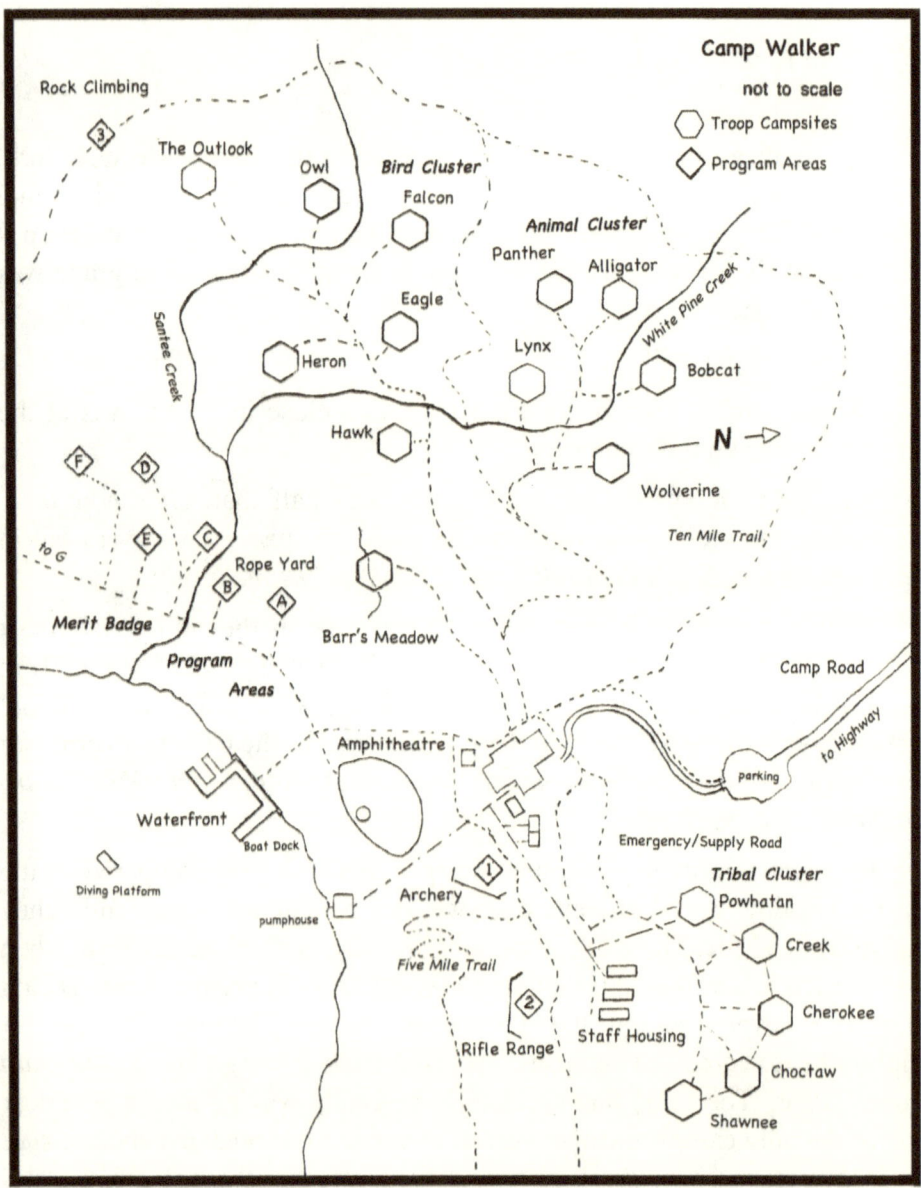

"There, in the Adirondack. It's the Fox Patrol, too. I stay with the Cranes, over to the right."

"So where's this perfect place?" *All these camps are almost within speaking distance of each other. They didn't have a separate leadership tent. No cabin. man...* He was reminded how deluxe the Meadow really was.

The others laughed. "We already walked past it," Geoff grinned. Tom's puzzled expression pleased them immensely.

Tom looked in every direction. Nothing. He looked at Geoff. "You got me, I guess." *what are these guys up to?*

"C'mon. It's back here." He backtracked about twenty feet and turned right.

The faint hint of a branching path dropped laterally down the slope to the south. The dense duff looked barely disturbed... *no wonder I missed it.* It was in the general direction of the Meadow... *the Meadow must be downhill quite a ways.* Only ten yards in, the rhododendron and ground shrubbery hid it completely: *the troop supply tent! looks exactly like ours in the Flaming Arrow camp.* Every campsite had one... *this is the first one I've seen separated from all the patrol-camps. these guys are absolutely right. it's perfect.*

Geoff led them inside.

Like the tent in the Meadow, a space behind the crates and boxes had been opened. It had a recently created look; the scrape marks on the ground showed where the crates had been.

Geoff stooped over and slid a footlocker out—he opened it with a flourish. He lifted the blanket on top to the side. A deck of cards, and a pile of white poker chips. He grinned wide. "Ready and waiting."

The tail end of a tube was visible under the jumble of chips. *excellent. they have KY on hand.* Tom kept a straight face. "Boys, you are so right! This is perfect." He looked at Geoff with admiration. "Did you pull this off yourself, or just luck out?" *His troop didn't use the tent at all—out of sight, out of mind.*

Geoff smiled with a sly glance. "Well, luck, mostly; but we did move the supplies we needed over to the scoutmaster's shelter. No one ever comes down here."

Tom gave him a magnanimous pat on the back. "Excellent work, my man." He made a show of looking at his watch. He paused ever so briefly and looked at the tablet. "Gentlemen, we only have about two hours and ten minutes until lunch… I suggest we play a little game."

Geoff looked at Jack and gave a whoop. Tom noticed Brian smile… a little too grim. *this is one guy not to piss off. looks like he could press 250, easy. I did that once… but I'm happy at 150. pecs and biceps aren't a way of life.*

Brian grabbed the blanket and shook it open. He handed one corner to Jack, and they spread it out.

Jack looked at Tom briefly and assessed his potential; Geoff's urgings to bring Tom into the club filled the hole this time, maybe—*no way to tell yet if Tom will play along… could just be a country hunk who doesn't know any better. he's plenty sure of himself—when the first shoe comes off, his reaction will tell the story… when that time comes he'll either be in or out. Tom doesn't look like the type to hesitate.*

Tom tore out the schedule sheet and handed Jack back his tablet. He folded the page and tucked it into his shirt pocket. He sat down cross-legged, thus establishing the fourth side of the square.

Geoff reached for the footlocker and pulled it over to his side. He scooped out the chips and put them in a mound in the center. "Everybody gets twenty. Help yourselves." He took out the deck of cards and placed it in front of Brian, who was sitting to his right. He watched Tom take his stash of chips. *yum: I get to sit right across from him. the stack will shrink away very fast… it's hard to wait.*

Tom was annoyed. This position didn't sit well. *pricklebutt doesn't like it.* He chuckled to himself. *pricklebutt. that's a good one; I'll make that the name from now on.* He changed position and sat on his heels. 'thank you,' PB seemed to say. He finished counting out his chips.

Brian took the deck out of its small box. Glancing at Tom, he did a cursory shuffle. The more he looked at Tom the more eager he got. He dealt everyone a single card. "High card picks the dealer." *let's see how he reacts.*

Tom picked up his card. A Jack of Hearts. *whoa! look at the thing! the Jack is a nude body builder.* He laughed and glanced around. "Where did you get these?" He grinned. Three faces smiled back.

"My little secret... glad you like." *that's a good sign. these are good at flushing out prudes. Geoff is sure itching to get going. maybe I shouldn't have made that deal before the meeting this morning.*

Tom glanced at Brian. *maybe I was hasty in judging this guy. not your standard jock. smile is still a bit grim. maybe that doesn't mean anything.*

Geoff put his card in front of him face up. It was a two of diamonds. He didn't mind. He didn't care who dealt. He was being good, too, controlling his eyes. Mostly.

Tom glanced at the other cards... Geoff's body builder was holding up a little card painted with a two of diamonds. *he's winking! these cards are wild.* Tom hadn't seen very many pictures of male nudes, actually... *kind of a turn-on.*

Jack put down a seven of clubs. The club was used as a fig leaf. Tom put his Jack down next. Brian flipped over his nine of spades. That made Tom high man: he could pick the dealer if he didn't want to deal.

"I think Brian's the man for this... he's doing just fine." The gesture pleased Brian, which was good—*besides, it places me strategically at the last card position. sometimes that's all the edge needed to win—or lose the hand, if I want to.* Tom knew what they thought he didn't know: losing is the goal here—no one had mentioned that little detail.

"Five Card Draw, Jacks or Better, Last Man Standing, Deal Moves Left." Brian flipped a chip into the center. "Ante up."

Everyone else put in a chip. Brian shuffled the deck a few times and had Tom do the cut. He dealt the cards. Good manners dictated that everyone wait until all five cards were in front of them, face down. They picked up their hands and sorted them. Brian looked to his left. "Geoff?"

"Nope." It was a terrible hand. He was perfectly happy. Tom's fascination with the cards was most revealing—and encouraging.

"I'll open." Jack flipped in a second chip.

Everyone put in another chip.

"How many?" Brian asked Geoff. Four fingers waved, happily.

Brian put down four cards in front of Geoff. He looked at Jack.

"Two, Brian."

He dealt two cards. "And our guest?"

Tom had too good a hand: three Queens. He'd gotten sidetracked examining the various models on the cards. The "Queens" were also body builders, posing grandly; their capes and crowns had an insignia that showed the suit. They had long eyelashes and lipstick… *gross*. He continued to play it cool. "Two for me, too."

"Dealer takes three. Jack? You opened. Your bet—oh, wait!" Brian stopped. "I forgot to mention something to Tom. Our club rule is a one chip limit on all bets. No raising or bluffing allowed. Okay?"

that's a new one. so much for strategy. "Sure…" *that will slow the game some. I'm not sure that's such a good idea.*

Jack put in a chip, and everyone else followed. Tom's reaction to the rule was very interesting; clearly he understood the implication. His opinion of Tom went up a notch.

"Call." Brian looked at Jack: he laid out three tens. He looked at Tom; out came the three Queens. Geoff whistled. Brian put down a pair of sevens. He looked at Geoff.

Geoff laid each one down separately. It looked like a straight: three, four, five, six… then a Jack. "Nada." Geoff smiled wide.

"Nice try." Tom was amused by Geoff's teasing approach. He was about to scoop up the pile when Brian beat him to it—he raked all but one chip to the side and nudged the one left behind over to Tom.

what's this? Tom looked at Brian, puzzled.

"Last Man Standing. The House takes all the winnings. You're the only one who didn't lose." Brian pointed to the lone chip. "That's to enter the next round with. Okay?"

"Oh… that's a new one on me." Tom thought about it for a second, then saw how brilliant it was: no one would gain a pile of chips. He tilted his head. "Okay." He nodded assent; he could see they were very relieved that he had agreed to this rule. *so, everyone will be showing it all, eventually. these new rules make sense… that's why no bluffing!*

Jack gave Brian a wink. The new recruit was working out well, so far.

Brian shuffled the deck and passed it to Geoff. Geoff had Brian do the cut. "Five Card Stud, Jacks or Better, Last Man Standing." He dealt three cards to each player, followed by two more, face up. Geoff preferred Stud; it had more style.

Tom had a pair of eights showing. Not enough to open. Everyone peeked at his face down cards.

"I can open." Brian put out a chip. Everyone followed. Brian flipped his hole cards: he had a full house—threes and Jacks.

Geoff flipped his cards: three sixes. Jack had nothing. Tom flipped his up: a pair of Kings. It was Brian's game; he kept a chip and pushed the stack to the side. Geoff shuffled the deck and passed it to Jack. He glanced at Tom… obviously Tom was an experienced poker player. *too soon to tell if he knows what's coming.*

"Blackjack!" Jack called out. He had Geoff cut. "One to play, one each hit. Dealer loses a tie. Last Man Standing." He dealt one card face down all around, then one face up. "Tom?"

Tom was to Jack's left; he had a seven showing. "Hit me." Tom put out a second chip. He received a three: that made ten showing. "I'll stand." He studied the cards some more… the lower numbers featured a rear view, mostly. *nice.*

"Brian?" Jack asked.

Brian had an ace showing. *a nine in the hole… I can stand at twenty or play at ten. obviously Tom's in a good position with ten showing. Tom knows how to play the game. better stand… safer that way.* "Stand."

Geoff and Jack looked at him; they were afraid he might have a Blackjack. Fortunately, Jack hadn't said "Jackpot Rule." The whole game could be stopped right here—on the first round that would be a disaster with someone new in the game.

Tom saw the strange look on their faces. *there's something I don't know. should I ask? nah. you'll find out eventually… keep your cool.*

Geoff had a four showing; he put out a chip. "Hit." He was dealt another four. He faked a frown, and flipped in another chip. "Hit me." This time he got a two. "Gaar!" Eight showing. He had to hit if he had under nine in the hole. He bowed his head and looked at Jack with a have pity on me grimace. "Hit me." He flipped in another chip. This one was a seven. In regular poker this could be nice. "Stand," he said, finally. It had cost him four chips! He wiggled his butt in delight.

Jack had a six showing. The dealer had to show first, so he flipped over his hole card: it was a King. He put in a chip and dealt himself another King. Bust.

Tom flipped over his hole card. He had a ten. Twenty points.

Brian had an Ace showing. He flipped over his nine in the hole— twenty: he and Tom had tied.

Geoff looked up to the roof and flipped over his hole card. Five. Twenty-two was a bust.

"What's the rule on a tie?" *whoa...* Tom just noticed: Brian's Ace of Diamonds had a hard-on!

"Playoff, or cut for high card." A playoff would speed up the end of the game. "A cut costs a chip, a playoff costs the same as a regular game."

Tom saw what had happened to Geoff. It would cost him his lead, but it was the least dangerous way: "I'll cut. Okay with you?"

Brian nodded yes. Jack put the deck in the center. They each put in a chip. Tom cut an eight. Brian cut a Queen; he smiled and took both chips.

"Huh?"

"One for the cut, one for the win." Brian grinned wide. He had taken the lead.

Jack shuffled the cards and passed them to Tom.

Tom asked Jack to make the cut. "Here goes. Five Card, No Draw..." he paused to see if they would remind him about the Last Man; their look indicated they would, more than likely. "Last Man Standing." He liked the sudden death aspect of no draw... only what was dealt could be used. He dealt the cards with a flourish, snapping each one by the corner. His grin was infectious. It seemed odd to not be able to bluff these guys out of their stash.

Each put a chip in the center and looked at his hand. Since Tom had not said Jacks or Better, no one had to open.

Brian was first. Down they came: 7, 6, 3, 3, J. A pair of threes.

Geoff was second: 9, J, 6, J, K. A pair of Jacks.

Jack was next: 7, 4, K, 8, A. Zero.

Tom was last. "Drum roll, please." 2, 4, J, 7, J. Another pair of Jacks!

Hmm." Brian frowned. "You're good at that."

"Sorry. Cut?" he asked Geoff. Geoff nodded. Tom cut a Queen. Geoff got an eight. Tom took his two chips and pushed the pile over to Brian.

"Rise and Report, round one results are in." Brian counted his remaining chips. "Fourteen." He was ahead—or behind, actually.

Geoff counted his. "Eight." He did a pretend sob.

"Eleven." Jack chuckled. *Geoff always lightens up the game.*

Tom saw the shrewdness of this. *I will steal this system, for sure.* "Twelve." Geoff will be the first to undress. *suits me just fine. I'll stay cool to the end. what I don't know is the action rules. prickle B keeps telling me there's a boundary still in effect. the front side is in service, though.* He squirmed for comfort; *where can I find a deck of cards like this?*

Brian shuffled the deck and called out: "Five Card Draw, Jacks or Better, Last Man Standing." That was his favorite game.

The second round went much as the first had, with a few close calls. At the end of Jack's third deal, it was clear what would happen during Tom's next deal: Geoff only had one chip left. Tom took the deck with great interest. All of them would be down to threads very soon. He saw no reason to dally any longer.

"Blackjack, again!" This had proven to be the most costly of all the games, and Tom wanted to speed things up. "One to play, one each hit, Last Man Standing!" He placed a card face down in front of everyone with definite pleasure in the snap. His second card, face up, he put down with delicate tender care. The others loved it.

Geoff started to squirm. He could hardly wait to shed his clothes. Tom didn't pick Blackjack by chance. *he isn't as green as he seems.*

Everyone put out a chip. For Geoff, it was the last.

Brian had a six showing. He put out a chip. "Hit me." A seven. "Stand." He watched Tom closely out of the corner of his eye... *Geoff will have to start the strip in this hand. how will Tom react?*

Geoff had a nine showing. He took off his right shoe, and put it in the center. "Hit me." A two. He wiggled happily, and took off his other shoe. "Hit me." A three— *this is my game!* He took off a sock. "Hit me!" He got a six this time. "Stand."

Tom pretended not to notice their intense look at him when Geoff was the first to take something off. He wanted to keep them guessing whether or not he understood what was going to happen, eventually. He reacted as if Geoff's articles of clothing were just another plastic chip. He pretended to be clueless. *I'll play poker as if I plan to win, and be the last man standing. I can sport a poker face as well as anyone.*

Geoff was as pleased as he could be: *Tom didn't bat an eyelash when I started taking things off.* That could only mean that he knew the score—the poker face gave him away. *ooo. I can hardly wait. now Brian has to follow through with his promise;* Geoff glanced across to Tom's crotch again. No changes yet...

Jack had a King showing. He put out his last chip. "Hit." Tom dealt him a five. "Stand!" He glanced at Tom again. *what a cool customer! he must know what's up now. I'm beginning to share Geoff's enthusiasm for the new recruit... looks like Brian is happy too.*

Tom had an eight showing. He put out a chip. That left one in his stack. "Dealer Hits." It was a four. In went his last chip, finally. "Hit." It was a five. "Dealer stands." He glanced at the growing pile of chips and clothing between Brian and Geoff. *my hunch was right—Geoff's plan all along has been to lose the fastest. I don't mind.*

Brian flipped over his hole card. It was a nine: twenty-two. "Bust. He glanced over—that was Tom's last chip. *will he be this cool in the next hand? he'll have to start taking off things too. he must have figured that out by now.*

Geoff turned over his hole card: a deuce. Twenty-two: "Bust!" he said cheerfully. He resisted the temptation to bat his eyelashes at Tom; he was certain that Tom knew what was coming up. He'd seen a few glances that told him that Tom was definitely interested.

Jack turned over a five. "Twenty!" *I might win this hand.*

Tom turned over his hole card: a five. "Bust; twenty three."

Brian made the announcement as he scooped the pile to the side, clothes and all. He tossed Jack his win chip. "Rise and Report, round three results are in." He counted his chips. "Two."

"Minus three." Geoff gave a pretend sad slump to the side.

"Zero." Jack was not unhappy. He was ready for the game to finish.

"Ditto for me. Zero." Tom got a kick out of Geoff's clowning. *this is it: either they declare Brian winner—he still has two chips left—or not. he is the Last Man Standing.* Tom passed him the deck to see what would happen.

Brian shuffled the deck three times, and put it in front of Tom to make the cut.

Now Tom knew for sure— *this is going where I thought, all right.* He was pleased at their cool. He could match it. As the game went on to the fourth round, Tom was intrigued—how would they handle the first "action" ante? The fact that it would be Geoff was **much** to his liking. *the undressing parade is going to be nice.* He suspected, no—he *knew* they were all waiting to see his particulars. *I will do my best to please. now: to watch Geoff take it all off.*

Brian made his usual call for Five Card Draw. He put in a chip; Geoff put in his other sock. Tom and Jack each would need to put in a shoe.

A pause was required; Tom had to shift around so that he could take off a shoe. He noticed how silent it had become; he kept cool.

Geoff licked his lips in anticipation; he envied the enjoyment Tom's pants must be having, restraining that enormous package. It was clear that Tom was going to shed them, and soon. *poor pants...*

"I can open." Tom stopped to remove his other shoe. "Three cards." He had a pair of Kings.

Brian spent his last chip, and took two cards. He winked at Jack; *the recruit is proving out as good or better than I expected. there's no stopping now!*

Geoff couldn't help himself. it's parade time. With ceremony he removed his kerchief and put it to the side, not in the pile. He unfastened the buttons on his shirt with flair, took the shirt off and folded it neatly and placed it on the pile. "One card, please."

Tom watched Geoff's performance with interest. *why didn't he play the kerchief instead of the shirt? maybe that's another rule or something—maybe playing a kerchief is forbidden. hmm.*

Everyone knew it was too late for Geoff's change in luck to matter any. Jack put in his second shoe and asked for three cards.

It was Tom's call; he flipped over his pair of Kings. His three new cards were worthless. As Brian showed his hand, Tom's glance traveled to Geoff's bare chest. The fine, clear hairless skin was a wonder—it was like ivory, or a pale cream. *must feel like velvet.* He hoped to find out before long. Prickle B seemed pleased as well; to gaze any longer was to hazard a premature elevation. He wanted to treat them all to that when the time came. He looked away.

Geoff turned over his two pairs: threes and eights. He rocked his shoulders contentedly. He had caught Tom checking him out.

Jack turned over his pair of aces. Tom's glance at Geoff was predictable. He looked forward to seeing Tom's chest... pecs were his main interest. *Geoff is substandard there.*

Tom observed that no one seemed to care if there was a winner. Brian shuffled the cards and passed the deck to Geoff. *this will be interesting: the dealer is down to his shorts. that means this hand will be the beginning. will Geoff stick with stud?*

"Five Card Draw... Jacks or Better, Last Man Standing." Geoff stood up, took off his shorts, and put them in the center. He did this without a flourish—that would come next.

Jack and Tom each put in a sock, and Brian gave up his first shoe. Geoff dealt.

"Open." Brian put in his other shoe. He glanced at Jack. They had been anticipating this moment: how will the new recruit react to this?

Tom had been waiting for this moment, of course. He tried to appear indifferent.

Geoff stood again and took off his underpants. He extended his hand over the pile and paused a moment. He glanced to see if Tom was paying full attention… a straight face. Geoff wasn't fooled! On to the pile the skivvies went. He was proud that he wasn't getting hard just yet. He moved slowly and gracefully, for effect. He had planned a pirouette, but chickened out.

Jack put in a second sock.

Tom noted Jack's disinterest in Geoff's particulars. *he knows from before, obviously. they know I have a hunch at least about what's ahead.* He had seen a few eye contacts between them, as if they were telepathically talking about him; placing side bets, probably. He put his second sock onto the pile.

Brian wanted two new cards; it cost him his first sock. He glanced over to Tom's lap. *hmm… looks the same down there. it won't stay that way very long.* Geoff dealt him the two cards.

It was Geoff's turn again. He wanted three cards, but he had no clothes remaining. He stood up and took a step to Jack's side. "May I have three cards?"

"Yes, you may," Jack said, with a polite nod.

aha! so that's how they do it. excellent.

Geoff stepped around Jack to Tom's side and stood inches away from his face. "May I have three cards?"

Tom looked at the very nice uncut cock, tantalizingly close to his face. An instant message about developments below arrived; *look away, now!* "Yes, you may." He looked up into Geoff's face. *yikes.* Another buzz. The smile there told him that Geoff had him figured out.

Geoff stepped around Tom's back to face Brian and asked the question. Tom could not resist. He had to look at that butt. *oh, yeah. yeah. think of anything else.*

Geoff sat back down and took three cards. He hummed lightly as he arranged his hand. He'd seen Tom's look. He tilted his head to the left, then to the right, as if he were paying attention to the cards. He had no idea what he had just dealt himself. *oops… I have them upside down.*

Jack took off his kerchief and followed Geoff's routine without the style. His shirt unbuttoning was matter of fact. Everyone watched politely.

"Two, please," he tossed his shirt on top. He turned his gaze to Tom. He kept a good poker face, but he wasn't about to miss the unwrapping of Tom's pectorals.

"Three please." Tom took off his kerchief. Clearly, the hosting trio had been waiting for this—they watched as he folded his kerchief carefully and put it to the side. They made no attempt to hide their interest in the first view of his bare chest. Tom was amused. He pretended to be unaware. The flitting glances were wonderful. He thought he heard Jack hum his approval. His ego liked this.

They went through the formality of showing their cards; everyone knew that for all practical purposes the last hand was about to be played.

Geoff shuffled the deck and passed it to Jack. He forced himself to remain calm. *this is it! Jack will do Blackjack as always. I'll get a peek, too, before the end.* Unconsciously he squirmed in anticipation.

Brian moved the pile of clothing off to the mound at his side. He glanced at Geoff: he gave a wink. *Geoff is more fun than usual today.*

Jack put the deck in front of Tom for the cut. "Don't you just love Blackjack?" he looked at him as if he were in on the conspiracy. "Last Man Standing, Jackpot Rule Applies!" he chuckled wickedly. He got the hole cards down, then the face cards. He and Tom stood and took off their shorts.

Brian tossed in his second sock. *no reason to think Jack hasn't dealt this right.*

Geoff stood. He faced Jack and asked. "May I join the game, please?"

Jack looked at the growing cock and said, "If you are at attention, yes."

He looked at Tom and asked, "May I join the game, please," and smiled demurely. He did not move around as he had before.

Tom looked at Jack. Then he looked at Brian. *I love this!* He looked at Geoff and said, "I'd appreciate it if you were at attention first." He watched the cock reach half-mast. The head poked out slightly. *look away, look away!*

Geoff asked Brian.

"Come to attention, please," Brian ordered.

Geoff began to stroke himself. He became hard in an instant. He smiled, and said, "Thank you all," and sat down.

Jack turned to Tom—there was a glint in his eye.

Tom had a six showing, and a Queen in the hole. "Hit me, please." This was it, at last: he stood and took off his underpants.

too bad... I'm about ten percent up. A muted 'Oh, my god' came from each side, punctuated by a gleeful giggle from Geoff. Tom moved slowly so they could enjoy the early stages of his cock growing... *I'll be hard before the next ante.* Jack dealt him a deuce. "Stand." His cock seemed to think it had just been given a command... it moved upward unassisted. Tom was particularly pleased with the appreciation he saw in Geoff's wide-eyed stare. Geoff looked away, then risked another glance and got caught. He smiled back.

Brian flipped over his hole card dramatically. "Blackjack!" The Ace of Hearts had been hiding under the Jack of Clubs. He grinned fiendishly.

Geoff and Jack applauded cheerfully.

Tom did not understand what had just happened. He looked around—*why are they all so happy?* "What?!"

"Jackpot Rules," Jack gave Tom a friendly tap on the knee. "Whoever gets a blackjack gets to end the deals and order punishments." They laughed merrily.

Tom frowned. *punishments?*

"Don't sweat it—you'll see." Tom had not seen him deal from the bottom of the deck, of course. Their plan had worked perfectly.

Brian had been enjoying Tom's confusion and discomfort. *better make my game call now or risk fouling everything up.* "The Judge says that first, the Club must officially welcome its new member to the Game."

Brian stood and reached out for Tom's hands; he pulled him to a standing position... he knelt down on one knee in front. Geoff and Jack stepped around behind Brian in a line. When they were all set, Brian leaned forward: "I hereby invite Tom to become a Member of the Club." He kissed Tom's cock. Reluctantly, he stood and moved aside. While the others greeted the inductee, he removed the rest of his clothes. He was burning hot after being the first to touch The Big One. He had mixed feelings about cutting that deal with Geoff. Now he sort of wanted to be first in line.

Geoff knelt down. He looked in awe at the pulsing masterpiece. "I hereby invite Tom to become a Member of The Club." He wet kissed the head, letting the tip of his tongue go around the rim. This had to be one of the most outstanding examples of manhood he had ever encountered. He looked up at Tom and winked his appreciation.

Tom's knees nearly gave in at the touch of that tongue. *my cock is harder than it's ever been, I swear... this whole thing just keeps getting better.*

Jack knelt down last. He took full advantage of the situation. He raised his right hand and pulled Tom's foreskin down to the base. "I hereby invite Tom to become a member of the Club." He squeezed gently and kissed the tip, puckering his lips with a pulsing massage. He stood and joined the others in a line.

Brian was envious of Jack's daring... *I should have done that.* "Do you accept the invitation to become a member of the Club?"

Tom was overwhelmed, and as horny as he had ever been. "I sure do, boys."

"Club cluster hug!" Brian extended his arms; the trio surrounded Tom and kissed him and each other on the lips. They all had to be sure to hug and kiss everyone and grab a handful of everyone else's buns. It took a little while. They broke off at last, and Brian took the lead again.

"The Judge decrees that the following punishments will be conducted: Brian is to suck Jack off. Jack is to suck Brian off. Tom is to fuck Geoff. Geoff is to stroke himself to the finish, and put the Game to rest. Let the punishment commence!" Brian and Jack went to one side of the blanket and began to do a sixty-nine, one of their favorite things.

Geoff stepped to the footlocker, took out the tube of K-Y and brought it to Tom. He looked into Tom's eyes with lust. His lips twitched, and he raised his eyebrows. He was unable to form words just now. He was certain Tom knew what to do.

Tom accepted the tube. He didn't know why they called this punishment, but he was ready to accept his.

Geoff lay down on his back, lifted up his knees, and spread his legs wide. He held up his arms. *I am so ready!*

'Thank you, Nick...' Tom remembered last night. Nick had given him perfect instruction in what he was about to do. He knelt down, took the cap off the tube, and greased his right forefinger. His left hand grasped the cock in front of him. He pulled down the foreskin and leaned forward to kiss it. It pulsed at his touch, and Tom put his finger to the beautiful, hairless anus that pursed itself. He slipped it in gently, and it grabbed back eagerly. He kissed the cock and pushed his finger in to the first knuckle. He pulled it out part way, and pushed it in farther as he sucked this exotic honey stick in earnest. The aromas were incredible.

Geoff was deliriously happy; he had been fantasizing this ever since he had seen Tom at the lake. *it's even better than I hoped... I want that monster to enter.* He wiggled a little; he was ready for more. Tom didn't need to be this tender about it.

Tom greased the next two fingers; he sensed that Geoff did this a lot, and wanted to speed up the pace. He leaned close again and took Geoff's balls into his mouth. *tasty. nearly hairless... the strands are straight instead of kinky curly.* The texture was exciting. He inserted two fingers in as he rolled the testicles back and forth. He felt his finger hit the prostate. Geoff bucked in ecstatic response. Tom released the balls and took the cock back in his mouth. He pulled on the foreskin gently, and inserted the third finger. The cock pulsed; he lessened the pressure because he didn't want Geoff to get too far along. He removed his fingers and took hold of Geoff's right knee. With his right hand he guided his cock in. It slipped in without argument. It was tight, but muscle tight. It felt glorious. He began to pump.

Geoff felt Tom enter. *wow, it is big.* It didn't hurt, though. He was delighted, because he had expected it to hurt some at first. Tom's prep was superb. *when I get my rhythm going, I know just what to do; I'm going to give Tom the best fuck he's ever had—it feels so fabulous already.* He hummed in pleasure. He reached down for his cock—still hard! Sometimes big guys made him go limp. Not Tom!

Tom leaned forward on his arms and kissed Geoff as he picked up his pace. He went all the way in—and he could feel his balls contact Geoff's butt. He hit the prostate and Geoff responded instantly. It made him constrict; the squeeze around Tom's cock was wonderful. He closed his eyes and concentrated. He followed this pattern and rhythm for some time: it worked perfectly... he had learned just what made Geoff respond, and Geoff had learned how to work with him. Never before had an anus grabbed him so well, and always at the right time. The intensity built gradually, but constantly. His eyes remained closed... he wanted no distractions.

Geoff was in heaven. He hadn't expected Tom to be so skilled! He flexed his thighs subtly to reinforce his hold on Tom's enormous cock as it pulled back... the next thrust was so **powerful**.

Tom took long thrusts, pulling out to the tip, then all the way in. His conscious mind reeled in ecstasy. He grasped Geoff by the shoulders and kissed him hard. Time and place faded... now he was in a strangely familiar place. He tried to find Nick's magic kiss, but it wouldn't appear. His ecstasy was intense, but strangely muddled—he had flashes of being Nick instead of himself as he worked. It was as if he were both on top and below. He broke contact with Geoff's lips—they eroded his concentration.

Tom's cock swelled at every inward thrust. He squeezed his buns together tightly as he drove in. He worked to reestablish the zone he had a moment before... he heard himself grunt. He tensed; his heartbeat was going crazy. His thrusts became hard, sudden, spaced by a brief stop at each end. His concentration was slipping—he increased the pace. He clenched his jaws: *I insist on being obeyed.* His cock head swelled as it slid past the prostate. He shot suddenly! It was huge. He grunted, and stopped breathing for a moment, straining with all his might. Something loosened in his reflexes, and he was able to pump again, and again, and again. He could feel Geoff coming at the same time, his anus squeezing with each of his shots. He was aware of being splashed on his stomach and chest. Tom raised his head and shouted victoriously— "Yah!" He collapsed and rested his head next to Geoff's.

They were drained... unable to move for a moment.

Tom was all the way in still, his cock pulsing. PB was pulsing again too. He had succeeded, but... *I feel like I just won a footrace or something...* He was cheek to cheek. They were still breathing hard. He didn't feel the familiar glow, the gradual easing and wonderful relaxing afterward. He didn't want to open his eyes. He wasn't sure why. Suddenly he thought of Nick. *that's why. ohmygosh...* He felt very bad all of a sudden. *I should be kissing Nick right now.* He felt his cock begin to shrink. He froze in place… he had not planned on this. He was confused. He felt all wrong… sour, or something.

I have to lighten up, somehow. He pulled out and sat up. *I have to clear my head.* He had never had this kind of feeling. It was scary, in a way. But he had to get in control. He shook his head. *what could be wrong, anyway? I just had one of the best fucks in my life. Geoff was fabulous! shape up, Tom!* After a few seconds he was better. *maybe something was wrong with breakfast.* He opened his eyes. *now I'm okay…* now he was ready to look at Geoff. *I can figure things out later.* He wanted these guys to like him, to invite him again. *their club is terrific.* Geoff's eyes are closed. Tom closed his again… *take some deep breaths… get back in shape. I don't want these guys to know anything was wrong.*

Geoff was in a trance. He had not expected it to be quite this good. He had to wrangle a re-match somehow. Tom may just have set a standard no one else could meet. He looked at him at last, as he was sitting above. *Tom is holding me by the knees… I'm so glad he did it this way. most big guys like the doggy position. I like that too, but it leaves the lips and cock out. this is so much better. my butt hole will be buzzing for a day or two at least… I love that.* An hour ago he had been thinking he might have to show Tom what to do. Boy oh boy was that ever wrong. They had both just earned a new notch on their experience belt.

Tom looked at Geoff again. He could tell this was mostly pleasure. No mush. Great. That might qualify him for another. *Nick comes first, though.* He felt much better about this now. He was over whatever it was that had upset him. He looked over at Jack and Brian. He had almost forgotten they even existed. Obviously they had gone all the way, and were happily wrapped in each other's arms. They looked back at him and smiled.

"Welcome to our little club," Brian said.

Somehow this hit Tom in the funny bone. He fell on his side and laughed. He rolled back, knees up, holding his sides, trying to stop. When he calmed, finally, he looked at them. They looked puzzled. He sat up on his heels and held out his arms to them and smiled. He beckoned with his hands. "Come here, you guys, please." He felt better… *I don't know what came over me.*

They approached, eyes wide. He insisted that they bump heads in a close hug. He released them to sit back. He had a few things to say, and to figure out. This game had introduced something to the summer he had not expected. He wasn't sure what it was. This game could become pretty regular. How often did these guys do this? He wasn't used to spending time "playing" with anyone outside of his own troop, for one thing.

6 *new faces at free swimming*

Julian had to find a Swim Buddy when he got to the lake. He didn't have much choice. His plan to practice with Danny had been ruined because of the sunburn; there wasn't time to look for anyone else. He had his sun cream along today with his sketchpad and towel—he certainly didn't want to get a burn like Danny had. He didn't plan to lie around in the sun anyway; getting a tan was not something he cared about, one way or the other. *what will Danny's buns look like when they're tan instead of pink?* Who would ever see them, anyway? *seems silly... must be boring, just lying around in the sun. more interesting to do a sketch or something.*

He looked around... no one else was coming to the lake all by himself yet. Someone was sure to, eventually. *I want to improve my diving and ability to stay underwater. if I work on that a little each swim period, by the end of camp I'll be a lot better. maybe next year I'll be good enough to work on the Swimming merit badge... I have a long way to go; be stupid not to use this opportunity. dummy: you should have gone over to the Wolves and grabbed someone after inspection. that's what I'll do next time, for sure.*

About halfway down the slope he sat on the grass off to the right. *I can see from here if anybody's looking for a Buddy.* This was where he had begun the lake sketch during Certification. He opened his tablet to the drawing he had started out on the canoe dock. *after I do some on that, I'll jot down a few ideas about that skit of Max's for the scrapbook.* That one was not appearing in his mind yet at all, and Nick would ask about it at supper. He giggled happily, recalling the image of Danny's shiny pink butt. *hey—no one is watching; why not start the page of buns while I'm waiting?*

Several Buddy pairs checked in... all from other troops. He watched them undress as well as he could; this is a poor place to sit for that. Their buns were on the wrong side of the cubbyholes.

okay, then; time to work on the dock sketch. how am I going to add all the swimmers? they'll have to be in the water. that way I won't have to worry about the scrapbook having nudes in it—that's probably a no-no. too many moms will be looking at this... Besides, he'd never even tried to draw a cock. They'd have to be pretty teeny in this drawing, but still... it wouldn't be a good idea. *I'll just put bathing suits on everyone that's out of the water.*

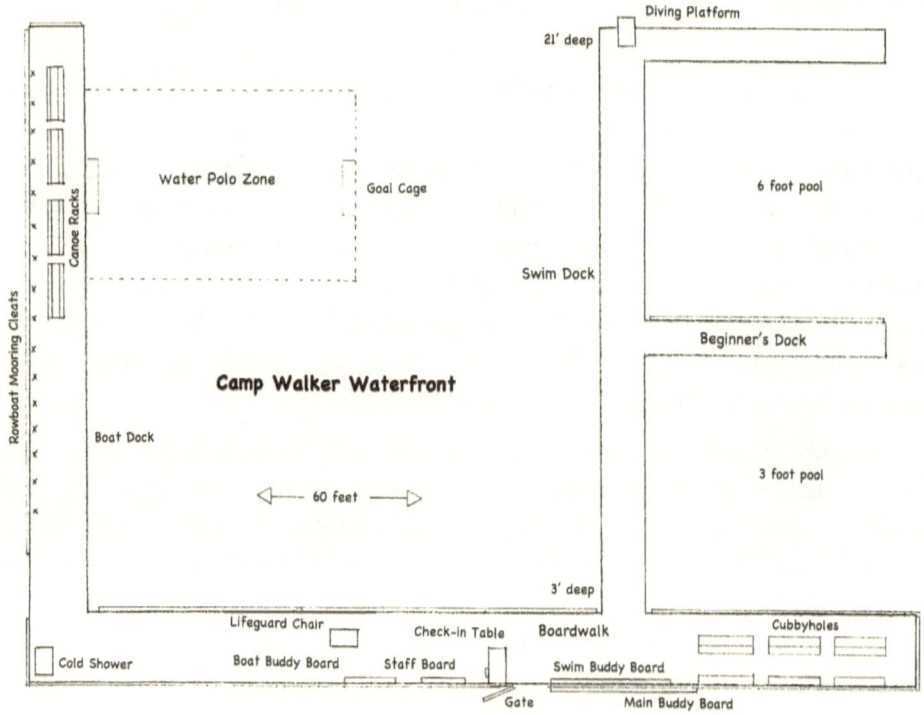

oh-oh. the top line... I didn't pay attention to what it looks like up slope behind where I'm sitting. probably just a row of trees... I'll have to go out on the dock again and add that in.

Julian sketched for a while; he was happy with his progress. The sun was annoying though. *too bad there isn't any shade around here.* The glare on the page made his eyes tired.

—⊸m⊷—

Bruce felt much better. The Trading Post had just what he needed after such a strenuous workout in the Swim Class. *these cheese crackers with peanut butter in between are so good. mmm...* he took itty bitty bites... *gotta make this last.* He was a good boy and only bought one package... at home he'd have two or three as well as a root beer. *I could have gotten some Oreos... but I'm supposed to lose a few pounds while I'm at camp.* It made sense to cut back some. Cutting back was hard though... he wanted another one already. *anyway, if I'm going to swim, a full tummy is a bad idea. luckily I'm closer to the lake now.* It was too much trouble to go back up there to buy another one. And, he enjoyed feeling virtuous.

Bruce was disappointed, but not discouraged. Nobody in the Badgers wanted to be his Swim Buddy this morning. He couldn't blame them. Why should they have to practice in the F when they could be out in the lake? No one in swim class wanted to stay and practice either. After class Mr. Smith said to ask Mr. Stafford at the check in table. Sometimes he could help find someone.

oh, look! there's Julian... he comes by mornings on the inspection. maybe he needs a Swim Buddy t'day. "Hi!"

Julian looked up. He blushed; he and Nick had joked about Bruce's weight yesterday at the Lifesaving Merit Badge test. "Hi, Bruce!"

Bruce sat down. *Julian is nice and friendly.* "I saw you yesterday. I got rescued, too!"

"Wow!" Julian pretended he didn't know; he wanted to make it up to Bruce. "Did you have as much fun as I did?"

"I dunno. It was okay. I heard they thought you drowned."

Julian laughed. "Yeah! They pulled me out of the water and started to pump the water out!" He shook his head. "It tickled so much it made me laugh."

"You were faking it?" Bruce was impressed.

"Well, sure! That's what they told us to do, remember?"Julian shrugged. "The instructor told me I ought to be an actor."

"Huh." Bruce was glad they didn't pull him out of the water. Most of the time he ignored his weight problem; he was aware his stomach looked pretty big when he was out of the lake. He'd just as soon leave his clothes on, but his dad had laid down the law. He had to get the Swimming Merit Badge or else!

"How long can you stay under water?" Julian just realized that Bruce might want to swim. He might go in as a Buddy today.

"I don't know. I've never timed it, I guess. I'm in Beginning. I'm still working on getting my First Class." Bruce's hair was still damp from his morning class. His fingertips weren't still all wrinkled up at least.

"Maybe we can go in and work together. I'm trying to get good enough to start work on the merit badge. I bet we could help each other out." He could make up for yesterday by helping Bruce! Besides, it would be nice to know him as a person.

"Would you?" Bruce was overjoyed. *I'll get to practice after all. and Julian is a Flaming Arrow, too!*

Seeing Bruce's face just now made Julian very happy. *this will be fun and good at the same time.* He stood and stretched out his left hand. "Put 'er there, Buddy!" *Bruce has dimples when he grins wide.*

Bruce gave Julian the Troop Shake. They went to the board and got their badges. Bruce showed Julian his Buddy Badge. The bottom was white.

Julian was surprised. *it isn't colored blue... oh, yeah. he said he was still a beginner. how come they let him be in the rescue group yesterday?*

Leonard looked up at the two scouts whose badges had just been placed before him. The names were familiar, but... He was startled. He was looking at opposites in an odd way—no, not Beauty and the Beast, but something like that. *the blond is the gorgeous kid I met yesterday! in a year or two, woof! the round one, well...* he'd hold his tongue. "I'm trying to remember you two. You're both new this year, right?"

Julian and Bruce nodded yes.

I know these names! frustrating. wait. the fat one was one of the rescues yesterday! "I remember! You two got rescued yesterday, right?"

Julian and Bruce nodded again. "I was number eight."

Leonard remembered in an instant! "Julian! Of course! Silly me. You talked to me yesterday, didn't you?"

"Yeah. About the shower." Julian looked at Leonard's hands; *he has long fingers. those would be interesting to draw.*

this is the lovely that got pulled onto the deck. buns of Adonis! This kid is like a Studebaker. he's gorgeous front and rear! coming and going!

Leonard chuckled at his unspoken witticism. *I will enjoy the next few minutes a great deal.* "Well boys, have a good splash!" He wrote their names down and handed their Buddy badges back.

"Thanks. Leonard." *I like Leonard. he seems to care about all the swimmers. the Archery counselor could stand a lesson or two from Leonard.*

Leonard gave his standard wink, and watched with great appreciation the hanging of the Badges on the west Buddy Board. *mmm. and now, the cubbyhole ritual. mercy, what eyes that boy has—the lashes look like a mascara advertisement.*

Julian found a cubbyhole for his clothes and undressed. He picked one up toward the top; he could keep his notepad and things safer from all the stray drops of water that flew around. He dabbed some sun cream on his nose and forehead and his shoulders. "Say, Bruce—do you want any sun cream?" He spread it outward.

Bruce looked over at Julian. It looked like he was putting on some white war paint. "Thanks, Julian!" He stepped over... *Julian is sure a nice guy.*

"Stand still; I'm good at this!" Julian rubbed cream on Bruce's face, then went behind and did the back of his neck and shoulders. "I'm just in time back here. Your neck is a little pink." Those are the areas where Danny was burned the worst—and the buns. Julian glanced down... *oo-ee:* Bruce's really white buns. Julian did not want to deal with those especially. Bruce isn't going to be lying around in the sun anyway. "There." *I like my tube better than Danny's bottle. it isn't runny and hard to control.* He screwed the cap on and tucked it into the cubbyhole.

Bruce was surprised at how friendly and nice Julian was. He didn't know anybody outside his patrol besides Tad over at Zebra. *this is a lucky day!*

"I want to practice some on my diving. What about you?"

"I could do that... I need to practice my distance. I'm supposed to practice over inside the F, actually." He needed to report to Mr. Smith about putting in some extra time, like he'd promised.

"Let's go over there, then!" They walked out on the F dock. It wasn't nearly as crowded today, at least. Julian looked out into the middle of the F. Half a dozen scouts were doing laps between the prongs of the F. "Hey, these guys must be doing that, too."

"Yeah. At Certification that's what they told us to do. When we can swim back and forth six times, they'll give the distance rating." Because he was trying so hard in the morning class, Mr. Smith had let him volunteer to be rescued yesterday—he only had to swim out a few yards to his rescue area. Mr. Smith was there in person, running the tests on this half of the boardwalk.

Julian thought about asking the Lifeguard if he could just practice in the F with Bruce. *nah. the other side would be best overall, even if it is pretty full.* "I know: I'll practice over there just on the other side. When they blow the whistle, that's where to look for me."

"Okay. I'll stay close to this end. Thanks, Julian." Bruce stepped to the edge. He did his usual studied squat and jumped forward.

> > ***ka-whumpp-ssh!*** < <

Julian would always remember what he had just seen. Bruce did a perfect cannonball. It was as impressive as it was funny. The sound! The splash shot straight up into the air. Bruce surfaced and Julian gave him a "perfect" gesture. *Bruce is fun to watch, but...* He turned to the other side of the dock; the sight of Bruce's buns stuck in his mind. He controlled the urge to laugh... *I just saw one end of the S/B scale!* That did it... he held his left hand over his mouth to muffle the urge to laugh and quickly sat down on the opposite edge of the dock.

It took a minute to calm down. *well, you said you wanted to study buns, smartypants!* He didn't want to attract attention, but it was **funny!** At last he was ready to move on. *so, what am I going to do?* Buns were put to the side for the present. He didn't want to bust out laughing all the time. He looked at the sky... the sun was well overhead now; *it must be somewhere between 10:30 and 11. I'll swim for an hour, and then sketch until the lunch whistle.* Julian watched a few others diving off the edge. *I'll follow their example—at first, anyway.*

Some pinched their nostrils with a finger and dove with one arm extended. A couple of guys had a pair of nose plugs. Others just dove as is. *that would be best, if I can.* At the pool he always got water up his nose, so he liked to pinch it shut. That was why he always did a one arm dive or the cannonball. *after watching Bruce, I'll concede there—that is Bruce's dive! I'll start with the way Tom showed me yesterday: both hands, pointed outward. I didn't get water up the nose yesterday. I'll count my time under water, too.* He stepped to the edge—the way was clear, so he took a deep breath and dove.

He opened his eyes almost at once; he didn't want to bump into anyone, so he turned outward. *water is colder all of a sudden... I must be farther out than I thought. maybe I should have ducked under that cold rinse. five. I keep forgetting to do that. it's supposed to keep you from being shocked when you hit cold water.* As he slowed he started to kick, then fan his arms down to his sides. *the instructor said yesterday that my arm movement is good. ten; I seem to be in better shape today.* He worked his arms again and again... *remember, legs kick better if you keep your knees straight. fifteen; I can go farther, I just know; he stroked again. twenty!* He felt the need, so he headed up. He burst up on the surface: "Twenty-eight!" No one close by was impressed. He turned around to see how far he had swum. Not bad. That jump must have helped a lot. It had to be over thirty feet. He was quite pleased with his start. *I'll do ten of these.*

The Buddy whistle blew just as he climbed out of the water. He looked over for Bruce. He was just approaching the inside arm of the F. When he stopped Julian waved at him. Bruce smiled and waved back. The lifeguard gave him a strange look.

"Hi... that's my Buddy over there." Julian pointed to Bruce. The Lifeguard nodded and moved along toward the end of the dock. Julian saw him signal to the chair; after the three others did that, the all's well signal blew. Julian gave the okay sign to Bruce, and stepped back to the other side. *here goes.* He extended his arms again. *that last one went well, and I didn't get any water up my nose, either. keeping my chin down must be why—the trouble is I can't see very far ahead when I do that. I don't want to bump into anyone.*

After six dives Julian's arms and legs complained too much. But he had gotten up to thirty seconds! He sat on the edge of the dock for a while, contented. He surveyed the crowd... *maybe I can spot some of the guys from Troop 9. funny... they must be around. I should see a Wolf, at least,*

or Nick, or Tom. ah, over at the far side of the shallow area near the canoe dock... it's Doug and another guy. are they practicing something? Doug is holding a stopwatch. huh... the other guy just popped out of the water and took the watch. Doug ducked under the water; who is that guy? I know: they're practicing holding their breath! what a great idea. maybe I could join them; I don't know anybody who has a stopwatch. He watched them for a while. *looks like they're having fun. maybe I better wait. don't want to just barge in... I don't know them personally. besides, I should keep close to where Bruce is practicing.*

oh, yeah—there were others here; they just looked different with their hair all wet, bobbing up and down in the lake. Casey and Robin were racing... headed out to the platform. *looks like Robin is gaining. yep...* Robin climbed up the ladder first. *they're going to rest up on the platform. hmm... maybe I'll swim out there this afternoon... be good a place to sketch the F dock from if I could get there with a dry tablet. kind of far off though...* The water was open in front of him now. *well, back to practice.*

—✺—

Robin swam as hard as he could... *maybe this time I can beat Casey. we're almost neck and neck...* the platform was just ahead... *blast! so close.* Casey won by about five seconds. *he's always lucky. at least I'll be first up the ladder.*

"Man, you are better than I thought!" Casey did not expect to work for it... saw Robin catching up just in the nick of time. This surprised Casey. After all, he had been one of the fastest in the Swimming merit badge class.

"Hey, if that little red-haired kid hadn't popped up out of nowhere, you'd never have caught up with me!" Robin's jump-off had been spoiled; *I'll demand a rematch tomorrow.*

They rested on the platform and caught their breath. They hadn't decided whether or not to race back. It was nice out here in the sun. They'd probably just hang out for a while, since they had the platform to themselves right now.

"So, how's it going so far?" Casey was curious... maybe Robin was interested in fooling around a little.

"Rowing will be a breeze. I'm not sure about Calvin, however." Robin hated to be snotty, but Calvin is not that enjoyable to look at for over an hour every day of the week.

"He's a Panther, isn't he?" *always has a load of stuff in his pockets. so, Robin isn't horny. that's okay. he paid his blackjack bill off very nicely yesterday.* Casey was four games up when the bus arrived at camp.

"Yeah. I feel sort of sorry for him… he's low man on the totem pole over there. Mark asked me to sort of help out… he couldn't get anyone else to partner with him in the Rowing badge. He's a nice enough guy… really big on his rifle range stuff." Rifles were something Robin wanted nothing to do with. Fishing with Grampa Wilson was one thing. Hunting was another.

"But zero looks." Casey nodded his head. The acne alone was enough to turn him off… not to mention the oddball arms and knees. *what could a guy like that do, sex-wise? play in the dark, what else?* Casey felt lucky all of a sudden. He looked over at Robin. *Robin is about the best friend anybody could want. he's about as opposite to Calvin as he could be. good looking, real good to "play" with, too—day or night.*

Casey Snyder and Robin Simmons had become good friends during the past year. It started by accident; Robin had seen Casey walking "that way" one afternoon an hour or so after school. He was coming from the direction of Hayden Park. Since they were both in Troop Nine, Robin figured that had to mean one thing: he was a fellow fuckee. He hurried to catch up.

"Hey, Casey."

Casey turned slightly and sort of smiled. "Hi, Robin." He looked down, embarrassed. Nobody knew about him and Tom, and he didn't want anybody to, either. This was about the fourth time, and it was a bad one for some reason. The time before had been pretty good.

Robin looked at him sympathetically. He wasn't positive, but it seemed to fit. He'd been here himself, not that long ago… he had to ask about it just right. "So, was Big Tom a little rough today?" He looked for the reaction. It was instant.

"How..." Casey started, shocked. How could Robin know what had just taken place? Must be... he looked into a knowing and very sympathetic face. He had to stop a minute. Besides, his butt hurt, and he wanted to rest up, anyway.

"Well, he's done that to me too, more than once." He looked at Casey sympathetically. "How long ago?"

"Ten minutes or so." He wasn't sure how much to say; the idea that Robin even knew about this was mind blowing enough.

"Listen. You want to come over to my house? I've got some cream that will really help. Besides, we should talk about this anyway."

They became very close friends after that. They learned how to elude Tom, and how to have a lot of fun on their own. They didn't think of themselves as steadies, but for most purposes they were. They weren't interested in playing the field. Each had had a couple chances to play, and did. That was okay; if it came their way, they wouldn't run away automatically. And they certainly didn't need Tom's little side trips into the woods. By sticking together, they'd brought that to a halt. Tom only jumped a yummy butt who was all alone.

Robin looked at Casey again. It was so easy to take his friendship for granted; being with him was like being with a brother, or a cousin. It was lucky they had so much in common. "How's Indian Legends?" Robin had considered signing up for that originally, but Chuck had talked him into Pioneering.

"I think it will be a good one... the instructor is from Atlanta. I think maybe he's a teacher or something. Seems real smart." Casey had expected an advanced Cub Scout course. No such deal. "It's a lot different than the stuff we used to do." He was just as glad. He liked a challenge. "You ready to race back?"

Robin looked toward the boardwalk. It was pretty crowded. "Nah... let's hang here a while longer." He wanted a rematch when he was really fresh.

7   *free swimming continues*

Julian pulled himself onto the dock. He needed to catch his breath again. That last one went very well, except at the very end. He had to pull up early because a swimmer cut across his path unexpectedly. He looked over to the six-foot pool— *Bruce is still slaving away... good for him.* He sat on the edge and surveyed the area. *not as busy as yesterday, but crowded enough.* He glanced at Bruce again... *maybe I should do a sketch of the F with some swimmers—*

Suddenly, Julian felt a tug on his left foot. He looked down and up came Nick with a whoosh and a laugh.

"I chickened out!" Nick laughed, a little out of breath. "I was gonna pull you in by the feet." He lifted himself out of the water and sat next to Julian on the edge.

Julian laughed. "I'm glad you didn't." *what luck! maybe Nick can advise me on how to hold my breath longer.*

"I wondered why you didn't say hello. You walked right by me."

Julian frowned. "Sorry, I didn't see you. Were you on the dock someplace?"

Nick chuckled. "Nope." He was bursting with pride, and couldn't hold it in any longer. "You had to look up to see me." He pointed to the lifeguard chair.

I don't get it. Nick was pointing over to the boardwalk. *up? what is up?* He looked at Nick and shrugged.

"In the chair! You walked right under me!"

Julian looked at the lifeguard chair. There were two lifeguards up there. He frowned and tilted his head. "But..."

"He just took over from me. I just finished my first training session as a lifeguard, thanks to you! I even got to blow the Buddy Whistle!"

"Really?" Julian grinned wide.

"Yeah! Everyone who qualified for the Lifesaving merit badge yesterday got assigned; we have to spend half an hour training with the regular guy. That way, if they need us, we know what to do! I could have two duty periods scheduled before camp is over. They're trying to even it out so that it doesn't become a regular job for anybody. Thanks to Mark. He raised a stink about it, I guess."

"So did Jay make it too?"

"Yeah, he did. Tugging Bruce along paid off!" They both laughed, recalling yesterday. They'd watched Jay bring Bruce in after the third rescue. It looked like work.

"Listen, I came in with Bruce." Julian felt guilty for laughing. "He's really nice, you know. We shouldn't make fun. He probably can't help it."

"Yeah, you're right. How far can he swim?"

"About two laps, I think. He said he has to get up to six over there to get the distance rating."

Nick had watched Julian and Bruce walk out the F dock. Julian's buns were half the size of Bruce's: he had seen them side by side. Julian's buns were award winners, for sure. He was **really** glad Tom was busy elsewhere this morning.

Talking about Bruce reminded Julian; he had not been looking at buns at all. They were all in the water, or too far away to see very well. He thought briefly… it would be okay to ask Nick; Danny said that he and Tom were—what did he say? Into boys? He took that to mean that they enjoyed playing around with each other. A question about buns wouldn't embarrass him, probably.

"Nick?"

"Yeah?"

"I've been wondering about something." Julian paused. "You remember, yesterday, you said I had choice buns?"

Just then the Buddy Whistle blew. The arm raising routine began. Nick raised both arms and joined his hands. That signaled that he was alone with permission. He was grateful for a chance to think about this while the lifeguards checked. Maybe he could figure out a way to change the subject. He was sorry he had made that comment yesterday. He glanced over and saw Bruce merrily waving an arm. *what can I do to divert Julian's attention? I didn't expect the subject to come up...* Nothing came to mind... *blast.* The all-clear whistle sounded—*too late. maybe Julian's mind has moved elsewhere.*

"Umm..." Julian paused. He sensed that Nick was reluctant to discuss the topic. *hmm.* He crossed his arms. *this time I want an answer.* "Choice?"

Nick blushed. He hadn't meant to spook Julian. "Yep. I said that. It's a true statement. Sorry, not my fault." *maybe making light of it will take the edge off.*

"Well, maybe. But I want to know what that **means**, really. I look around here at all these buns," he laughed at how silly that sounded. "I mean I never thought about that before." He paused. He wanted some of Nick's expertise. "So, I wondered, maybe, if you could help me out a little."

Nick looked at Julian. What an odd turn. Why in the world would Julian give a hoot about buns? Had Tom gotten to him after all?

Julian looked at him. "I mean, some time, could you show me others who you think are 'choice'?"

"Show you?" Nick laughed

"No, no, silly. Just point them out if you think of it. Maybe you could think of somebody else, you know, off the top of your head. I'd like to know a little better about it is all. I never thought about it before yesterday. It's probably sort of cool; I never see them myself, you know. They're back there," he chuckled and reached behind to poke his left cheek. "What's so choice, anyway?"

Nick was amazed. *the kid is so pristine. where has he been all his life?* This reconfirmed his intent to keep Tom clean away. Julian was simply curious. Nick felt a sense of responsibility; but this is something he didn't know about— *I don't have a younger brother. try your best... steer clear of sex talk.*

"Hmm. I can't say I'm an expert, you know. But I can give you my opinion, I guess." *how do I do this... it would be better to avoid topics like this with Julian... I hope this isn't a mistake.*

Julian grinned; he wanted to know if Nick thought Mark had choice buns. Or Danny. He looked at Nick eagerly.

"Lessee, now. I'd have to say Tony Johnson has a nice pair."

pair. Julian giggled. *that's funny.*

Nick giggled too. He was glad this had turned light—*that will help. aha!* He just had a thought. *go through Tom's "I got him" list. choice buns are his only thought most of the time.*

"Andy Ashbaugh, there's another; oh! Chris Smith—now he is in your league, for sure," Nick nodded.

Julian didn't know any of these names. "These guys are all in the troop?"

"Yeah, sure." *that's right: Julian has only been in the troop a little over year; of course he wouldn't know too many guys.* "I'll point them out to you some time—maybe tonight, at the campfire!"

"Wow!" *that would be a help.* "Thanks, Nick. I hope you don't think I'm being stupid or anything."

"Nah. Think nothing of it." *change the subject, now!* he commanded himself. "So, tell me about your swimming; you were practicing swimming under water."

"Oh, yeah!" Julian enthused. "I got up to thirty seconds! I'm trying to learn how to hold my breath longer."

Thirty seconds? Nick doubted that... *twenty, maybe. I can help out here.* "You don't need to worry about that to get the merit badge, you know."

"Oh." Julian thought of the stopwatch. "I wonder why Doug is working on it, then." *maybe there's a different badge.*

Nick looked at Julian sharply. "What do you mean?"

Julian pointed over to boat dock. "He has a stopwatch; I was just watching him for a minute. He takes turns timing with that guy. I thought about asking them to help me sometime. I don't have a stopwatch."

Nick looked over. He saw Paul holding a stopwatch. He laughed at once. He knew what they were **really** doing. The stopwatch was not what it seemed.

"What's so funny?" Obviously Nick knew something special.

Nick had to cover for this somehow. Julian wasn't quite ready to find out about those two. He hadn't noticed them when he was in the lifeguard chair, because they were in shallow water by the boat dock. They were playing one of their favorite games. They weren't just holding their breath under the water. They had a game challenge going to see who could come first while they were being sucked under water. Supposedly it took a long time… *I don't remember who told me about that… it was last summer.*

"Nothing. The other guy is Paul from Lynx patrol. But I don't think you should butt in, if you know what I mean." He smiled without thinking. He hadn't expected to see them do their thing in public like this. The lifeguard was looking right over the top of their heads… *he doesn't see a thing. amazing.*

Julian **didn't** know what Nick meant: he made an instant decision. This was the sort of thing that needed a little careful listening and paying attention. *I'll keep an eye out. must be a reason Nick is being mysterious. big kids always did that—they always clam up when I'm around.* He'd learned a few ways to get around that.

Nick looked over at Doug and Paul. "Though, come to think of it, you might want to check **them** out if you get a chance. They both have choice buns." *very choice.* They had driven Tom up the wall once; he did them over two years ago—*the same year Tom pounced on me.* That was back in the seven and a half inch days.

hmm… Julian narrowed his eyes and looked; Paul was holding the stopwatch again. *that's two reasons to keep my eye out for those guys.*

From the left they heard the impact of several feet running on the dock. They turned to look. Tom raced toward them ahead of three other guys. The thundering noise caused everyone to stop and watch. They swept past and dove off the end. They were in a race out to the floating platform.

"I betcha Tom wins." Julian's butt tickled from the vibrating boards. Watching Tom leap off the small diving platform was thrilling. He went farther out than the other guys. It wasn't a contest. Tom beat them by a body length, at least.

"Wow… Those guys are good!" Running like that on the dock was frowned on. Tom might be in trouble for that… the Lifeguards didn't stop them though. Nick glanced around. *they aren't doing anything… huh.*

"Yeah," Julian's mind played back the image of four waving cocks coming at them a minute or two ago. *Tom sure won that one, too.* "Who are those guys?"

"Dunno." Nick watched them horse around on the platform. One of them looked Chinese. "Now there: see that Chinese guy?"

"Yeah," Julian thought he was Japanese.

"When he turns around again, look. He has choice ones, for sure." *Tom would be partial to him... looks like another rival. ask me if I'm surprised.*

Julian focused on the Asian. *huh.* They looked sort of like Danny's... same nifty dents in the sides. *are my dents like that?* He squinted, hoping to see clearer. The Chinese guy was uncircumcised too, but a lot smaller than Tom. *well, duh! everybody's that, I bet.* The cold water had shrunk them all up, including Tom. Julian thought for a second about the sight he saw this morning just before breakfast. *man alive, that's a huge one—even when it's limp.*

Nick watched Julian study the group on the platform. He was curious—he looked down at Julian's crotch. He hadn't paid attention to Julian's equipment before. *hmm... not much to pay attention to. the kid's a typical hairless. not at all ready for the big league, that's for sure. that makes no difference to Tom, though.*

"Too far to see real clear," Julian stopped squinting. "'Cept I can tell some difference between those guys. Tom's are a lot more muscular; so are that other guy's—he looks like a football player or something." *he has major dents, too. but they don't look as nice as the Chinese guy's. not even close. so it isn't just dents.*

"Yeah. He's what they call a **Beefcake**."

Julian laughed. "Beefcake? That's funny!" He tried to make sense out of putting those two words together.

please don't ask me what that means! Nick crossed his fingers.

Julian was about to ask about that word, but he saw the grimace... it was like the one about Doug and his stopwatch. *I better not ask.* Julian knew that if he asked too many stupid questions guys started to think he was a pest. Big guys, older guys, were always like that for some reason. It was a pain in the neck, but he had learned to put up with it. *I'm glad*

Nick is my friend. he's so smart, and knows so much. I won't be a pest, though. I know better than to badger him with stupid questions all the time. he already told about choice buns, sort of. enough for one day, I guess. maybe I can find out about Beefcake from Sid. I wonder if I should ask Mark? I'll put that on my list.

Nick changed the subject. "You want to swim out there?"

Julian thought about it a minute. "Nah." He didn't know why, exactly. Something held him back. He wanted to wait a little. These big guys… well, he wasn't always comfortable being the little kid all the time. He felt a little guilty, maybe a little chicken. *maybe I can get over that by the end of camp. I'd rather swim some more and then do some sketches.* "Maybe later."

Nick was just as glad. *in time I'll find out who those guys are. Tom must have met them this morning at that meeting.* He looked out at the swimmers, then back to the boardwalk; he didn't have anything special in mind. *what to do? nearly thirty minutes until the whistle… no way to tell if Tom is going to stay with those guys or not.* Keeping Julian out of harm's way leapt to the front of his mind.

"So you want to swim?"

"Yeah! I'd like to see how far you can go under water. How 'bout giving me a pointer or two, now that you're the expert and everything."

"You're on. You go first. I'll watch and come along right behind."

They stood on the edge of the dock. Julian took a deep breath, and jumped.

I'll give him a tip or two on his form, for a start. Nick counted to ten and jumped in.

—ᴍᴍ—

Robin and Casey were resting on the platform, not in a hurry to do anything. The sound of a speed swimmer's hands slicing into the water drew their attention. The approaching splashes from several arms swiftly striking the water ended with a pair of hands grasping the platform edge. Tom vaulted himself onto the platform, landing just inches away. They sat back, startled. Three other guys followed up the ladder, one at a time. Tom had just won a race.

"Hey! Good to see you guys." Tom shook the water out of his hair. He grinned wide; he put his hands on his knees and caught his breath. Finding a couple of old favorites out here was a nice surprise.

Casey and Robin made room for the new arrivals. They sat cross-legged. They couldn't very well leave—and Tom seemed very cheerful.

Geoff punched Tom on the arm and laughed. "No fair! You started running first. We didn't stand a chance. I demand a rematch, with a proper start." He wasn't serious—he just wanted to reinforce his position in Tom's universe. There was a lot of time ahead in this camp, and he didn't need a poker game to have a good time with Tom.

Brian and Jack stood beside Tom, hands on knees, catching their breath. They didn't care who won. They were just happy to have found Tom; they were looking forward to having another poker game. They didn't want Geoff to have exclusive rights; finders keepers did not apply.

Tom was delighted to see Casey and Robin. They were ideal candidates for the 'poker club!' It had been a while since he had messed with either of them, but that was okay; he had a healthy sized stable. He wasn't greedy— just horny. Something had happened last night, though, which he had not sorted out yet. He liked Casey and Robin; they would enjoy the poker club experience. He started with a basic introduction.

"Brian, Jack, Geoff… Let me introduce you to a couple of guys from my troop." Tom raised his eyebrows meaningfully. He made certain they saw that. "This is Casey, and this is Robin." He looked at Casey and Robin and gave the same eyebrow message.

Everybody checked out everybody else. Jack was pleased with the view—**especially** the one on the right. Brian was less impressed; he wanted Tom next.

Geoff was at ease and friendly with both—but he was still savoring the event just concluded in his supply tent. It would be a while before he'd want to play again. He wanted to swim some more; he might have a little more flushing to do. *hee-hee.*

Robin was in danger of blushing—Jack had just given him the sexiest double take. He'd been caught checking Jack out—seriously checking.

Casey gave Geoff the eye—he hadn't ever seen one of these guys up close: he looked part Japanese or something. Casey and Robin exchanged glances: they were somewhat surprised. Tom was known for chasing the young bubble butts. These guys are his own age—and there are three of them. They thought of Tom as a one victim at a time kind of guy. Things were improving all the way around, evidently. They looked at each other and shrugged; might as well hang around.

The racers sat down. A rough circle took shape; this simplified the almost casual surveying of crotches: Tom had made being furtive about it pointless.

Jack would have preferred to be in Geoff's spot—that would make checking out the one on the right easier. *very nice indeed.*

Casey and Robin were in danger of showing their potential. They ignored their crotch alarms for now... no one else was on their way out here.

"Brian... has the club ever met with more than four players?"

Brian looked at Jack and Geoff. This question was not expected. He raised his eyebrows. "No, I can't say it has; always three or four." Four was better by far, too. Three ways were never any good; someone always got left out of the act.

Tom looked at Geoff's deep black eyes; his lips made a faint pucker. "Are those all the chips you have?"

That pucker worked a minor miracle. Incredibly, Geoff now had a blinking green light in front. He tipped his head slightly, wondering what Tom was getting at. "Ahh, yes. That's all I have. Eighty chips."

There was a brief silence while Tom calculated. Jack's eyes focused on Robin's biceps... *nicely defined, not bulbous...*

Brian saw what Tom was implying. "Not much point in chips then, is there? They'd be gone at the end of the first hand, almost."

"Hmm. Yeah, but ya gotta have the chips. The suspense is essential." It wouldn't be half as fun if they had to take it all off in the second hand. He thought about it a little. "Any of you good at math?"

Brian gestured to Jack. Jack had been trying to not watch Robin's slowly raising cock, without success. "What do you need?"

"There must be a rule or formula that factors in number of players plus number of chips to open the game. We each had twenty today. It was ideal when you look at it. But if there were six of us, or seven, or even five, it wouldn't work as well."

"That's **right**, Tom." Jack pondered for a moment. "We never had to face that one." *that's a good point: when we had a threesome, there were too many chips. it takes forever to get to the action. is it a calculus problem, or what, exactly?*

Casey and Robin had a pretty good hunch that what these guys were talking about was going to be a good time. Given the situation they now found themselves in, they stayed tuned. They exchanged grins. They had gotten hard. Couldn't be helped. They could see that the other three and Tom were on the way to join the upstanding.

A ragged, sparse sideburn was developing in front of Jack's right ear. Robin was glad it hadn't been shaved. The mole on the right cheek looked exotic. He wanted to touch it. He was getting seriously turned on.

"I could use a calculator; or a pencil and paper at least." Jack frowned. He didn't want to deal with this right now, actually. *the yummy sitting diagonally to my right is vastly more interesting.* "Okay. Let's try this out for size: Each player gets a chip for each hand—let's say three hands. Each player gets a chip for the number of players in the game. If there are four players, that means everyone starts with seven. That means thirteen to bet with, if there are four. Everyone has twenty. If you have six players, you have to add two more for the number in the game; that means twenty two chips, right?" Jack was confused… embarrassed by his clumsy calculation. His mind was distracted by the tugging in his stomach—he wanted to check Robin… *must be hard by now.*

Brian and Geoff thought about it. It seemed like too few.

Tom could see that Jack was in a muddle. "What about this: everybody has five chips for the number of people in the game. Three players would be fifteen, four players twenty. Five players twenty five, six players, thirty."

They pondered that briefly.

"I believe you're right." Jack nodded, resisting the urge to look across at Robin. "You need the extras to hold out long enough. You'd never get everyone around twice, otherwise. You might not be able to go with the Jackpot Rule, either." He understood what Tom was up to— figuring out how to include these guys in the next game. *outstanding!*

He sensed Robin watching him—his peripheral view tantalized, tempted, teased. It was making him grow hard.

"Guess there's only one way to tell." Geoff raised his eyebrows. He was starting to swell. Casey looked sort of tasty.

Brian was delighted: Tom was engineering the next game. *my turn with Tom is next.* "I may be able to come up with some."

"We're gonna need what, another… wait a minute. That can't be right…" Jack scratched his head. "Another hundred chips?" They looked at him. "Well, figure it out: four times five is twenty, and four times twenty is eighty. That's what we have now."

Robin wasn't interested in the details being discussed by these guys, but he was glad they were busy—it made it possible to study Jack more closely. *mmm… his eyes. hazel eyes… exciting.*

Jack continued, "Six times five is thirty, and six times thirty is a hundred eighty. We'll need a hundred more chips, right?" It sounded right. But why would adding half their number more than double the total pot? Jack looked over at Robin, ostensibly to check his opinion on all this. He felt a rush… Robin was staring right at him. *maybe, just maybe, we'll be playing poker together.*

"I'll check." Brian wanted to guarantee this new session. "You guys check too."

Tom was eager to get a game going for tomorrow. "Well, there's always good old matchsticks. 'Course, nowadays those are fairly scarce too." Because of the fire danger, carrying matches was restricted.

Brian looked at Casey and Robin. "You guys like to play poker?" Obviously they were qualified—he didn't need to glance down to check.

Casey and Robin grinned at each other. They looked at Brian. "Sure do." They had figured it out already. They had played strip poker before, and the players here looked mighty fine. Besides, they liked the way Tom had mellowed out, too—that was most welcome.

The group did a mutual grin. Geoff made a point of licking his chops. That broke everyone up. They were all quite hard now. Suddenly, the whistle blew from the shore. Free Swimming was over. They looked at one another. Somebody had to take charge.

Tom spoke up. "Raise your hand if you're free tomorrow morning during free swim time." Everyone raised a hand. "Okay. Everyone check around; see if you can borrow some poker chips. We'll meet tomorrow morning at the HQ building instead of here. Brian is in charge of the game. Bring your towel and… well, you know."

They laughed at that.

"Okay, guys. We gotta shrink down for lunch. Cold water, here I come!" Tom stood, stepped to the edge and spread his arms grandly. He performed a perfect pike.

Robin hesitated; he wanted to say something to Jack, but he didn't know what, exactly. Casey tugged at his arm, so that was that. They got set to race, and dove.

Brian gave a thumb up to Geoff and Jack. *what a great day!* He jumped in.

"Was I right, or what?" Geoff punched Jack's arm. He was so pleased with himself for discovering Tom.

"For sure." Geoff was referring to Tom. *fine; Robin is far more interesting. tomorrow morning… I need to huddle with Brian beforehand and get that set up.* He nodded to Geoff. A race to the boardwalk was in order. "On three…"

8   *afternoon developments*

Danny sat on the short bench outside the office at HQ. He'd been sent there by Scoutmaster Taylor, the Backpacking merit badge instructor. Five guys wanted to drop, but only two did, finally. The problem was, Taylor explained, there was no way to start any of the other badge programs late. But he agreed, at last, to send Danny and Geoff to HQ, because they did have good reasons. Danny had a note from Taylor to give to the Camp Director.

"Nasty burn, there." Geoff looked at Danny's red neck and the top of his ears. The curly dark hair above the ear was unusually fine.

"Boy, you don't know the half of it. I got toasted yesterday at the lake."

"Oh yes, I think I saw you out there on the platform, come to think of it." Geoff looked at Danny more closely. *the curly black hair is nice... much nicer dry.* He recalled admiring Danny's backside when he was lying on his stomach... *that was after I spotted Tom sitting in the Lifeguard chair.* "So you got burned..." he raised his eyebrows.

"Everywhere! My shoulders and back are the worst." Danny looked at Geoff and shrugged. He hadn't met an Oriental before... *seems very nice.* "Front side is okay, though." He tested the burn with a small twist. "I plan on staying out of the sun for a while, that's for sure."

"What's up, boys?" Jorgensen, the Camp Director, came out of the foods office.

Danny stood at attention. He gave the scout salute: "Danny Laskey, Sir, Troop 9. I have a note from Scoutmaster Taylor." He held out the note in his left hand. After a minute, he dropped the salute; it had not been returned.

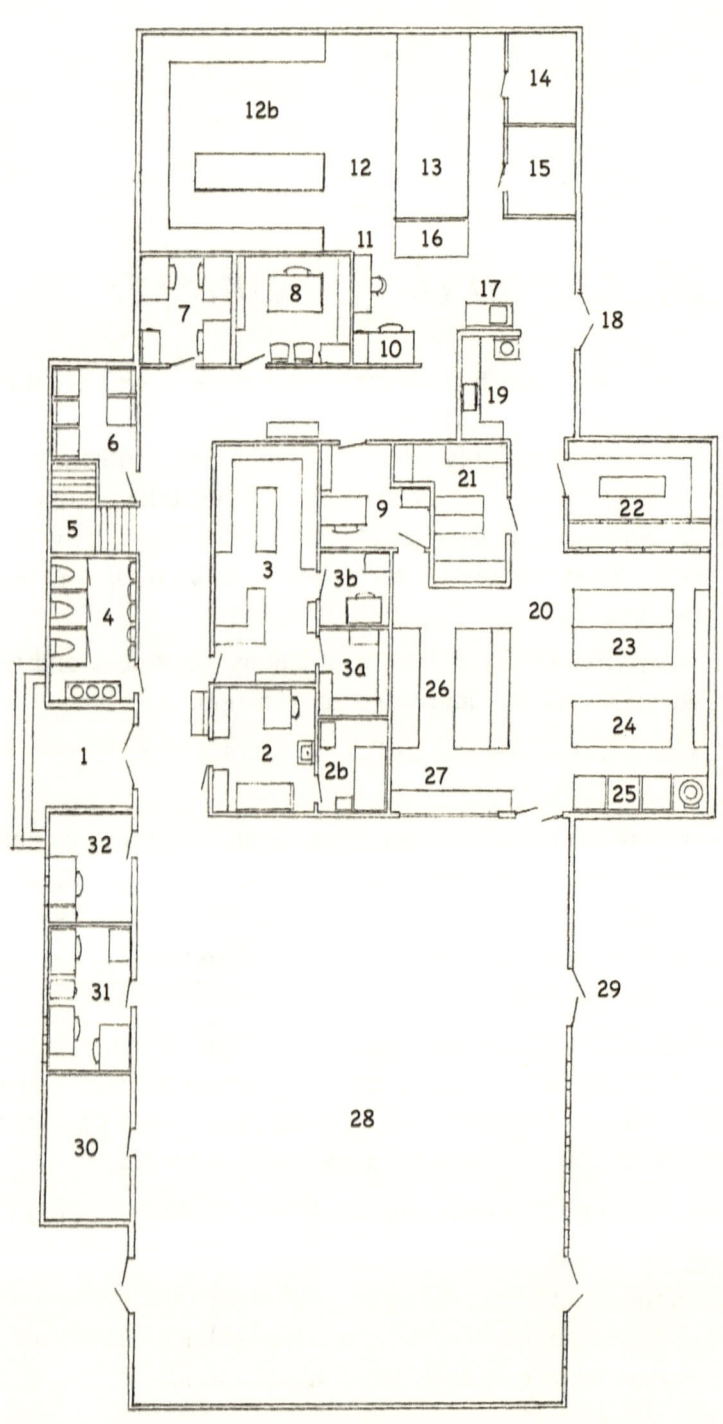

Camp Walker Headquarters

1	Main Entrance	15	Pillows, Blankets, Tarps
2	First Aid	16	Moveable Worktable
2b	Recovery	17	Sink
3	Trading Post	18	Delivery Entrance
3b	Supply Room	19	Dishwashing
3c	Office/Security	20	Kitchen
4	Rest Room	21	Dry good Stores
5	Stairway up	22	Walk-in Cooler/Freezer
6	Laundry	23	Prep Tables
7	Instructor's Office	24	Grills
8	Camp Director Office	25	Ovens
9	Foods Office	26	Food Assembly
10	Camp Ranger's Office	27	Pass Through
11	Workbench	28	Assembly/Dining Hall
12	Supplies and Equipment Warehouse	29	Safety Exit
12b	Hand Carts	30	Table Storage
13	Tool Cage	31	Waterfront Director
14	Featherbed Storage	32	Activity Director

Jorgensen was impressed. Troop 9… *it figures. Schaefer's boys always look sharp. this one is rather pink.* "At ease, son." He looked over at Geoff, who had tried to follow Danny's example. Obviously, spit and polish was not a part of his program. Jorgensen looked at him, expecting to be told who he was looking at.

"Oh. Excuse me, sir." Geoff felt a little lame. He had just realized that Danny was from Tom's troop. "I'm Geoff Staley, Troop 419. I believe the note includes me as well." He was slightly embarrassed. "I'm from the Atlanta Area Council." Danny's precise military manner had surprised him as much as anything, and had thrown him off guard.

Jorgensen looked at him kindly, but with some sympathy. Obviously, Troop 419 was as opposite from Troop 9 as it could possibly be. Jorgensen doubted if his scoutmaster had ever saluted in his life—he noticed Geoff's JA patch. He had to work at not rolling his eyes. *incredible.* He doubted if Geoff had any notion of how unprepared he appeared next to the Troop 9 boy. He had just been presented with a discussion topic for the next meeting. Scoutmaster Olson was going to get a prod about this. He was tempted to give Schaefer extra points, but that wouldn't be necessary—

Mark didn't need any patronage to win his awards. He earned them honestly, the hard way. He read the note.

"C'mon into my office." As they entered he gestured toward the two chairs that faced his desk.

"Geoff, I assume you are working for your Eagle?"

"Yes, sir. I have the Service Project to complete."

"And you, Danny?" He looked at the sunburn more closely. *ouch.*

"Sure, but I'm pretty much just starting. I'm working on my Life rank now. I have seven badges finished." He shrugged.

"And you're **Senior** Patrol Leader?" The proper patch was on his shirt.

Danny blushed. "Yeah, I thought a couple of other guys deserved it more, but Mark... I mean, Mr. Schaefer..."

"Say no more, Danny, I know **exactly** what you mean. But you should know that if Mark Schaefer thinks it's right, it probably darn sure is. Well done." Telling Danny how lucky he was would be bad form. He glanced down at the note again. It wasn't very specific. He looked at Geoff. "I'm surprised you want to drop this badge. What seems to be the problem?"

"The overnight requirement most of all, but the time commitment generally is greater than I expected. My Junior Assistant duties require my presence." Geoff didn't have a second in command ready to pick up the slack.

Jorgensen was impressed. This boy's speech pattern was unusually adult—almost British; *accent is curious... west of the Rockies or somewhere in the north. reasoning is sound and responsible... the same rationale doubtless fit the younger scout.* "Well, boys, the problem is that we can't get you into another badge workshop. They're too tightly run and set up, and all the equipment is in use. You'll have to make do with one less. He looked for a reaction. There was none. Taylor must have informed them of this already.

"But you are in luck. It so happens that our Quartermaster could use some help. One of his assistants didn't show this year, and he's having a time of it with supplies."

Danny and Geoff gave a big sigh of relief.

"Of course, there's no badge in it, or even points. But it's more interesting than having to shadow your scoutmaster or sit here in the office for ninety minutes every day."

"I don't understand, sir." Geoff didn't see what his scoutmaster...

"Well, you see, it's against regulations for any camper to be unscheduled or unsupervised while they are here. You knew that, surely?" *strike two, Olson.* "I doubt that your scoutmaster needs you to be right alongside him, for whatever he's doing every day after two o'clock."

"Oh... yeah, of course... naturally." Geoff fidgeted. He did know that. *I can be so stupid at times. even free swimming is supervised; being glued to Scoutmaster Olson every afternoon? no thanks.*

"Mr. Oliver will be happy to have you aboard. You will help him distribute supplies to the camps, and keep the HQ building outfitted properly. Wait here while I check his board." The Quartermaster kept a chart on the warehouse wall that told where he was at any given time. Jorgensen went to check.

Danny looked at Geoff and smiled weakly. He was proud of the way Mr. Jorgensen had talked about Mark. He didn't deserve any credit himself, though.

"Troop 9? Really?"

Danny nodded his head, simply. *what's the big deal about that, anyway?*

Geoff was impressed. First there was Tom. Then there were the two hotties out on the platform. Now, this pink dumpling. *is there something in the water where they come from? I'll have to see what else is hanging around in that troop.* He looked a little closer at Danny, past the sunburn. *mercy. has Tom made any visits to this one? must have done...* he recalled the posterior lying in the sun again. *face and hair are primo. he's about two years younger... that's old enough. best for private stock, however; poker would be a waste.*

"He's filling stores up at the Tribal Cluster right now." Jorgensen came back into the room. "That's not too far; come on along, and I'll walk you to him. I'm sure he'd like to do some briefing along the way, so the sooner we get you to his rig, the better he's going to like it."

That's one man Jorgensen liked to please and keep happy. Gaining two helpers would make his disposition improve a bunch. He led them out the door. *Powhatan is only half a mile... the hike will do me good.*

Geoff deferred, and let Danny go in front. *mercy me! looky there! I have just the thing for that sunburn, too.* Geoff clicked into his planning mode; *who said this camp would be out of it? Jackson, back in Atlanta. the laugh is on him this time.*

Danny would have appreciated a slower pace with this burn. But he didn't complain; they had lucked out. Helping out around the HQ sounded like fun, actually. *the other guy is interesting... it's hard not to stare. no Orientals in my whole town, I don't think... talks fancy enough.*

Julian walked down the trail, thinking about Forestry; he had just said 'bye now to Justin—he had Indian Legends next. Julian was worried a little about Forestry. *I'll be okay as long as I don't have to memorize all that stuff.* There was a whole new sheet on trees today: "All there is to know about insect damage." It made his head spin. One reason he liked Forestry, he had to admit, was Justin. The only person that he got to spend any time with who was shorter or younger, was Justin. It was such a pleasure; he didn't have to worry, or impress, or feel so stupid all the time. It felt good to have Justin look up to him. Actually, in Forestry, it was Justin who had all the brains.

No complaints though. The day was going great... during lunch he and Nick made a lot of plans for the newsletter—two patrol leaders brought some items over. *we'll work on that after swimming this afternoon.* He had a good start on a couple of sketches. *Bruce suggested a drawing of him being "rescued" during the Lifesaving test. trouble is I can't frame it in my mind; the view Nick and I had wasn't very interesting. I like Bruce; I'll remember him when I need a Buddy for swimming.* He'd never tried to draw anybody swimming before. *one idea I have is better, but it's going to be a little tricky—especially the elbows as they come up out of the water.* Elbows were the hardest thing to get right.

He thought about the archery situation. *maybe it won't be as tough today;* he looked forward to seeing the row of guys standing there, pulling on their bows. A solid row of buns, like in his dream, except they'll have clothes on. *how easy is it to tell if buns are choice if they're under cloth? Danny? yes. Mark? no.* Mark's short pants completely disguised what they covered. *wow. I just thought of something. I bet I'm one of the only people who ever got to see those buns.* He called up the image of Mark disappearing behind the shower curtain. It was only a peek, but... *tonight Julian, see if you can get a better look. say, now... will Mark ever be at the lake? watching him swim... mmm.*

what do you know! got here before Cory today. Julian signed in and selected his equipment. He asked for a ten pounder. The Counselor smiled back. *hmm. so the he knew I picked wrong yesterday. well, not everyone is nice.* He went back to the target where he and Cory were yesterday. It was lucky they were at the end; it made seeing the entire row automatic. He put his bow and three arrows down and sat cross-legged to wait. He flipped his tablet open to the drawing he started last night. *after working on this I'll start a special one on a new page: the bun row.* He chuckled and started to draw.

9   *a helping hand*

"Need some help?" Calvin asked hopefully. He wanted to make a favorable impression, and he didn't get a chance like this very often.

Mark looked up. "Hey, Calvin. You bet! Good for you." He waved at Rick Strauss, the marksmanship instructor. "I've got two more arms over here." *this will make things easier.* "You can help put on slip cases for a start." He pointed to the cases piled on the center table.

Calvin hopped to. He knew how to take care of a rifle. *these zip up cases are cool.*

Mark watched. Calvin checked the breech to see if the chamber was clear. *excellent* He'd paid attention. Mark was confident he had, but it always felt good to see things done correctly. "You want to help take them to the warehouse?"

"Sure!"

Mark was pleased that Calvin had stepped forward. Additional chances to talk with his scouts one-on-one were always welcome. *Calvin could use a little attention; he hasn't got any close buddies in the troop yet. we'll find a fix; camp is a great place for that.*

"Any used target sheets over there, Mark?" Strauss called.

Mark looked around. "Don't see any... who are you missing?"

"Davy Spencer. I forget his troop number." Strauss leafed through the stack again to see if he'd missed it.

"Here it is..." Ron bent down to grab. It had fallen between the table joins. Ron Carville was the Senior Counselor assistant this season.

"Great! Thanks, Ron." Strauss tucked them into his free period folder. These extra credit targets were helpful in measuring a scout's daily progress. He hated to evaluate performance without these at hand.

Soon all the rifles were tucked into their travel cases. Strauss and the camp counselors led the way up the trail; each carried three or four .22 long Winchesters. Mark and Calvin fell in behind. "Where did you learn how to use one of these?" Mark guessed that Calvin knew his way around firearms pretty well.

"My uncle takes me duck hunting sometimes. He has lots of guns." It was a sore point at times; his father didn't approve of hunting.

"So, you enjoy hunting?"

"I guess. Mostly I like to shoot at targets." He understood why his uncle liked to hunt. He didn't feel one way or the other about it. He realized it was killing, but… well, his father was so extreme about it he tended to side with his uncle. Uncle Keith was level headed about it, at least. Anyway, it was the skill that appealed to him, not the killing. And being with his uncle.

"It makes sense for you to get the badge, then." The skills and knowledge are transferable. "How many different guns have you used?"

"Not that many," Calvin complained. "I was hoping maybe we'd get to use a 30-06." His uncle wouldn't let him use that one.

"Those have quite a kick. You can get a nasty bruise—or dislocate a shoulder. We have to be careful at camp. The .22 is the biggest we take on. A big rifle like a 30-06 is trouble if you don't know what you're doing."

Calvin had heard that already. *one of these days I'll get the chance.* The range was what intrigued him most. He wanted to see how far he could shoot with accuracy.

Mark looked at Calvin's slender rather gangly arms. "I doubt if you could control the recoil. The weapon pulls up so fast there's nothing you can do unless you have it hard mounted somehow. They weigh ten pounds, you know. These are only six. Big difference."

Calvin was impressed. "How many guns do you own?"

Mark laughed. "I have a squirt gun somewhere, I think."

Calvin gave him a puzzled look.

"I have to be honest, Calvin. You probably know more about guns than I do. Most of my experience is two years of college ROTC. We used the standard M-1 army issue. That is a 30-06. We had required firing range once a week, so I got to know that thing inside and out."

wow… "You must be an Expert, then."

Mark wasn't inclined to boast. "I was, as a matter of fact. But that was a while ago. I could still make Sharpshooter, I think." *I don't want to test it, actually.* He didn't relish the prospect of a sore shoulder and ears ringing for hours.

"In a year or two, you might want to join Explorer Post 15. They have a firearms program. I think they train for competitions."

"I heard they do pistols mostly." *they're sponsored by the Sherriff's Mounted Posse.* Calvin wasn't planning a career in law enforcement.

"Could be." Mark didn't know any details. "I have a flyer from them somewhere… I'll check that out when we get back home." Mark noticed the soft jingling sound coming from Calvin's pockets. *I've been wondering about that.* "Say, what all do you have on board, anyway?"

"On board?" Calvin didn't understand the question.

"Your pockets. Maybe you need a pouch. No telling what might fall out along the trail." Mark had overheard a comment some weeks ago. Calvin usually looked okay in a formation, but his pocket bulges today looked comical—like a third grader on the way to a marble tournament after school.

Calvin blushed. "Just habit, I guess… never know when I might need something, y'know?" He'd always had stuff in his pockets.

"Be Prepared," Mark laughed. "Can't knock that, I guess."

Calvin chuckled. *Mark always has a positive way to look at things.* He thought for a minute, and glanced down. *handkerchief sort of makes the left pocket puff out… the right pocket makes a little racket. keys are whacking the pocket knives again. s'pose I should do something about it; the guys in the patrol give me a bad time. thing is, I feel practically naked without some of this stuff.* Empty pockets always made him feel vulnerable somehow. *I guess it's a phobia or something. that's what Ryan said. maybe he's right.*

Mark didn't press the issue. Usually, if he waited, the scout would bring it up on his own. That removed the pressure. *he needs to be a little more conscious of his appearance. it's a shame to be judged by superficialities, but if you make it easy, well… when he's not on the defense, he'll be receptive.* Mark ran through the troop roster in his mind.

I need to find one or two that might make a good buddy. someone his own age or older. maybe a mentoring assignment… put that on your list, Mark.

As the group approached the HQ complex, the cheerful activity down at the lake became audible. Mark felt drawn at once. *what I wouldn't give for a good swim right now! unfortunately, I'll have to settle for a shower at bedtime.* That seemed very second best right now: Strauss had taken the short route to the warehouse, which meant the stairway. just as well. His legs needed a workout; there wasn't much exercise in rifle range duty.

Long steep stairways are a good thing if you need a workout, or if you're in a hurry. Otherwise, they were a chore. Mark rarely used this route, since he rarely needed to go to the warehouse. As he neared the top he was grateful the opportunity was rare. The straight line of the steps forced a steeper than normal pitch. Carrying thirty odd pounds of firearms didn't ease the task, either. Luckily, this was a rotating duty; tomorrow, someone else would have the pleasure.

"Non non non!" a loud nasal voice exclaimed.

As they reached the top, Mark looked to the left. Chef Pièrre was supervising a potato peeling crew. Grateful for an excuse to rest a minute, Mark stopped to watch. Three kitchen crew were in a semi-circle hard at work; it looked like they'd been at it a while. *must be over a hundred pounds of potatoes.*

"'Ere, 'ere, let me show you…" He took the peeler from the crewmember and demonstrated how to use the tip to remove the eye. "Do zees first! Always first. Zen you don't waste so much when you peel."

Calvin watched with awe as the camp chef peeled the potato. His hand was nearly a blur. *how can he do that so fast?*

"Voila!" Pierre handed Greg the potato. He pointed at the pan full of peels and shook his head in disgust. "Regarde: you waste 'aff ze potato."

Greg hung his head. "Sorry…" Sometimes he wished he'd been assigned a different duty, like one of the merit badges. He was always fouling up. He carefully excavated the eye of a potato and waited for a judgment.

"Oui, oui, much better." He patted the boy on the shoulder. "We keep you after all." He looked up and gave Mark a wink. He smiled wide and moved over to look at the next boy's output. "Ah, zis is good." He could tell at a glance by the relative size of the peelings to the finished pile. He glanced at his watch. "**Zut!**" *so little time left.* "'Urry, 'urry... fifteen minute, zen evari-zing put away." They had to do the supper setup next.

Mark glanced at Calvin and smiled. "Now you know how zat is done," he said softly. "And zo do I!" He winked and hurried to catch up with the others. They'd gone in the back door already.

"Remember, boys, match the case number with the number on the slot." The rifles were stored horizontally in a honeycombed set of shelves. Strauss had learned to make the boys attend to this detail. He didn't need another dressing down from Sarge. *he may be gruff, but Sarge is the man who keeps this place up and running.* Amazing, for a man his age. He did the work of three men. And he knew where everything belonged, including these carefully, purposely, numbered rifles.

While he and Calvin waited to put their rifles away, Mark glanced back at Sarge. They'd passed by him without noticing he was there. He was at his workbench repairing something... a propane stove like those in some of the patrol camps. Mark just realized his good fortune: *I need to beg or borrow a few things for the cabin. I can get those checked off my list in a minute or two.*

Sarge tried to blow through the fuel line—still clogged. He'd isolated the problem finally, but fixing it was not going well: *need more pressure.* Something in there didn't want to budge. *I hate to get out the compressor... might not have a choice.*

He hadn't been paying the rifle crew any mind—they knew what to do; but someone was standing just behind with a question. It annoyed him when anyone did that. He put the line down and swiveled around.

He drew a deep breath as if about to utter an oath; instead he delivered a silent challenge.

"Sorry, I didn't want to interrupt. Looks like you've found the problem." Mark nodded his congratulations. He knew the curmudgeonly attitude of the Camp Ranger/Quartermaster was mostly show.

Sarge looked at the man facing him. *I've seen him around. looks sharp enough. the boy at his side is new. I suppose he needs something.* He regarded Mark again. Sarge appreciated his comment. "Ruddy fuel line is half plugged." He shook his head. "Blamed if I can figure how anything could get in there, though." He scratched his chin. "So, which one of you needs something? Or is it both?" He looked at Calvin suspiciously, as if he was a no account pest. He couldn't do his usual ogre routine with a scoutmaster right by his side. But it was policy to look dangerous. Saved a lot of time in the end; cut down on nonsense requests.

"Afraid I'm the pest. Mark Schaefer." He reached out to shake hands. "I'm up at Barr's Meadow."

Sarge controlled his reaction. He shook hands. *good grip; John told me about this fella. one of the good ones.* He looked at him closer… *yep. I can see that from here.* He stood off his stool and did a minor stretch. *I need to move around anyway.* "So, what do you need up there?" *that camp is about the best one at Walker. latrines are showing their age, but…*

"I need an extra chair, if you've got something. There's just the one, and I'd like to be able to conference, you know? I hate to flip a coin for who gets to sit."

this one is easy. Sarge appreciated Mark's approach and his sense of humor. "You're in luck; I've got a few army surplus folding units." He gestured for Mark to tag along. He headed down a corridor to the left of the back door. At the end he opened what looked like a closet door.

"See if one of these will work." He stood back so Mark could pick one out.

Mark looked into the small storage space. It was back to back with the rifles. A stack of… he had not seen this kind of chair. It looked like half a chair. He lifted off the top unit.

Sarge's eyes twinkled with amusement. He figured this would be a puzzle. *let's see if he can figure it out.* He crossed his arms to watch.

Mark turned it over and examined it from every side. He looked up at Sarge with a smile. "Reminds me of a turtle. Army, you say?"

Sarge nodded with a smile. He was wagering with himself; *odds are, this fella can figure it out.*

Mark held it at arms length and looked at it carefully. Looked like a giant clam. He tucked his fingers between the two pieces of curved plywood and pulled them apart. It opened so easily he was startled. He smiled and tilted his head. *this is clever!* He sat down. The built in curve of the seat and back made it quite comfortable. He looked up at Sarge with an approving smile.

Sarge nodded. "Don't know why they quit making these. For my money, best folding chair there is."

"I agree. I've never seen one before. Odd, really. They're not any heavier than a regular folding chair."

"Man up in Wisconsin… or was it Michigan? Don't know for sure. Invented it during the war. He did other things out of wood too. Never caught on afterward, I guess. Too bad. I use one over at my cabin."

Mark stood and folded it up. "Sold." He lifted it to test the weight. Not bad… about ten or eleven pounds.

Sarge assumed the man would ask to have it delivered. Annoying, but that camp is a quick run. "Just one, then?" He half expected the scoutmaster to ask for two while he was at it.

"Yes, that's all I need. Besides, I don't have my packboard handy. I get to carry this under my arm."

That impressed Sarge. "Need anything else?" He'd just decided to make the run.

Mark paused… *this is awkward. Calvin is right here.* "Well, I did wonder if you had a way to deal with Louise." He chuckled.

Sarge returned a blank look.

Mark laughed. "That's my name for that mattress up there: Lumpy Louise."

"Haw!" Sarge guffawed. "That's a good 'un. I never slept up there, myself, but I have turned the thing a few times." *thing's stuffed with shavings and kapok. must be twenty years old.* "Lumpy Louise!" That really tickled Sarge. Felt good to laugh for a change.

"If I'd known, I'd have brought along an air mattress. Getting a good solid sleep isn't gonna happen." He'd had two nights of tossing already.

Sarge knew at once what to do. "C'mere," he gestured for Mark to step across the passageway. He opened the first partition door and stepped in to a space about eight feet square. He pointed to a tall pile of rolled up featherbed mattresses. "We rent these out in the winter. Reckon I could spare one or two." He bounced on his toes proudly. He knew he had just made this man's day.

Mark could hardly believe his luck. *this is perfect!* Only... he looked at Sarge with a big grin. "This is a trick, right? All I have to do is figure out a way to get one of these up there."

Sarge laughed heartily. That would cut a funny picture. He and this lad could each take an end. "Never you mind that. I can run one up there right now." He paused. "These have seen some use... might need a couple. You might want to fluff 'em up every two or three days. You just pick one or two out and bring 'em to the door." He stopped suddenly. "There's one condition." He looked at Mark seriously.

Mark saw that Sarge meant this. He nodded. "Of course." He waited to be told.

"Mum's the word on this. I reckon there'd be a dozen other scoutmasters back here making demands. What they don't know won't hurt 'em any, y'hear?"

Mark was slightly uncomfortable about this, but he knew all about the better part of valor. He nodded his consent.

Sarge pointed his finger at Calvin and pushed it into his chest. He gave his best Long John Silver squint. "That goes double for you, boy." He grabbed the chair and headed toward the door.

Mark was amused by the shocked look on Calvin's face. But there was a side benefit. "He's got a point. I'd appreciate it if you didn't mention this back at camp, either." He raised his eyebrows.

"No, no!" Calvin protested. *not a word. who would I tell, anyway?*

"Good boy. Now, then." He tugged at the top roll. "I've never used one of these." It was neatly tied with twine. *no need to unroll it.* He sniffed at it. No problem smells, no dampness. He looked at Calvin and shrugged. He pulled out a second one. *Sarge said two, didn't he?*

Calvin grabbed the first one and headed toward the door. Mark followed right behind.

Sarge had his rig standing ready—a modified Indian Scout 500 motorcycle. He'd made a trailer especially for use up here to make supply deliveries. It wasn't huge, but it could handle this job. He had a sidecar too, but it was in the shop. He'd detached it so that he could work on the wheel bearings. He gestured to the empty trailer. "Stuff 'em in crosswise. I'll put the chair on top." He was glad to do this, actually. The meadow run was always a pleasure. He'd taken supplies up there earlier today, in fact.

Mark wedged in his roll and reached for the other. Amazingly, they squeezed in without protest. He reached for the chair. It fit into the depression in the center nicely, but the load looked precarious. He tilted his head, assessing the tie down hooks. He looked at Sarge. "Rope, you think?"

Sarge held out a small loop of rope he had brought out for this very thing. He watched Mark secure the load. *you can tell a lot about a man by how he does that.* He was impressed. No showoff extras. *reminds me of Cap, a little.*

Mark finished with a bowline, and looked at Sarge. Mark was a trained lashing instructor, so this was child's play.

Sarge nodded his approval. Two yanks and it's free; *this fella knows his stuff.* He stepped over to the kickstand. "I reckon you know the way. I'll head out now." He glanced at his watch. *plenty of time. the spud crew is done, though.* He mounted the bike and kicked the start pedal in one move. It started with a soft purr. Bessie always made him feel good. He started off at once without another word.

Mark looked after him gratefully. *what a character.* He turned to Calvin. "When I was a scout, he scared the daylights out of me more than once." Calvin's wide eyed stare was wonderful. "He's the backbone of this place. And his bark is all there is—no bite." Mark held up his right hand in the scout salute. "That is another thing you are to keep secret." He waited for Calvin to return the salute. He knew that spooking scouts was one of Sarge's favorite things.

"Hey—I just remembered. We don't have to go up to camp empty handed after all." *I'll touch base with Pierre and get a couple of small tumblers for the cabin. Julian will be pleased.* "Ready to hear some more French?" He didn't wait for an answer.

Calvin tagged along eagerly. He had just had one of the most interesting afternoons in a long time—and it wasn't over yet. *man, what a lucky day.*

10   *second troop campfire*

Nick sat with Julian in nearly the same spot as last night—it was an excellent as well as a safe vantage point. They'd decided how to treat these skits in the Newsletter and Scrapbook. They had agreed to work together on both; Nick's typing would revolutionize the Scrapbook when they got back home. *too bad I don't have a typewriter here.*

Nick maintained his vigilance, keeping one eye on Tom, as usual. But something was different tonight—Tom was not behaving according to expectations, at all. At supper he hadn't even glanced at Julian. He was preoccupied with something; he didn't try even once to make a move on Julian this afternoon, and he could have, easily. Instead, he did long distance laps out to the buoy. The afternoon had gone surprisingly well; Nick had been able to give Julian some rigorous swimming lessons. Julian was a good learner. Afterwards, he and Tom had made macaroni and cheese with Spam for supper... it was not one of their prizewinners. He watched Tom build the fire, efficiently as usual. *hmm. I'll find out what I can after the campfire.*

something else could be up: Mark is at the back talking to some official. looks like the bigwig who has an office at HQ. maybe Tom is just being on his best behavior or something. Nick remained alert—the troop was all assembled now, waiting to see the new skit. They had positioned themselves by patrol, just in case.

"Troop 9: Attention!" Tom commanded. They stood at attention in place, not in neat rows. "Tiger Patrol: two paces forward."

The Tigers were in the front rank, at Tom's right, where they were last night. They stepped forward as a group.

"About face." The seven Tigers faced the rest of the troop. Tom stepped over next to the patrol leader. "Congratulations, Tigers. You have won the patrol of the day." He turned to the rest of the Troop. "A total of forty-five points was awarded to the Tigers after the first day. Most of these were passed on by merit badge instructor reports. Troop, salute your outstanding patrol." The troop saluted, following Tom's lead. He broke off the salute and led them in a brief applause. He brought that to a close. "The Tigers will lead the Scout Pledge." Tom gestured to Dale Baker, the patrol leader.

Dale stepped forward, held up his right arm in the scout salute and began to recite: "I, Dale Baker… " The troop followed, in unison. At the finish he faced Tom. "The Tigers thank the troop."

"Troop, at rest." They sat down in place. Tom gestured, "Danny, you're up."

Danny stood and read the news and announcements—there weren't many. "Last of all, we drew Saturday for our laundry slot. Patrol leaders need to have their stuff ready early, because we have to be there at the ten in the morning. Let me know Friday who will have your patrol's duty." He kept a straight face. He'd seen Tony duck down. *afraid he'll get the duty for the whole troop. Tony always has demerits to work off.* "And now, here's Mark."

Mark came forward. "Thanks, Danny. Tonight we'll have a look at the second nominee for our closing night presentation. The Badger entry will be introduced by Tommy Carlysle. After their skit we'll dismiss to Patrol Camps until lights out." He gestured to Tommy, who was sitting right before him.

Tommy was a skinny, five foot eight blond, whose hair refused to be controlled. His ears, nearly perfect semi-circles, poked straight out. He only lacked having buck teeth to be a perfect cartoon. His voice was in the cracking stage; he couldn't control whether it would come out soprano or baritone. Most of his sentences alternated between the two, randomly, especially when he raised his voice. That's why he had been selected; he was the narrator, and the effect of his uncontrolled yodel was hilarious. His patrol had brainstormed a **Gunsmoke** parody.

"Okay. Now, you gotta understand that we'll have on some better costumes. We made some temporaries for now. They won't be fancy— we haven't figured out exactly how to do those yet. After you pick us, everybody gets to pitch in, okay?" He looked around. No comments. "Okay." He stood to one side and unrolled a makeshift scroll.

108

"Shootout at the Dodge Saloon, episode one." The characters lined up to parade by when introduced. "Protector of the weak, and defender of justice, Sheriff Dilly!"

Bruce strutted across the open area and paused to straighten his paper gun belt. He had a large star pinned to his shirt, and a paper hat that wanted to blow away. The troop was delighted. Their laughter covered his entry line completely. He failed to repeat it. His hat had blown off, headed east.

Chuck Nelson walked out next with his thumbs tucked into his belt. Tommy described him. "Doc Apple has been patchin' up folks here for many years. When he's not protecting the Sheriff from...." he gestured for Arnie to enter... "Miss Kitty Katt."

Arnie Shaw was the Badger patrol leader; gangly and awkward, he pranced out behind Doc. He had a couple pair of socks tied in a knot at one end to serve as a wig, and two T-shirts tied at the sleeves into a makeshift skirt. A big beauty dot was painted below his right eye, and he chewed a mouthful of bubblegum. He paused and wagged his butt back and forth.

"Hi, there!" He gave a mini wave to the audience with his fingers. He walked over to Sheriff Dilly and bumped with his hip. Arnie had a very deep voice, and his falsetto was a big hit.

The Doc forced himself between. The audience ate it up. Words were unimportant. Those three walked off left, and Don Felton came on pushing an invisible broom. His sleeves were rolled up and shirt untucked. He pretended to have buck teeth.

"This is Fester, the jail keeper. He's always sweeping up and bringing messages to the Sheriff." Fester finished sweeping up and moved off to the side.

Out jumped the shortest scout in the troop, Freddy Scott. He opened his arms in a 'ta-daa!' flourish. He had a cutout cardboard six-gun in each hand.

"This is Billy the Kid Jones. He just got a set of guns from his grandpa, and he's come into town to make his name. He's been down at the saloon all day saying the most awful things about One Eyed Joe, the town drunk!" Billy made some firing sounds and shot into the air as he walked off.

Tommy lowered a paper patch over his right eye and staggered forward. "One Eye ain't takin' any more, either! He's gonna go over there and call him out, that's what!" Tommy staggered off after Billy, waving the scroll as if it were a six-gun.

The troop applauded and waited for act one. The Sheriff swaggered on, tucking in his shirt and adjusting his belt. He had retrieved the hat, but kept it in his left hand. It had been torn during the hasty rescue.

Mark walked back to stand with the Camp Director.

Director Jorgensen had decided to pay an unscheduled visit. He had been so impressed with Danny, and with everything else he had heard and seen, that he wanted to get a direct feel of what this outfit was like. So far he was amazed. He didn't want to distract the boys, or to miss anything. So when Mark came back to stand with him, he simply nodded. He was thoroughly enjoying himself.

In the final scene, Bruce, the really round and heavy kid was smiling at Arnie, who had bumped his hip again. "Aw, Kitty Katt, you oughtenta do things like that when I'm on duty, and all…"

The Troop erupted in hysterics; the more Kitty bumped, the louder they laughed.

Doc came from one side to defend the Sheriff's honor, and Fester came running from the other side—they collided head on. Fester stood back up; while the Doc brushed himself off, Fester said with alarm: "Sheriff Dilly, Sheriff Dilly, you gotta come quick! One Eye has called out Billy the Kid Jones. There's gonna be blood in the streets!"

The audience loved every minute.

Mark laughed. It was so special when the boys were merry. Letting their hair down was essential at day's end.

"Schaefer, this is wonderful." Jorgensen had to say a couple of things. Then he planned to stand back and sort of fade away. "Where did that opening come from?"

"The Patrol of the Day? The Junior Assistant. It's all his. He asked me first, of course. We've been doing that off and on for six months or so. It's a great device. We use it only when a patrol has a genuine brag coming."

"Hmm. And it was your JA's idea?" He remembered now—that was the scout that had impressed him this morning after the JA meeting.

Mark nodded. "I helped him shape it a little, but the idea was his. I think the practice will stay with the troop long after he's moved on."

They watched the skit finish. One Eyed Joe was facing east, waiting to draw. Billy tiptoed around behind him. When it looked like he might point the gun and shoot One Eye in the back, he put his gun barrel into his pocket and reached forward to One Eye's waist. He faced the audience and winked. Then he pulled One Eye's gun belt and pants down around his ankles. When One Eye tripped and fell face down, Billy the Kid Jones stepped on his back with one foot and performed a Tarzan chest thump and yell.

The Troop cheered and applauded.

"Did you want to say anything to the boys?"

"No, not really. But you can tell them later, from me, that I'm impressed. You do good work, Mark. Thanks. I'll just take off." He extended his hand and gave a strong shake. He had enjoyed himself tonight.

"Thanks, John. I appreciate that. I'm glad you stopped by."

Tom stood and looked at his watch. "Troop 9: lights out in twenty-eight minutes. Dismissed!"

The gang all took off, many running for the latrine, as usual. Mark moved down to the fire circle and began to put out the remaining fire. He was methodical and careful.

Jorgensen paused to let the crowd of scouts run by… it looked like half the troop was doing a sprint for the latrine. He noticed Mark speak briefly to a scout that had remained behind. Mark fetched the water pail and drenched the fire to the last spark. This surprised him. Mark did this last task, himself, alone. He had not delegated it, as Jorgensen presumed every other scoutmaster did. He watched Mark make certain, personally, that it was out: feeling through the cold wet ashes with his bare hands. Impressed, he turned and walked down the trail to his quarters. *this visit was a good idea. I should see a few others… Thompson's troop… that would be a good*

*one to visit, too. Taylor and Simmons probably have something to show…
and Soames. Soames is the big critic. Soames will be next.*

Tom walked slowly up the path from the latrine to the Flaming Arrow camp. He didn't even think about racing down there after the campfire tonight; he just waited his turn, like everyone else… that was okay. He'd had such a full day—he was looking forward to some thinking time. He waved at Danny… *he's on his way down to wait in the line back there. good. maybe Nick is by himself… I haven't had a minute to talk to him since this morning…* He didn't understand why, but he wanted to talk with Nick. *oh… he's with Julian at the table comparing notes or something… hmm. have to wait a little… Nick is busy writing something.*

He went to the stove and felt the side of the coffee pot: borderline warm. He was glad it hadn't been tossed out; he poured half a cup. He sipped… *mmm. kinda blah.* He pitched it out… *stupid to drink coffee at this time of night anyway.* He turned around just as Julian stood up. Julian waved at him. Tom waved back and watched him step down the path toward the Farting Post… *on his way to the cabin. good deal.* Tom went over to the table and sat down next to Nick.

"Hey," Nick looked up with a brief smile, and went back to finish writing a sentence.

Tom looked at him a minute. He felt warm and sentimental all of a sudden. He leaned against Nick, sort of an extended nudge. Words were not forming in his mind. His eyes weren't focused on anything in particular.

Nick was a little slow on the uptake; he completed a thought in the rough draft he was working on about the skit. He glanced at Tom. Tom's mind was somewhere inside itself… it gave him a new kind of expression. It was a good kind, and not what Nick would have expected to see. He leaned back against Tom and held the contact. *why not? it felt good.*

Tom leaned his head against Nick. It was an automatic, unconscious act. He took a deep breath and exhaled as if relieved.

Nick felt a rush—but he was wary. Tom had never done this before. Never done anything close to this. *what is going on?* He waited. *it's smart to wait.*

"Hey," Tom answered at last. He felt good right now. He did not understand why. *maybe I'm just tired.*

"You okay?" Nick remembered that the day had started with a bit of uneasiness below; that must have cleared up by now… it was only considerate to inquire.

"Oh yeah. I've had a really good day." *it feels so damn good to sit here. why is that?* "Nick?"

"Mm-hmm?"

"I don't know how to say this. No, that isn't right… I don't know what I don't know how to say, is…" he frowned. Abstractions were rare to him, uncomfortable.

Nick reached over with this left hand and felt Tom's forehead. "No temperature," he remarked to no one in particular. "Just checking," he smiled at Tom.

Tom sat up straight suddenly. "Something weird just happened, and I didn't even notice it until this minute." His eyes were batting back and forth. He was on to something.

"O-kay," Nick said, slowly. "I must have missed it; mind telling me?"

Tom turned and looked him directly. "I just now saw Julian. All I did was nod and wave at him."

"What's weird about that?"

"Yesterday, all I could think about was getting my hands on that cute little butt that he wags around everywhere he goes. He's got one of the best looking sets of buns I have ever seen. Today, I didn't even notice them. You gotta admit that's weird. Weird for me, at least."

wow… weird, and most welcome. "Well, different…" Nick sensed that this was a big deal… he had to be careful. "Any theories?" *play this light as can be.*

"Well, I don't know, for sure. It's been weird all day." Tom shook his head. "You're such a brain, I …" Tom stopped himself, and looked directly at Nick. "I'm sorry. I didn't mean it that way. I mean you are a brain, and all, but you can see into stuff." He slugged himself on the jaw. It was more than a tap. "I don't know how to talk about things, y'know?" Suddenly, and unexpectedly, he realized that he cared very deeply about how Nick felt. He did not want to hurt his feelings.

Nick looked at Tom with sympathy and affection. *Tom is just a big puppy right now.* He had a hunch. He reached out and embraced him. That was just the right thing to do. Tom hugged him hard—so hard, it almost hurt. He held it for an amazing length of time. When Tom released him at last and sat back, Nick swiveled on the bench to face him directly.

"So tell me about your day." Nick smiled a friend's smile. He looked Tom right in the eye... he didn't usually do that.

11   Lumpy Louise

Julian opened the cabin door and flipped on the light. He was all business. He had a lot to do, and not much time. *Mark will be here for our conference before long, and I haven't even thought about it. not only that, Nick wants to see something about the skits—I haven't even started the sketch for last night.* He went straight to the table and pulled out the chair. He turned the clock face around... that way he could keep an eye on it. *twenty-three 'til. no telling when Mark will get here. ten minutes maybe.* He turned on the desk lamp. *that's better... Mark was right about this lamp! wow.* He opened the notepad to a new page. *I'll make two lists— one for tonight and one for tomorrow.* He allocated a half page to each. *the sketches can wait for now.*

which one first? ...better start with tonight— okay:

1: Questions to ask Mark

   Forestry words; Archery words

2: —

hmm... Julian wanted to ask Mark about Choice Buns, but maybe that would be stupid. *you don't want to get a quick ticket back to the Wolf camp. if only Nick wasn't so... what's the word?* Julian frowned. Sometimes it was so frustrating when he didn't know the word for something like that. *how are you supposed to learn those words, anyway?* There it was again: words! Julian was fine when it came to drawing stuff, but when he had to talk about things, he felt like a dodo or something. He wrote down "buns" and put parentheses around it...

See if you can figure a way, nagged his inside wise guy critic. "Something will come along," he chimed aloud. That was his clever new motto. He giggled... *I came up with that the first day here.*

He sat up straight: **buns!** *I just remembered... Mark will take his shower...* A crafty grin appeared. *tonight, Julian, pay attention for a change.* He wanted a better look. He'd seen so many buns at the lake that he needed a fresh picture in his memory. This item, of course, couldn't be on the written list. He had an unwritten list on hand at all times.

Except when you're not paying attention!

True; he'd nearly missed out the first night, and the second night he was clear across the room, way out of sight. *tonight will be different.*

He slouched back in the chair... he'd lost his concentration all of a sudden. That happened whenever he thought about Mark. His eyes blurred as his mind groped around for something else to put on the list. *you should do that during the day, dum-dum.*

Something in his peripheral vision caught his attention. He looked to the left... *what is that?* Two large puffy rolls were sitting on Mark's bed. Something made him think of Sid's air mattress. *I didn't see those before.* He stood and reached over to touch... *soft.* He pinched it. *kinda like a pillow. huh. must be a mattress.* He reached down and pushed on the bed... oh. He nodded, understanding. *makes sense to do something about that, all right.*

I didn't know Mark's bed was so hard. it looks okay, except it sort of sags in the middle. why is it so big, anyway? there's room enough for two or three... he stopped in mid question.

Because sometimes more than one person sleeps there, stupid. Once in awhile his 'Inside guy" self got a little sarcastic.

maybe in the winter they rent this out to the hunters or something. Julian's fantasy dream machine started up. Two people could sleep there in the summertime, too... *ooo, if only.*

—⁂—

Mark strolled toward the Panther camp. He swung his arms wide to speed drying his hands. The campfire was more stubborn to quench than usual. He hadn't had much time today to collect his thoughts. A short tour around the meadow would help make up for that. I'll have Julian to occupy me in a few minutes; I'm looking forward to hearing his news report. last night we didn't have much time. Mark smiled at the image of

Julian mimicking his shaving just before lights out. *when all is said and done, Julian is entertaining.*

He paused to look over at the Panther camp... Calvin was talking to Ben and Don—the Tenderfoot. Mark appreciated the moment; it was always a boost to see his efforts make a difference. The brief talk we had after the hike up was just the ticket. *Calvin is engaged and enthusiastic— must be talking about Pièrre.*

Barr's Meadow

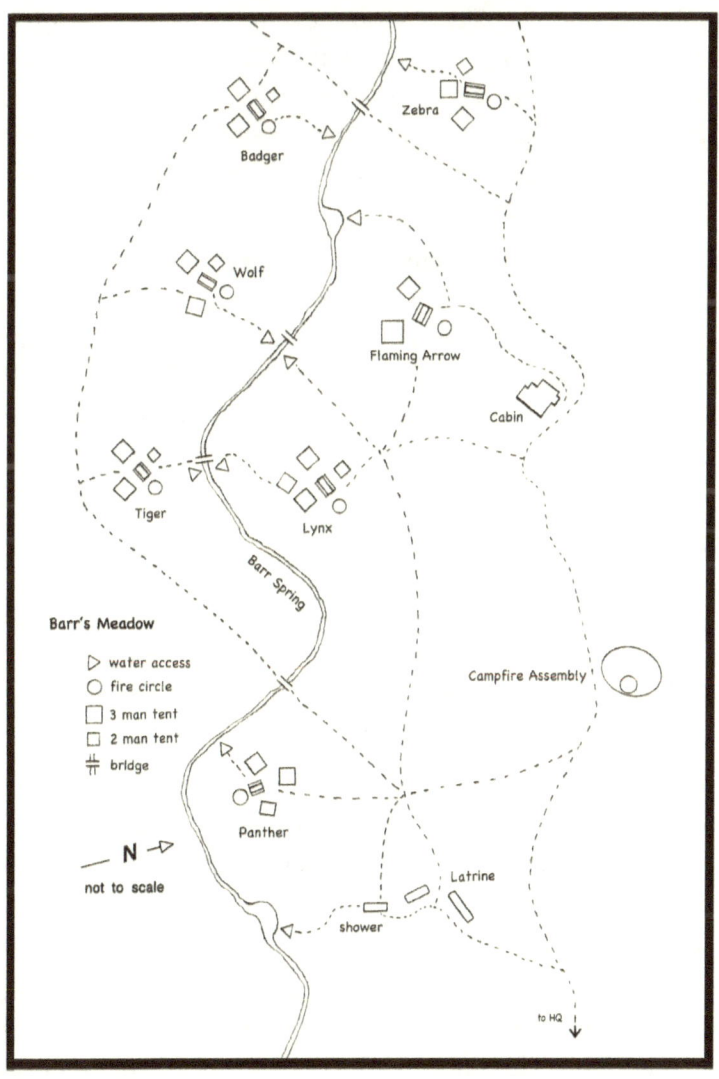

Mark recalled Pièrre's enthusiastic response to his inquiry about small tumblers for the cabin. "Mais oui, I 'ave just ze teeng!" He commanded one of the crew to fetch a stool and open an overhead cupboard near the bread mixer. He patted his very healthy tummy and shrugged his shoulders apologetically. Standing on stools was something he no longer risked. Obviously Calvin was amused by Pièrre's manner. He was also pleased by the gift of a couple of freshly baked cookies. *one of the staff perks tonight, evidently.* Mark moved on across the footbridge. *the overstuffed pockets solution will come along eventually.*

He looked up at the sky. *moon is up longer every night now... should be full next week.* The meadow always looked special in the moonlight... *the grass turns silver—when there is a breeze, it's transporting. I'll walk along the perimeter trail and be seen—I don't need to do any drop-ins tonight. tomorrow and the next day, be a good idea to visit a couple or three patrols.*

speaking of drop-ins... why had Jorgensen popped in? Mark was happy that he had, because the boys were in great form tonight. This was the first ever visit by the Camp Director. My fifth camp as a scoutmaster. Last night's skit would have impressed more, probably. Max Webster's spoken choral fable was first class. *I should have extended an invitation; I've never thought about doing that.*

"Hi, Mark!" came a call from the Tiger camp. He turned and waved. The other camps had probably heard; likely most or all would give him a wave. That's fine; he wasn't trying to surprise anyone. He never did that anyway. He believed in being up front, always. He returned a wave from the Lynx camp. If one of the boys needed him, they would wave him over. Otherwise, just being seen lent the boys a feeling of security. This part of the job he found extremely rewarding.

The air is still and quiet... voices carry remarkably well. That's one nice feature of the Meadow—each patrol had its own space, yet its still within earshot of the next one. The afternoon breeze usually declined after sunset, which seemed to enhance the acoustics.

Tom and Nick came into view—sitting at the Flaming Arrow table across the creek. He laughed... right behind them he could see the Farting Post branch stabbed into the ground. *that's right! I haven't thought about that little situation.* He stopped to ponder. *at supper they were very cool.* But he was certain about what he had heard this morning—he was pleased as could be, actually. He was still surprised that it was Tom, not Nick, who had to recuperate. Nick's smiling blush had cinched it. Mark had long suspected that Tom might be a butt puncher; he'd seen him giving an appreciative glance more than once, certainly. Mark swung his arms behind and back again absent mindedly; he had to admit that he himself didn't always observe his policy of "don't even look." He had never heard of anything going on, of course—he didn't want to, either.

There would be little choice but to be the bad guy. He recalled that sound from this morning, and laughed aloud. He had never seen Tom try to shrink out of sight before. It was wonderful. *maybe, a few years down the road we can talk about it.* He continued up the path past the Wolf camp. He returned a wave... Norman or Stuart. Too dark to say for sure.

Tom's "accident" forced him to think of Erik for a minute. He remembered the first time Erik had done him. *man...* It had changed his life forever, of course. The next morning he'd had his own first gurglefart. He'd become accustomed to them once in a while during that brief time of heaven on earth. If only Erik hadn't taken that doomed flight to Boston. Life would have taken him far away from here, and he'd probably still be contentedly tooting away. Lord, how he had missed Erik; he was sure there would never be anyone who could replace him. Until a few months ago, life had been like living in a desert. Something had changed that; he wasn't sure what. Time, probably, the great cure-all; he was grateful, nonetheless. *if it hadn't been for scouting I don't know what I would have done to keep my mind occupied.*

He stepped off trail to bypass the Badger camp and went straight to the junction. He glanced at the Zebra camp and returned Cory's wave. To the right, Tom and Nick were still talking... *having a heart to heart, looks like. I won't interrupt.* He glanced at his watch... *almost fifteen 'til.* He picked up his pace and headed for the cabin.

now that we have a second chair, we should be able to cover more ground. I'll allow for a fifteen minute conference. that should be plenty. if we need it all, I can shower after lights out.

The cabin door was wide open... It told him that he was welcome. He didn't need to be told that, but it was nice, anyway. *there's Julian, sitting at the table, working at his sketchpad—total concentration.* Several of his scouts had a good work ethic, but none more so than Julian. *he has such total focus at times. remarkable. it's been a while since I've seen his work. I should look at what he's done since we arrived—I'd like to know if the workspace in here helps.* He stepped in and closed the door.

"Ooo..." Julian complained. He wanted to finish this one sentence. "In a jiffy..."

Mark chuckled. "Take your time, Julian. It's alright." Mark closed the widow and curtains above the counter.

"There!" Julian slapped down his pencil proudly and turned around.

"Sounds like you just achieved something."

Julian nodded enthusiastically. "I just wrote down some stuff about Tommy's skit." Bruce in particular amused Julian. "Nick gave me an assignment on that." A cartoon of it was taking shape in his mind—Bruce chasing after his paper hat.

"Excellent. Pull your chair over here and we can talk about it." Mark grabbed the folding chair. Sarge had placed it in front of the built in cabinet next to the door.

Julian grabbed his tablet and pulled the chair over by the fireplace, where Mark had on the first night. "Wow, you got another chair!" He watched Mark open it up. *huh.*

"They have these in the warehouse, isn't that lucky?" He settled in. It still felt awkward, but it was better than sitting on the floor. "So, you're reporting already. What do you think of the scribe business?" Mark wasn't worried about Julian's talent. His writing in the scrapbook was usually very descriptive. He rarely made a grammatical slip.

Julian considered briefly. "Depends. The skit is easy, because it was so funny. Other stuff..." Julian wrinkled his face.

Mark returned an inquisitive look.

"Well, how do you make a story about insects eating up the trees around here interesting?" That handout was the most boring thing he had ever seen. "I was trying to write on the Forestry badge, but..." he shook his head.

"I see your point." Mark sat back and relaxed, crossing his left leg over the right.

Julian wasn't expecting to sit directly opposite Mark, and so close. He had not devised a plan for catching glimpses from this distance. He didn't dare look directly down… his peripheral vision would have to do. Prospects improved when Mark sat back, but… this won't be much good.

You hafta pay attention to what he's talking about, anyway. Julian was glad his Inside guy was on duty at a time like this.

"That's the kind that has to be put aside to ripen a little. In a day or so, look at it again. If nothing comes to mind, move on to something else. Maybe Nick has an idea or an alternate assignment." Julian's earnest expression impressed Mark. *it's not only drawing that engages Julian.* "So, tell me what was fun today, what you enjoyed. You're not supposed to work all the time, you know."

Julian pondered that… he didn't usually have fun as a goal. Fun was a byproduct. "I was at the lake most of the time." Julian laughed. "Bruce was my buddy this morning. He's fun. You oughta see his cannonball!" He could still hear that **whoomp!—spshh** sound. "The water shoots straight up in the air." *I can't get mine to do that.*

Mark pictured it. He'd seen a few splashes like that. "Sounds like an idea for the scrapbook."

Julian's eyes opened wide. "Yeah! I never thought about that…" a cartoon began to form in his mind. "Thanks, Mark!" That will go nice with the racing one…

Mark wondered if there were any problems. Nothing seemed to be wrong. He liked to let those subjects appear unasked for; big problems almost always show somehow. So far it looked like having too much to do was Julian's only problem. He glanced at Julian's tablet. "Your turn. What's on your list?"

Julian glanced down at the tablet. He was embarrassed that the list was so short. He frowned. *what the heck.* He made a snap decision. "Words."

Mark waited for more.

"Everywhere I turn I have trouble with words. He looked at the tablet. "In Forestry they have lists and lists of these words. Who can remember all those? And in Archery there's goofy words like nocks and fletches and ends and pounds—they don't use words that make sense, like notches and feathers. And then there's…" Julian paused. He was losing control here—he had almost said buns.

Mark was impressed by Julian's intensity and his fervor. His frustration was easy to understand and sympathize with. "And there is..." Mark repeated. He could see that Julian had hit a stumbling block. *This is more than a vocabulary problem.* "Something to do with writing your report?" *Perhaps Nick is pushing Julian too hard.* "If Nick isn't able to explain something, maybe I can help."

Julian looked at Mark directly. *how did he know that? is he a mind reader? no, that's silly. on the other hand, maybe I'm too chicken.* He nodded yes to that and to the fact that Nick was one source of his frustration. He still felt uneasy about this. He wasn't ready. His inner boss had held up a red flag. He needed a strategy. *I have to figure a way to get Mark to talk about stuff that Nick won't, but I don't want Mark to be afraid or to be mad at me. this is really tricky. too tricky for tonight. how do I back up?* He spotted a way out over on Mark's bed. "What are those, anyway?" He pointed at the big rolls.

Mark turned around. "Oh! I almost forgot!" He turned to Julian. "That's my new mattress! Thank you for reminding me." Mark looked at the clock—it was facing the bathroom. "I have to get that set up before lights out." He looked at his watch. "Where did the time go?!" He looked at Julian. "Want to give me a hand?"

"Sure!" He stood up, awaiting instructions. *This looked like fun. Besides... getting inside information about that object was very much a part of his overall plan. Changing the subject had been the perfect thing to do.*

"The Quartermaster has a small room full of these!" He went around to the dresser side of the bed. "Let's roll these out of the way while I strip the bed." He rolled the first featherbed toward Julian.

Julian took the roll and put it over by the chairs. *This is real light.* "What's a Quartermaster?" Another odd word. *this place is buried in odd words.* Mark passed him the other roll.

"That's what they call the person in charge of supplies and equipment. Here he runs practically everything—food, tools, tents, you name it, he's got it somewhere." Mark pulled back the covers and grabbed the corner of the form fit mattress pad. "Go to the other side and loosen the top like this."

Julian hurried over to the other side of the bed. *my bed at home has a thing like this.*

122

"Now, we roll it or fold it all the way down. That way we can put it back on real easy." Four hands made this job a cinch. In no time, the covers and sheets were folded neatly into a horizontal strip and placed carefully on the floor by the foot of the bed.

Mark went to one of the featherbed rolls. He was about to pull out his pocketknife when he thought again. *I'll bet Sarge has this tied so that it can be reused.* Cutting it would be a mistake. This had to go back to the warehouse at some point. He examined the twine as he rolled the mattress a few feet. *thought so... a simple slipknot. this was trussed with a single piece of string.* He pulled the end of the twine and the roll began to open itself.

"Whoa..." Julian was intrigued by what Mark had just done.

Mark looked at Julian—he had such a terrific expression when he saw something new. "If you study any of the rope tying or lashing methods, you can learn how to do a simple truss like this. It's a handy thing to know." He wound the twine around his elbow as he pulled it from the featherbed.

Julian had figured this out before, but he asked anyway. "What do you need these for?"

Mark laughed. "To protect me from Louise."

Julian tilted his head. That didn't make any sense.

"Go and lie down on that bed. Tell me what you think."

Julian felt a rush. He knew what Mark meant, unfortunately. He went over by the table and sat on the edge. He flopped onto his back and twisted so that he was stretched out lengthwise. "Eew!" He looked at Mark.

"Go ahead and roll over a couple of times. See if you can find a comfortable spot." Mark folded his arms and watched Julian erase any guilty feeling he had for getting this special favor from Sarge.

Julian struggled and squirmed for a while, to no avail. "Wow." *I thought he had it lucky. wrong.* He climbed off the bed at last. "How do you ever get to sleep?"

"It takes some doing. I wake up about a hundred times a night. I couldn't believe my luck when I found out about these." He grabbed one end and pulled it out. "Grab the other end. We're supposed to give it a good fluffing up."

They fluffed up both mattresses and spread them out on the bed. They were smaller, so there was a six inch margin left around all four sides. Next they reinstalled the mattress pad and covers. The newly made bed looked very inviting. Neither Mark or Julian commented.

Julian did remember one thing, though. "Who is Louise?" The idea of a female sneaking into bed with Mark did not rest well.

Mark laughed. "You were rolling around on her a minute ago. I call that thing Lumpy Louise."

"Oh!" Julian laughed weakly. He saw the humor, but still... He wasn't over the dark thought he had a minute ago. He was relieved, but it was a big scare.

Don't be stupid, stupid.

Mark looked at his watch. "Oh-oh," he warned.

Just then came the nightly announcement. Tonight it was a freak stereophonic "Two minutes, you have two minutes..." Simultaneously, both Tom and Danny had called out from different ends of the meadow.

Mark pointed to the bathroom. "Teeth." In an instant, the nightly ritual was hurriedly underway. While Julian dashed into the bathroom to brush his teeth, Mark finished securing the windows and returned the big chair to the table.

Julian worked very fast. He was bending down to rinse his mouth when he saw two small plastic tumblers sitting beside the washbasin. "Ooow! Oo gaw a gaaa!" He selected one and put it to use.

Mark heard the frothy exclamation from the clothes rack. The words were impossible to discern, but the sentiment was terrific. *thank you, Pièrre.* Mark hung his shirt on the rack. As he sat on the edge of the bed to remove his shoes and socks, he reflected back on the day. It had been very busy, as usual, and much was accomplished; *yep, a good day.* He stood and tossed the socks into the laundry drawer.

>> scree—eep! <<

stupid man! you forgot to ask Sarge about sandpaper. The drawer had won another round. He shook his head and pulled out a fresh pair of briefs. He heard Julian running across the room. He snagged an empty hanger and handed it to him on his way to the shower.

Julian was unable to witness Mark's entry into the shower as he had planned. But the wink he got from Mark as he went to the bathroom was fabulous! He hung up his shirt, savoring the moment. He turned to look, just in case… it's safe… Mark is scrubbing away. He stepped to the right and gently whiffed the other recently hung shirt. He hadn't gotten a good dose of that aroma for a long time. *ohhh.* He took another. *mmm. catnip.* He floated over to the light switch on the way to his cot.

He scootched to get comfy. He was used to the cot, but he wouldn't mind a chance to test out those featherbeds. *someday, Julian… some day.* He was in position for the winding of the clock and turning off of the bathroom light. Both were very nice tonight. As he heard Mark flap back the covers, he laughed softly… *Lumpy Louise. that's funny, actually.*

12 *Tom and Nick, again*

Nick could hear Danny and Tom in the distance giving the lights out command to the patrols. yow… *running out of time…* His heart was beating hard from the hurried effort, and from the unusual nervous state he was in. He was making the final adjustments to the special accommodation he had thrown together in the supply tent. His sleeping bag was spread out open full, face up, and Tom's was opened and laying face down on top. Their pillows and towels were at the end near the east wall. To the right he had placed his flashlight and his tube of K-Y, should either be wanted. He undressed and settled in. He turned back the top corner on the other side so that Tom could slide right in. *the ground isn't too bad; the bumps have been worked out, mostly. the tarps underneath help some.*

Hands behind his head, he lay on his back, waiting for Tom to arrive. It would be only a minute; the shadows in front of the lantern on the table outside would alert him that it was about go dark. *Tom will come straight in.* He replayed the extraordinary conversation he'd had with Tom less than twenty minutes ago…

He sat straddling the bench, facing Tom directly; he wanted Tom to know that he had his complete attention.

Tom rotated on the bench and faced Nick. He didn't have the faintest idea of what he was going to say. The only thing he knew was that he wanted desperately to be right here, right now, with Nick. He was so grateful that Nick was patient and understanding. And so damn smart, too. He glanced up and looked at Nick's face. It was in sharp contrast, being lit from the side by the Coleman Lantern. He had to look a second time to see the kind open trust that was in front of him.

"See, there are these guys I met today…" Tom wasn't sure where to start. "I met them this morning at HQ. They're all Junior Assistants too." He laughed. "We had **some** morning!"

Nick figured that must be the bunch that he had seen with Tom at the lake when he was swimming with Julian. He didn't want to interrupt.

"You remember, two, three years ago, that campout during spring vacation?"

It took Nick a minute. "You mean…oh, yeah, who could forget that!" Nick laughed. *how could I forget; I lost my "innocence" on that trip.* "My very first experience, actually." He punched Tom on the knee lightly and smiled. That was one of the most thrilling times he had ever had. *my one and only circle jerk. that's when Tom was only seven inches. I could hardly see it because it was so dark. it seemed gigantic at the time. Tom wasn't the oldest scout on the trip, but he was among the biggest, even then. that was when I fell in love with Tom…* Nick had not ever told him that, either.

"Well, we played that this morning. These guys have perfected that game like you wouldn't **believe**." Tom laughed… how they had played cat and mouse with him.

Nick observed that while Tom described the game in some detail, he danced around whatever it was that was bugging him. It was interesting, to be sure, but Nick sensed it was not really what Tom wanted to talk about. *smart to pay complete attention, though.* At the point that he was describing the clothing removals beginning, Nick saw Danny approaching from the latrine. *not good.* He put his hand on Tom's knee.

"Danny's coming," he whispered. "You want him to hear any of this?"

"Oh no…" Tom was only at the point of describing the clothing being taken off. He looked at his watch and grimaced: "Five minutes! Cripes, I want to talk a lot longer than that." He felt forlorn, almost desperate. He did not want to put this off until tomorrow. *what am I going to do?*

Nick saw his discomfort—he had an idea: "How about I set up for a Code Green again? I can line it up when you guys go to give lights out." The supply tent space was still there, he assumed. *it was ideal last night.*

"Yes! That's perfect!" Tom looked over his shoulder to see how close Danny was. He turned back and said, quietly, "set it up for an all-nighter." He looked Nick straight in the eye.

Nick blushed. He could count on one hand the number of times Tom had allowed himself to make solid eye contact. And they had never spent an entire night together. *something is up, for sure.*

Tom and Danny's shadows crossed the passageway. Nick heard Tom say something softly, and the light went out.

Seconds later, Tom came into the tent. His eyes had not adjusted to the dark. "You here?" He felt his way along the stack of boxes.

"Yeah; you need a light?" Nick reached for his flashlight.

"Umm…" Tom hesitated, still groping his way. He did want a light, but didn't want to say so. *that Coleman blinded me good.*

Nick clicked on his flashlight and aimed at the turned down corner.

"Perfect; thanks." Tom stepped to the side of the bag and undressed.

Nick left the light on. He always liked to look at Tom. At times he was barely able to remain stoic about his lopsided relationship. *good grief! Tom is up two thirds already. whoa… I'm going to get stuffed good tonight, for sure. well: I won't mind that one bit. Tom's in…* he turned off the flashlight and put it back on his side.

Tom wiggled briefly in search of a lump free spot… as close to Nick as he could get. *I'm so glad it's this dark. the moon will be down before too long, too.* Tom hated to admit it, but he was a coward about this. He had to talk to Nick, he had to be with Nick. But he was chicken to look at him in the face. He was fighting something, but it was futile; he realized that he had already lost. He was so darn used to being the big man, the big boss, he didn't know how to ask. All he knew how to do was tell. His feelings toward Nick had turned upside down, ever since last night. He didn't know what or how to tell him that, either. All he knew was that he couldn't blow it. He was not used to being afraid. Funny, though, it didn't make him mad; it made him feel… tender. Like a little kid, or something. *I'm all screwed up. Nick has to help, that's all.*

Nick was genuinely puzzled. He had expected to be pounced on by now. *Tom is just lying there, breathing. Should I say something? Do something?* Tom's unfinished tale about the poker game was no help. He had only started it, really. Suddenly, he felt Tom's hand reach over. It touched his arm, then slid down to his hand. Tom held his hand, and squeezed it gently. *how odd.* What a rush it gave him. He squeezed back. *is that what's needed?* He lifted their hands to his face and kissed the back of Tom's hand.

Tom exhaled a giant breath and turned over to embrace Nick. It was as desperate as it was erotic. He still couldn't find the words he had to say. *please, Nick… please kiss me.*

Nick sensed Tom's need. He took his head into his hands and kissed him on the lips. It became passionate at once. Tom let it all flood out; something had been pent up, and the doors burst open. Nick responded in kind, letting the depth he had long felt express itself at last. His stoic control had been shattered. He realized, that for the first time, Tom had kissed **him**. *man, he really kissed me…* It was before having sex, as usual, but it was so **intense**. He now felt very vulnerable. He had always feared that if he told Tom he loved him, he'd be discarded instantly. Now, he dared to think maybe that wasn't true. He would still wait to say the words—though he knew his kiss was telling all. *but isn't Tom's kiss saying the same thing?*

Tom broke off to get a breath of air. He rested his head on Nick's chest. He breathed deeply for a while. *Here goes…*

"Nick?"

"Yeah?"

"Will you fuck me?"

whoa! That's the last thing he expected to hear. *I thought the opposite was on the schedule.* In fact, he thought he even had a promise last night. His mind was racing over this.

"Well, sure, of course. But I thought you wanted to do me tonight."

"So did I, for a while." The ice was broken at last. *maybe now I can talk about it… a little anyway.*

"See, a real weird thing happened this morning. I didn't finish telling you about that poker game. I was boffing this hot, **really** hot Oriental guy. I mean, he was a real **prize**, you know? And he was really digging it, too. In some ways, it was the best one I ever had—this guy has a lot of experience. He was able to handle me easy, no sweat." Tom paused to enjoy the memory; it was a sensational one, for sure.

Nick listened intently; he didn't quite understand where this was going; Tom had boasted about his conquests many times, so that wasn't anything new. He remembered pointing out this guy's cute buns to Julian, in fact. He was not at all surprised that he had been added to the list.

"See, after I finished, this weird thing happened." He was a little afraid to tell this. But he had to. "I thought of you. I didn't want to look at Geoff— that's his name, Geoff Staples. I wanted to see you there, not him. I felt a little bad all of a sudden…" He had to pause; *this is tough.* He'd felt awful, in fact… he was verbalizing this for the first time to himself, as well as to Nick. He was only just now starting to see things. "Part of the time I thought it was you, just before we were done." *Geoff didn't begin to kiss like Nick, though. the kiss just now showed that—it's Nick's kisses that mean everything.* He just put that together this minute.

Nick could not imagine what he could say to this. He stroked Tom's back and shoulder, gently, lovingly. He had to show that he cared, somehow.

"I never felt that way before. I felt like it was all wrong or something. I felt like I was sorry. I wanted you to be there, and it was my fault you weren't."

Nick was thunderstruck. Tom had all but said 'I love you.' He probably didn't know that yet. *this is so important. I have to be very careful…* He turned to Tom and kissed him tenderly. He sensed that Tom had to work this out, and that all he could do was support, maybe nudge. This was not the time for a comic touch, or for a bold grab. All he dared do was hold Tom's hand as he crossed this threshold. He hugged Tom; he did not have any words handy for this; non-verbal proofs would have to do.

"I think something happened last night, Nick… I don't really understand it. But everything's different now. Like when I saw Julian. It made me think of what you said last night, too. I don't want to jump him any more. I feel bad that I even planned to. And then I think of all the guys I have—jeez, I don't even know how many."

Nick kissed his cheek; he nuzzled over to his ear, and licked his earlobe lightly.

Tom felt a warm blush and tickle that ran right down his back; the underside of his scrotum tingled. He shivered—a wave of some kind had just passed down all the way to his feet. Nick had found a new magic place. He pressed his hard member against Nick's side. It pulsed, it dripped... He clenched his buns and pressed hard against Nick and kissed him on the mouth again.

"You are **really** turning me on!" Tom was ready. "Did you bring everything?"

"Mmm-hmm," Nick caressed Tom's left bun.

"Will you please do what you did last night?" Tom pressed himself tight against Nick. **"Please?"**

Wednesday

Fourth Day

The roles of protector and protected are reversed unexpectedly in the Flaming Arrow Patrol. **Julian** and **Danny** find themselves cast as guardians.

Julian makes strides in his artistic ability while he continues to explore the marvels of adolescence.

Danny takes his second major step in learning about who he is and where he wants to go in life. **Geoff** emerges as a shaper of events; he undertakes the further education of **Danny** .

The Poker Club's second game runs into unexpected complications. **Nick** is forced out of his back row comfort zone, and **Tom** discovers how difficult it is to change. **Robin** and **Casey** are right at home.

Paul Harris and **Doug** Tucker are another pair from Troop Nine that was initiated in past years by Tom. They were not happy with that experience like some, and have struck out on their own.

Julian and **Sid** discover Doug and Paul's secret activity, and their long friendship takes on a new dimension.

Tom decides to make a permanent change in sleeping arrangements; **Mark** and **Julian** have a major breakthrough conference.

After hours in Barr's Meadow on Wednesday night is very special; relationships and perceptions develop and grow; reflections on the day's activity keep several minds occupied; a lot has to be sorted out before morning.

13   *gatekeepers*

Julian skipped toward the Flaming Arrow to start breakfast. He giggled softly... he had just refreshed his visual files for a terrific start of the day. Mark was busily looking for something in one of his manuals. Julian didn't pay any attention to the book—it was the extraordinary view of Mark's lap that occupied his full attention. For the second time he'd been in just the right place at the right time. *luckily, Mark doesn't put on his pants until he's all done in the bathroom and everything else. he puts them and his shirt on last thing. I think it's because he tries to keep them from as much wear and tear as he can. I never see any kind of spots or wrinkles on his clothes.*

His underwear, however... *must last a long time.* He doesn't have a mom who's always tossing it out and putting new ones in the dresser drawer. Well, sometimes that was okay, if the old ones were getting too small. Usually, though, they would last longer if they had the chance.

Julian was about to pass by the Farting Post—he stopped to look at it. It was a very funny idea, really. What would be the best way to use it? Lift a leg, or just bend over? *I wonder who will be the first one.* He chuckled again at the memory of Tom's accident at the table yesterday. He skipped on toward the Flaming Arrow camp.

oh! am I late? Danny was already at the stove. The coffee was started and everything! He hurried up.

Danny saw Julian coming—he put down the skillet with care to keep it silent. He had to meet Julian before he got all the way to camp.

what the...? why is Danny rushing toward me? Julian stopped cold; that seemed to be what Danny wanted.

Putting his finger to his lips, Danny led Julian into the camp tiptoe—directly to the three-man tent. He pointed to the empty cots and grinned wide. Julian's puzzled expression was terrific. He stifled a laugh and gestured with his finger for Julian to follow—he tiptoed over to the supply tent and pointed in.

Julian tiptoed along behind, though it seemed silly—regular footsteps didn't make any noise. But it was fun, so he snuck into the passageway, where Danny had pointed—the sun hitting the tan canvas on the east side subdued and softened the morning light, making it amber and dreamlike... *whoa*. Julian braced himself against a crate: Tom and Nick were asleep in each other's arms... The beauty and love he saw astounded him. It was the most sublime scene... it took his breath away. He was frozen in place. He felt a glow spread through him—he never expected to see something like this.

ow! Julian's trance shattered: Danny hissed at him, poking him in the back. He was supposed to go back out. *darn.* It took a minute to react—he wanted to watch some more. Julian backed out as slowly as he could. His instinct was to hold his reaction very close. He made a mental snapshot for later. Back outside, he turned around and looked directly at Danny. Silently, he mouthed "WOW!"

They broke up. Trying to stifle their laughter, Danny grabbed Julian by the arm and pulled him over to the Farting Post—he didn't want Tom to hear. They calmed themselves down. Danny was envious, but didn't want Julian to know that. Julian was both happy and proud, and didn't want Danny to know. So they both had to pretend to be shocked and amused.

Julian knew, but asked anyway. "All night?"

"Yeah! Tom told me at lights out they were gonna do it. We gotta get them up before Mark comes over."

"What do we do? Make a lot of racket, or something?" Julian wanted to go in and wake them himself, of course. Partly because he wanted see some personal equipment again. Somehow he didn't think he should tell Danny that, either.

Danny thought about it for a minute. *Tom didn't tell me what to do last night; I have to wing it. Tom and Nick trust me to know what's up... they think Julian is still as pure as he looks.*

"Go back toward the cabin and crouch down so you can't be seen. I'll go wake them up. I'll wave when you should come back."

"Okay." Julian returned down the trail toward the cabin. Danny knew best. He would have liked to see them again, though. It was **wonderful**. Of course, he could not tell anyone that. *I'll ask Danny later whether or not I should tell Mark. but maybe those guys deserve to have it secret. besides, I don't want to get Nick in trouble. I like Nick a lot. hmm...* he didn't want anyone to know what he and Danny had done either, come to think about it.

someday I'm going to see that again... I still can't believe it's that big. I want to see it fire! that would be a day to remember.

He waited, crouched down behind a tuft of swamp grass. Danny waved at last, and went back to the stove. Julian jogged toward the camp, pretending he was late. As he scurried up next to Danny, he had to force himself to not glance over at the three-man tent. I have a job now: *I have to pretend I don't know! that will be fun.*

The last hour and a half was very strange. Julian wasn't used to mysterious goings on. He understood why no one could talk during breakfast about Nick and Tom spending the night together: Mark was there. He understood why Nick and Tom didn't want to talk about it with him and Danny, either—they probably didn't want anybody to know, actually. But he didn't understand why Danny didn't want to talk about it after everyone had left camp.

there... that's better. He had just figured out how to show the splash the feet made. The new lake sketch was going surprisingly fast: two guys swimming out to the platform. He remembered it from yesterday, when he had seen Casey and Robin racing. *still have trouble with elbows though.*

The cabin was kind of dark; the overhead light didn't do much good. Pulling the curtains all the way open helped some, and so did the desk lamp. *too darn breezy today...* working at the camp table after inspections just wasn't possible. Besides, Danny didn't want to talk about Nick and Tom at all. "You're not supposed to know, blah blah blah..." *well, I do know! so why not talk about it?*

From what little he did see, he could tell Nick and Tom were in love. It was wonderful, but it had to be kept a secret. *I understand that part.*

everyone treats me as if I was a little kid, which can be a pain sometimes. why can't people just talk about stuff? after everyone was gone, after KP, after inspections, Danny couldn't wait to get rid of me, it seemed like. at first I thought it was because he was afraid I might tell Mark or something. but the more I think about it, the more I think something else is going on—something else I'm not supposed to know about. weird and mysterious.

At least this drawing was coming along. *it's so quiet in here... huh: I just realized—the radio isn't on like always.* At home, he'd be keeping track of how many times they played the same song, or what was on sale at Piggly Wiggly's. *I like this a lot better.* The breeze flapping the curtains around was about the only sound except for the clock. He kept an eye on that, because he was waiting to go to free swimming and work more on his underwater time. Danny had something else to do after inspection today; it was obvious he didn't want to fool around.

that's okay—I want to work on these sketches anyway. Maybe Danny's sunburn was still bothering him. *I gave him a good coat of lotion after inspections. going to the lake is still off his list. he has a new job that sounds like fun... maybe it has to do with that. no, the job is after lunch... oh well.*

what's Mark doing today? Julian went over to the chart on the wall: Lashing demonstration and workshop. *man. something different every day. this place would probably fall on its face if they didn't have Mark around. do they know how lucky they are?* He sat back down to draw some more.

He flipped down to the new bun page. Buns were harder to draw than he expected. *problem is, they don't stand still long enough in one place. there's such a range.* Nick tried to help there. He pointed out some of the choice ones last night. The problem was they were wearing clothes and being sat on, and it was dark. *but I got an idea at least... I glanced at a few during inspection. I'll keep an eye out at the lake, for sure. first: an outline of Danny's... I ought to be able to draw those: I greased them up with sun cream yesterday.* He guided the pencil along the page... *hmm. yes... hmmm.* How it **felt** was part of his memory as well. *I don't mind... it was fun to see Danny's contour reappear... dents: don't forget the dents.*

after I do this one I'll start sketching other buns I remember. trouble is, until a couple of days ago, I didn't really notice buns—or pay them any attention, anyway...

Julian glanced at the clock. Almost half an hour had gone by... ten minutes before free swimming. Seven sets of buns; he shook his head—*I need to see the real thing. the only ones that look right are Danny's. He looked at the clock again: maybe I'll go a little early. sit on the slope for a while and sketch from there. I can practice holding my breath in the water later. I forgot to set up being buddy with Bruce. he'll probably show up anyway, since he has to keep practicing his distances.*

> > giggle < < The idea of Bruce as Sheriff Dillon was a howler.

Danny stood just out of sight in the supply tent. He had been watching for two things, and they were now happening. Julian just headed for the lake and free swimming. He felt a little guilty about this, but he believed Julian was not ready for... for what he knew was coming. He still had plans for being with Julian, and he figured that this little session with Geoff would be beneficial, in the long run. He didn't want to admit that Geoff really excited him, but... *there!* Now the other scouts were breaking from their camps to go swimming or to one of the other free period activities. Tom and Nick had gone a while ago... they had huddled for a long time in the Panther Camp about something or other, then headed for the latrine. *it's going according to plan... in a few minutes I'll be the only one left in camp.*

Geoff came up with a special idea yesterday afternoon. Danny had fantasized about it all night. Seeing Tom and Nick this morning had really cinched it for him. He just knew this was going to be a big day.

He carefully peered around the tent corner... west, toward the Zebra camp... *empty.* South... Badgers? *yes!* Wolves were long gone. The coast was clear at last; he stepped over to his tent. *now I understand why the Flaming Arrow camp is located at this exact spot: I can see all the camps from here.* He gathered his sleeping bag, pillow and a towel. He took them over to the supply tent. He arranged it the same way he had for Julian the other day. Tom and Nick left everything in perfect shape. He removed his shoes and sat down cross-legged on the puffy plaid flannel. He fussed with his socks absentmindedly. He'd shown Geoff this place yesterday when they were helping the Quartermaster. Geoff had some arrangements he had to make; he said it might take ten minutes or so at HQ, and then he'd rush up the trail. *all I have to do is wait.* He remembered those incredibly hot few minutes yesterday…

Mr. Jorgensen led them up the trail to the Powhatan camp where Troop 118 was located; that's where they met the Quartermaster. He was a nice enough old guy, a little gruff maybe. But he showed them the ropes quick and easy: all they would have to do was check the delivery chart, assemble the food and ice packs listed for two of the five camps in the Bird Cluster plus the Meadow—it had the shortest trail. They only had ninety minutes to do their job, so they would have to hustle. They'd use this two-wheel handcart with large bicycle tires. Danny worried that it would be too wide for some of those trails. *Sarge's motorbike made it okay.* It had a small trailer—he had five camps now, so he had it a little easier—he'd been doing three on the west side plus the east five. A couple of guys from the Yellow Shirt crew did the north five camps with the other cart. The upper three Bird camps were a pack-in; Danny hadn't met that crew yet; they were out on their route. They must be from the Yellow crew.

Sarge gave them each a map that showed the trails to all the camps. They rode along with him yesterday to see what all they had to do. Beginning today they would go to HQ and see what supplies they were assigned to deliver. Now they'd be a team, and every day after Canoeing, instead of going to Backpacking merit badge, they would deliver supplies like eggs, milk, hamburger and fresh veggies. Everybody got the same thing, just different amounts, depending on how many scouts were in the campsite. *man, what a deal it is to supply all these camps.* A lot of food and ice moved through that warehouse. Big trucks delivered stuff almost every day.

Danny wiggled his butt unconsciously; he recalled the surprise he got at the Shawnee camp... the path back to the motorbike was narrow, and they had to walk right next to each other for a few yards. They were a few feet behind Sarge, so it was sort of slow going through there. *all of a sudden, I felt Geoff's hand slide across my butt! he gave me a really quick and nice feel. I couldn't believe it! I looked over and he gave me the sexiest smile! what a rush*—his cock seemed to like it too, because it sent that wonderful tickle pulse that always signaled it was about to wake up. *I smiled back, automatically.* Geoff raised his eyebrows and puckered his lips. *stupid me! I was slow at the switch. I finally realized he was asking a question. I nodded my head yes. what else could I do? this hot guy, super hot guy makes a pass at me?! of course yes!* Sarge didn't turn around, luckily.

They had no way to talk for a long time. The Quartermaster kept them close company and busy right up to the last minute. Danny sat in the funny little seat on the side, and Geoff rode in the trailer. The trails were a real bumpy ride. *I was surprised the motorbike could carry all that weight, it's so old.* It had to work awful hard, but made it just fine—the trailer hitch held too. *after we got back to HQ and Sarge dismissed us, Geoff talked to me out front.*

"Are you tied up during free swimming tomorrow morning?"

"No plans at all, except to keep out of the sun."

"Well. I'm supposed to play host at my camp to a special event, sort of. But I'd rather get acquainted with you. Is that okay?"

Danny blushed when he remembered this. "Yeah, sure." *my heart was beating. I didn't want to wait, to tell the truth.*

"It looked like your supply tent is just like mine. Is anybody going to be around there, do you think?"

"Nobody."

"Okay. Wait right there during free swimming. It will take me a little time, but not much; you might want to, you know, set things up a little," Geoff added with a wink.

I couldn't believe my luck. at least I nodded my head. I felt so stupid... I didn't know what to say.

∽⊙⊱∾

Ten minutes had gone by already. It was getting harder to just sit; his hands wanted to play… he sat on them. *I'll wait this way for a while.*

Danny just remembered: *Geoff and I both have Canoeing first.   it seems we were fated to meet…*

14   *second poker game*

The HQ building was a beehive of activity, for which Tom was truly grateful. *easier to avoid attention when this many guys are around.* A crowd waited to get into the Trading Post, jamming the entrance and hallway. He nodded his head to the right, indicating that Nick should follow; he made his way past the clot and went to the far side of the large room—it was set up for lunch already. He was not at all comfortable with what was coming up, and meeting those guys in a crowded place appealed to him for some reason… but he needed a little space.

He was all for backing out of the game today. He was still in a storm about Nick. He didn't want to mess around with anybody else. It wasn't because he was afraid it would screw his own mind up; he was afraid it would make Nick think less of him. Tom was afraid—and he did not want to admit this—that Nick might want to start liking somebody else. That had never even entered his mind before now.

He rattled the shaving kit. He borrowed it from Doug over at the Panthers this morning. It had fifty poker chips inside. They weren't all white, but that didn't matter in this game. He looked inside… *these chips go way back in Panther Patrol history… a lot fewer now.*

He glanced at Nick; he had always taken Nick for granted. For a long time he was afraid Nick might get mushy, or something, and he hated that. *well… I used to hate that.* After last night, he realized that Nick loved him. He may have thought that before, but he didn't let it bother him. Nick was always so cool about everything. He never got pushy, or jealous, or possessive. Or mushy. He was always there, and he was always terrific with sex. He was always just right. Tom wouldn't tell him this, but he could go right ahead and get mushy. *any time, actually.*

Tom had not understood how valuable or important Nick was until last night. He finally realized how lucky he was. He started to notice little things, too. And those kisses! They had always been a turn-on—but now!

but when we talked about the game they had set up for today, Nick was against me pulling out of it... really faked me out. Nick said it was a matter of honor. *come on! honor?* Nick was worried about Casey and Robin, for some reason. *well, Nick is pretty darn smart, so I had to go ahead with it—but I made Nick come along himself: maybe when he sees these guys, he'll see why we should go back to the Flaming Arrow, just the two of us, and skip the poker game. that's all I want to do. I wanted to just stay there all day, in the first place.*

"Where are those guys, anyway?" Tom was impatient.

"We could be early... their camps are farther away." Nick had glanced at Tom from time to time as they walked to the HQ. He had never seen Tom so on edge. Things were sure a lot different from yesterday—or the day before, even more. He knew now that Tom loved him. He still didn't understand why. What a feeling it gave him! But he knew Tom pretty well... at least he thought he did. The prospect of actually keeping Tom was a very new thing, and he was paying full attention. He didn't want to take it as fact, yet. And, he sensed that he would somehow get the blame later if he let Tom back out of this.

Tom probably doesn't know that I've never had sex with anyone else. never felt the need. there haven't been a bunch of guys chasing after me, anyway. I'm very ho-hum in the looks department. He had always thought it was a miracle that Tom jumped on him in the first place.

Nick was a little scared. He had only been in one of these poker games once, over two years ago now. He didn't know if he could actually do it. He wanted to try, sort of. But that time all they did was jack off at the end. This one will be very different.

What he told Tom was all theory, of course. *but I think it's right.* His real reason for coming along wasn't sex at all: *if we share something like this, it will show Tom that he is not in a trap—that I am his friend as well as his love. I'm so used to Tom boffing every pair of cheeks that passes by, getting upset about it makes no sense anyway.* Actually, watching Tom doing somebody else might be exciting... *maybe I'll need that to get turned on, even. I could never go to one of these things alone.*

And he was worried about Casey... if Tom didn't show up, Casey and Robin would be on the loose, and word might spread. *Tom has a peacemaking job to do with them anyway.* His conquest was not remembered with any fondness. *for some time those two have made certain not to be alone whenever Tom was near—or if they were alone, take the long way around rather than take a chance.* Tom was completely ignorant of what others thought about him. *I've had to cover for him a lot over the last couple of years.*

> > *rattle-rattle rattle* < <

The sound from the leather shaving kit indicated the level of Tom's impatience.

Nick checked the room again. *we seem to be the first ones here, all right. oh... Casey and Robin are just coming in—talking to the Oriental over by the entrance.* He nudged Tom and pointed. Tom's description last night had certainly made Nick curious.

Tom stood and waved. *about time...* He rattled the chips again. He was not at all comfortable.

"Hey, Tom!" Geoff gave him a thumbs up. "Pretend that was a pat on the butt," he chuckled. "We have to be polite in public." Geoff led the other two around to the other side of the table and they all sat down. hmm... a new face... he glanced at Nick. *who's this? he wasn't on the platform yesterday.*

Casey looked at Nick and smiled; he elbowed Robin. Robin glanced back to see why, and saw that he was looking at Nick. He looked too; Nick was blushing.

"Hey, Nick." Robin had known Nick a long time, ever since grade school. He was a little surprised to see him here, in fact. *wait a minute. I'm a lot surprised.* He looked back at Casey: his typical superior know-it-all grin was in place. *so Casey knew about this? hmm.*

Robin looked back at Nick, who returned his greeting with a small wave of the hand just over the edge of the table.

Geoff needed to get things going. "Have you seen Brian, or Jack?" No nods came back... *what's all this quiet about? these guys are supposed to be old friends.* Geoff sensed a complication—he didn't need that: he was counting on being able to exit without any problems. *must be a Troop 9 thing. I'll fix whatever it is while we wait for Brian and Jack.*

"I was trying to get these hotties to tell about how you ravished them, but they won't reveal a thing." He looked at them playfully; all four were blushing, now. "Well, don't deny it!" He winked at Robin. "With a set of buns like you parade around with, what do you expect?"

They all laughed.

"And don't you laugh, Bubble Butt," he nudged Casey. "You came so close to getting grabbed on the left side when I came up behind you this morning! I deserve an award for my restraint."

Casey felt a rush... *maybe I'll get paired with this guy.*

"But you: you I don't know yet." He looked directly at Nick. It was a penetrating look, with a very subtle pursing of the lips, framed in a small smile. "Tom, who is this man of mystery?" His eyes sparkled with mischief.

Nick was red faced and frightened. He had not expected to be noticed. What could he do?

To the astonishment of the Troop 9 boys, Tom wrapped his arm around Nick and hugged him like a football player hugs a teammate.

"Geoff, this is Nick." He didn't elaborate.

wow. Geoff took notice. Clearly, Nick was Tom's property. *well. this is even better. now I have a sub. he's not that cute, but he'll do.* He reached across.

"Nick, I'm glad to meet you." Geoff shook Nick's hand firmly; he tucked his middle finger back under and tickled Nick's palm at the same time. This was an old trick that Geoff loved to pull—*it's fabulous to see the reaction; it feels so naughty.* How long will Nick blush? *what a delicious color!* He let go finally, after winking at Tom.

"I'm here at last!" Jack approached, full of cheer. *he's on the far end. excellent. I won't stare. I still need to set up things with Brian.* He sat across from Geoff, next to Nick. *hmm?* He looked at the new face. *what do we have here? another one from Troop Horny? an orgy instead of a poker game, perhaps. not a bad idea. I'm ready, ready, ready.* He stuck out his hand. "I'm Jack."

Nick shook his hand. "Nick. Glad to meet you." He felt clumsy and stupid. *that darn Geoff started to get me hard!* That handshake was a shock. It was nice though. His hand felt very sexy... *so does this one.*

146

"Beware of that one, Jack," Geoff indicated Nick. "He's actually very horny today. He's a pro at hiding it. He wants to jump on your bones, actually."

Geoff's wisecrack made Robin blush. He wanted to do exactly that—he'd been fantasizing about doing that to Jack since he arrived. Luckily, no one was looking at him.

"Seriously. Don't sit next to him in the game. You're so drop dead gorgeous, he'll never make it to the end. He'll be forced to pounce and ruin just everything."

even Tom's laughing now. good. and Nick is blushing again. Geoff loved this. "Well, I see Brian is his usual early bird self." He scanned the room. "He probably stopped for a quickie along the way." He looked at Nick again. "He's the one you have to watch out for." He paused for effect. "He's not full of laughs, unfortunately. But he's overstocked in the **lust** department. Watch your back when he's around. Uh, backside, that is!"

Nick had never been paid attention to like this! It scared him to death, but he **loved** it. He wanted to grab Tom's hand, or something. He didn't dare do that.

oh goody! Another blush… Geoff was on a roll this morning. *I'll bet he's half hard, too. if I were sitting next to him… well, I'd better not trespass, anyway. Nick is Tom's, for sure.* Those messages sure came through from Tom's eyes. *interesting. I did not expect this at all. maybe it's just as well; I wouldn't want to be the one who gets to play with the precious one later on.*

"Sit tight, everybody. I'll just go look." Geoff got up and scurried out. He peeked back at the table. *yes! they're all abuzz. they'll be fast friends by the time I get back…* Geoff had come up with a hot idea, and he had to get to Brian before he arrived. *I have to sic him on Nick. Nick is the key, I can just tell.* He knew that Brian wanted what he had gotten yesterday: Tom's nine inches. He was going to help that happen. He went outside and looked up the northwest trail. Yep. There he is. He ran to intercept.

"Yo, Geoff!" Brian called.

terrific. he's in a good mood. "Brian, my man. A word in your ear." He nodded to the right. He led Brian over next to the building. Just in case one of the others came outside, he wanted to be out of sight.

Brian looked at him for an explanation.

"First, I want to thank you for granting my wish at the last game." He punched him in the arm lightly, and grinned.

"Good, eh?"

Geoff could tell Brian wanted to be next in that line. "**Better** than good. **Much** better. You must have some."

mmmm... Brian mulled. He had wanted it out on that platform. He never did get completely soft before getting ashore. He could almost feel his butt pucker. "Kinda big, though."

"Don't sweat it. He knows how to take care of that, believe me."

"So, what's up?"

Geoff checked to verify that they were secure. "I've got a super hot one all lined up, and it has to be now. Regretfully, I must drop out of the game today."

"What!?" Brian did not like that at all.

"Wait a minute, wait a minute—I have a sub." He grinned his best Tasty Grin. That usually got Brian's attention.

"I'm ears..."

Geoff explained who Nick was, and how to play things. He pulled a 3 by 5 card out of his pocket. It had some names on it. He had figured a match-up last night. He took out a pencil and wrote Nick's name over his. He handed the card to Brian.

Brian was prepared to tell Geoff to go jump, but then he looked at the list. *hmm.* Just what he wanted for himself. He didn't much care about the others.

"Wait a minute." Brian frowned. "How come there's two sets?"

"I knew you'd ask! Another brilliant invention of mine: that's round two. When Jack declares 'Jackpot Rule,' he just adds the phrase, 'two-layered cake.' That way, you get to command both sets, and nobody has to stop."

Brian's eyes grew wide. He growled hungrily. He looked at the second layer: it looked okay—he didn't remember the new ones too well. He licked his chops. *Geoff is some kind of a genius. crazy, but a genius.* "Can we get this all in by lunch?" Brian was going to try, in any case.

"Sure, as long as you hightail it up there right away. Okay: everyone is here. Let me take you in and tell them—they don't know yet. When you get the chance, fill Jack in—make sure he deals you the blackjack, and that he adds the two-layered cake. Remember: flirt with Nick a little. Make Tom want to jump you good. I think Nick is private property. We're gonna need to **fix** that."

"Right." Brian put the card in his pocket.

Geoff tugged at Brian's arm, and hurried back inside with him in tow.

"Here he is, men... I knew it: what did I tell you? Fresh in from his morning's, ah, **workout**." He waited for the laugh. "But he tells me he's saved plenty for the tournament." On that laugh, he stepped behind Nick and put his hands on his shoulders. He rubbed the back of his neck just a little more than was proper. Another blush. *this boy is so much fun!*

"Brian, this is Nick. Nick, this is Brian. He bent down and spoke in Nick's ear, not in a whisper. "Be careful. Be very careful." He gave a naughty smile, pinched Nick's shoulder just below his ear, and went back around the table to sit.

Nick looked at Brian and smiled a little. "Hi, Brian." He was petrified: *it's the Beefcake!* Geoff had pushed some kind of magic button. His pinch was electric; it sent a chill up his spine and a tingle down to his scrotum. He had gotten completely hard. He was astonished and delighted. *I need to get out of the house more often!*

"Hi Nick, glad to meet you." Brian extended his hand and shook warmly. He held it too long, on purpose. He assumed Geoff had this figured right; he always did. He sat down on the other side of Tom. He glanced at his face, then at his crotch. *is Tom half hard already? or just that big? I have to think of something else, quick—I'm in trouble already. I'll be hard in seconds.*

"Boys, I have some good news, and some bad news." Geoff took charge of the group. He had their full attention. "The good news is that the game room is all ready and waiting. There is a gallon canteen so you can have a refreshing sip when you get thirsty—sorry, no cups provided. The joy jelly is handy, as usual, and there are a couple of fresh towels; I hope you have brought your own? Good. I was able to get another twenty chips. Tom?"

"Fifty." Tom rattled the kit.

"Jack?" Geoff asked.

"Twenty-five." Jack raised a paper lunch bag up and set it in front of him on the table. He snuck another glance—*Robin is looking at me. oh boy.*

"Brian?"

"Sorry."

Geoff had been calculating the total; five short. "No matter! Just make the first hand ante free. You'll still be one extra. Take the odd chip out at the beginning. Everybody starts with twenty nine instead of thirty."

"But..." Jack started.

Geoff cut him off. "Which leads me to the bad news. It's not **awfully** bad, really. You see, it so happens that something has come up, and I will not be in the game today."

They were stunned by this news—except Brian, who leapt into the opening. "Come up?" he asked, suggestively.

They all looked at Brian, puzzled.

"Guilty, alas. It always happens when I see a plum that needs plucking. I am nearly up now, just thinking about him."

They had swung their gaze back to Geoff. Smiles replaced the puzzled looks.

"You see," Geoff said conspiratorially, "yesterday afternoon I was fortunate enough to arrange for this little **assignation**; and it is **not** to be missed. And fortune has been kind, because Nick has come to take my place in the game!" He clapped his hands merrily, and flashed his eyebrows up and down at Nick. *another blush! delightful. I should have been keeping count.*

Tom sat up; he saw this as a way out. "How can we be there without you?" *now Nick and I can—*

"No problem, believe me. Everyone in the troop will be far, far away all morning. Just be sure to tidy up, so the next event, *whenever* that may be, will be good to go. I hereby appoint Brian temporary host." Geoff got up from the table, and looked directly at Nick. He couldn't resist. "Thank you so much for helping me out today, Nick. I can't tell you what it means to me. Someday, who knows, maybe we can play another, **special** game."

He gave him a pucker and a wink. *yes! he's red again!* He glanced at Jack with a conspiratorial smile.

Geoff went around the table and bent down to Tom's left ear. "You naughty, lucky man. See you later." He pinched Tom's shoulder and took off. He waved at everyone as he went out the door.

Tom had a buzz he didn't understand from Geoff's pinch and whisper. He was stuck after all. He leaned his thigh against Nick's. It was strange not to be in charge. *at least Nick is here.*

Casey was disappointed; he watched Geoff leave. *too bad... choice buns.*

Brian stood up. "Mount up, guys. Time's a wastin'!" He led them out the door and over to Geoff's camp trail.

15   *the snorkel*

wow… the lake is going to be busy today… a big crowd at the gate. Leonard's just now letting them in. so, I'm not early after all… Julian wasn't in a hurry, anyway. He had a flash inspiration on the trail just now about the racing swimmers: make the forearm shorter. Maybe that would help fix that elbow. He sat on the slope on the opposite side from the cubbyhole cabinet. This vantage point was a lot better than yesterday's. Casually, he looked both ways… no one was paying him any mind. He flipped open to the bun page. *drat it! wind is just as bad here as it is in the meadow*—it tugged at the page. Drawing much was going to be difficult. *I'll study what I see for a while.* As scouts arrived and undressed, he compared the drawings to what he was looking at. He had a few sort of right. He made a tick mark by the ones that really looked bad; those would have to be fixed. *boy… what a lot of buns.* When they put their clothes and towels in a cubbyhole slot and moved off to jump in the water, he saw the other side too. *hmm.* He wasn't interested in drawing that, especially.

After twenty minutes, the boardwalk had become crowded—not everyone jumped right in. Clumps of guys sometimes stood around and talked. He liked that, because it made it easy to compare the dents. Most guys have them… yet they still look different from each other. *this isn't that easy to figure out.* Nobody seemed to be paying any attention to him, which was a good thing, because he was starting to get that tingle feeling again. Maybe it wouldn't get hard all the way. He was glad he had taken advantage of the opportunity. *hmm…* He flipped back to the dock drawing… *it's getting populated around here. too easy for somebody to see the buns page now. too breezy to do much anyway.*

oh, look! Paul and Doug! Nick said they had choice ones. He watched them undress and put their clothes in a cubbyhole. *so those are choice… hard to study them when they keep moving around so much… they do have interesting dents. Doug is a little more hairy.* He imagined touching them. *they don't look as nice as Danny's.* Doug was clicking the stopwatch. *ooo-ee, watch out! Paul's getting a stiffy!* They turned and jumped off the boardwalk. Paul's half-mast was a whole lot more intriguing than his buns. Julian's tingle had gotten a little worse. It was hard to see this forest of buns and not be affected. *say, now! Leonard is watching them, too. ooo! Leonard just adjusted himself. well.* A fellow bun watcher!

"Hey, if it isn't Doodles!" Sid plopped down next to Julian. "Taking advantage of the view, eh? Lessee." He took the tablet from Julian and examined the drawing of the dock. "Looks just like what I see out there, too." He flipped to the next page. He nodded his head in appreciation. "Man, you know how to draw the splashes really well. I can just see these guys moving." He examined it close up. *not that many eraser marks, either.* He had underestimated his pal. He handed Julian back the pad. "I may have to start calling you Michelangelo."

Julian sighed a big silent relief. He was afraid Sid might keep flipping the pages. "Thanks, Sid. I'm not that good." *I read a little about that guy*—painting an entire church ceiling lying on his back wasn't Julian's idea of fun, actually.

Playful, Sid swung his left leg and bumped Julian's thigh. "I thought maybe you were checking out the other scenery, too." He gave Julian an eyebrow dance, and looked out at the lake.

Whoa… Julian did not know what to say to that.

Sid looked back and saw the confusion and the beginnings of a blush. He smiled, "I may be the world's most extreme nerd, but I've got an eye too, y'know."

Julian warmed to Sid in a new way. He had just shown a bit if his inner self. Julian was pleased—a bit honored. He still didn't know what to say, though. He bumped his thigh back against Sid's to show that Sid could trust him. He didn't even consider that Sid might like to look at boys like he did. *I better not jump to any conclusions.*

good old Julian. "We miss you over at Wolf. Ever gonna come back?"

"Nope, don't think so. It's weird, though. Sometimes I feel like I shouldn't be there. Those guys are so smart I can't believe it. I feel like a little kid at times."

"That's no good; ya gotta set 'em straight."

"No, no, it isn't them—they treat me super! It's me. I know how stupid and green I am. It's a job trying to pretend I'm not, sometimes." Keeping his mouth shut was his best trick… his only trick, actually.

"Oh. Well, you'll get used to it. Those guys impress me as all right, except maybe Tom. What do you think of him?" Sid had heard a juicy rumor about him just the other day. Maybe Julian knew something.

Julian couldn't tell Sid what he really thought—especially after this morning. That scene in the supply tent had changed his opinion completely, and he had not had time to think about it. And Nick! He'd really like to talk to Nick about it. He didn't think he could, though.

"Tom? Well, I can't say I know him yet, very well. I've spent all my time with Danny and Nick. He's not as scary as I first thought." *Oh: I just remembered.* He looked at Sid. "I gotta tell you this, though." He put his hands over his mouth and muffled his chuckle.

"What!? Tell me." Sid knew that look; this had to be good.

"Okay. Yesterday after breakfast—Mark was leading the meeting as usual." Julian broke up again.

Sid punched him lightly. "What?!"

"Sorry. Well, it was quiet for a minute, you know, one of those minutes when nobody happens to be talking?"

Sid fidgeted, "yeah, yeah?"

"Tom let this fart…" Julian laughed loud. "It gurgled at the end, you know? Like maybe he had messed his pants."

"Eew!" Sid grimaced.

Julian held Sid's shoulder… "But that's not the funny part!"

Sid nodded his head, waiting.

"Mark says, 'that can't be good.'" Julian fell back on the slope and kicked his feet up and down. He hadn't been able to give vent until now—he rolled back and forth, pounding his fists on the ground.

It was infectious. Sid roared right along with him.

Julian sat up and put his hand on Sid's leg. "But then, and this is the best part!" He told Sid about the Farting Post.

They laughed a long time. Julian was relieved. Telling Sid was fun; besides, it helped him lose the stiffy he'd almost developed. He reckoned it was time to swim. *Oh...* he just noticed that Sid had a diving mask with a snorkel.

"Hey, I didn't know you had one of these!" He picked it up and looked it over. "I've never used one. Do they really work?"

"Yeah, for some things. They come in more handy over at the beach, but, yeah, they're okay."

"Can you show me? I've seen kids with them at the pool, but I never knew anybody who had one." Julian had just had an inspiration. This could provide a unique underwater view of some of those buns.

"Sure, no big deal. C'mon." He stood.

"Who's your Buddy?"

"You are, now." Sid didn't have one today. He figured he'd find someone, and he figured right.

Julian glanced around to see if Bruce was coming down the trail—*nope.* He didn't want to leave him in the lurch. *maybe he's already here.* He followed Sid down to the Buddy Badge Board.

At the check in table he paid closer attention to Leonard. *looks about Mark's age. interesting face: long and narrow nose, really full lips—long eyelashes.* His eyes made contact with Leonard's. Julian saw him smile. It made him blush for some reason.

Leonard was delighted to see this one again. *today's companion is the opposite of yesterday! today he's with the skinniest kid in the camp.* He admired Julian's judgment—either or both made him look even more irresistible.

Julian put his badge on the hook next to Sid's. He just realized... Leonard had given him a look of admiration. He felt flattered. He couldn't think of anyone else who looked at him that way. It was different from Danny. It made him feel good; *I like Leonard.* He tucked his towel and tablet into a top row cubbyhole. There were more empty ones than he expected; he undressed. As he took off his socks he happened to glance at Sid's mid-section—it kind of looked like Sid was starting to grow one. He pretended not to have noticed. It looked kind of big... he had never looked at Sid before.

They ran to the edge and jumped in. Sid showed Julian how to clear the lens and strap it on. "Remember, now, keep the hook pointed down. That way, when you go clear under, the tube won't fill up with as much water. And you gotta breathe with your mouth only." After giving a brief demonstration, he gave the snorkel to Julian. "Remember to blow out all the water in the tube before taking a breath."

Julian put it on and squatted down to test it. He turned his head back and forth and took a breath, then submerged and sat on the bottom. *whoa... I can see really good... up to about six feet before things get fuzzy. this is wonderful! much better than the naked eye. hmm... no buns close by...* he looked at Sid's cock by accident... *shrunk up again. wow... Sid has hair down there!* Julian was quite jealous of that. He stood up and broke the surface.

"Cool, Sid," he grinned. "Can you swim with it, and everything?" He took the snorkel off.

"Sure—as long as you clear the pipe when you come up for air. Otherwise, you'll go glug-glug in a big way. If you can't blow the water out, just pull out the mouthpiece. O'course, what it's meant for is shallow water... it's not like a scuba setup."

"Show me, will you? I'll swim alongside and watch."

Sid put the unit on and launched himself forward. He dog paddled for a few feet, just barely under the surface.

Julian followed at his side. He ducked his head down to watch from below. The lens looked the same, but there was a little water inside... He watched Sid tilt his head and dive at a slight slant downward. He fanned his arms wide and moved a lot faster, then held them at his sides and glided to a stop. He carefully rose to the surface. Julian followed the whole thing. *whoops! we're out in the deep already.*

Sid blew the water from the pipe and removed the mouthpiece. "See? Real simple," he grinned. "You want to try? We can go back to the boardwalk. I'll tag along." He took the unit off and handed it to Julian.

"Cool! Is it okay to have water in the lens?" He strapped it on.

"Yeah. It's hard not to have a little. It looks a little funny, but you get used to it."

Julian followed Sid's example. *works fine, as far as I can tell...* He swam where there were bodies to glance at. *this is cool! buns and cocks and balls. wow. staying close to the surface is tricky. hmm... this is pretty good, but the buns move around even more in the water than they do on the boardwalk. no way could I study any of these... I could barely get a glimpse. oop...* the boardwalk loomed ahead. He surfaced. It went too fast. He blew the water out of the tube.

"That is so cool, Sid." Julian was just about to take it off and hand it back when the sun glinted off something several feet away. He looked over—it was the side of Doug's stopwatch! He got an idea... *Sid won't mind.* "Could I do just one solo before I give these back? I want to check something."

"Sure, no problem. You want to use them for a while? I'll hang out along the dock. Take as long as you want."

"You can't dive, though, can you? I mean, like jump off and get a fast start, or anything." *It's quite a distance over to Doug.*

"I don't think so, no. I've never tried it, but the tube might pull out."

"Yeah. I'll just poke along, then. See ya in a minute." Julian submerged. He did a breaststroke out toward Paul and Doug. Nick's comment about these guys intrigued him. *what is so mysterious?*

He practiced using the snorkel as he made his way. He looked from side to side—breathing deep through the mouthpiece was weird. He practiced surfacing and blowing out the water. *just pretend you're a whale.* He peeked out of the water to see how far he had come. There they were, off to the left a little: they were in deeper water today, shoulder depth. That meant he had to submerge a lot more than he expected. He took as deep a breath as possible and submerged. He stroked toward them, kicking his feet as strongly as he could. He ignored the view along the way for the most part. *everyone has tight balls out here, too.* Soon the population thinned out to zero.

Depth perception was distorted... *not sure how far off things are...* **whoa!** He came up on them faster than he had anticipated. *there they are: Paul's buns... they look odd; seem to be jiggling or something. no... those are fingertips. they're squeezing Paul's buns! what is going on?!* He swung to the left quick—he was close to bumping right into them. He kept his eyes glued, because he had a sudden hunch. *ohmygosh!* Doug was sucking away on Paul's cock. Julian started to get a tingle at once. He kept

158

turning, and swam as far away as he could. *was I close enough for Doug to see me?* He wasn't sure… *I didn't check to see if Doug's eyes were open.*

He went up for air. He blew out the water and swam forward a few feet to be in the middle of a small group; he wanted to glance back without being caught. After a minute he looked back. Doug's head was out of the water now. *too blurry to see out here with the mask on*—he lifted them up to his forehead. Doug sure looked happy—*his eyes are glassy, not looking at anything. I never expected to see anything like that. hot! that's why Nick was laughing—he knew what they were doing.*

what should I do? Julian wanted to go back and watch; he was torn. He had to get the snorkel back to Sid. *I don't want to get caught spying. if you had any sense, Julian you would wait. compromise: submerge deep and swim slowly over that way until you can just barely see them… then watch as long as you can. yeah. when I run out of breath, I'll turn around and face away, then surface. I'll be far enough away… they won't notice.*

While he was pondering, they switched places. *of course! they're taking turns!* That did it. He put the snorkel back on and swam back. He got there quickly. He submerged and squatted on the lake bottom. They were about eight feet ahead. He crept to the side. He wanted to see some more—he'd never thought about doing anything like this. He'd completely forgotten about studying their buns. *there they are… it's so hot the way Doug kneads Paul's buns while he sucks! huh. Doug is down on him so far most of the time I can't tell very well exactly how long it is… I want to get closer! darn! I'm all out of air.* He turned around and floated up slowly to the surface.

He blew out the water, and took several deep breaths. He submerged as quietly as he could, and turned around just in time to see them swap places. *wow! Doug is big! and it bends down, not up.* He saw Paul grab the shaft and take it into his mouth. Paul's head went back and forth vigorously as he sucked. His eyes were closed. He handled Doug's balls with his right hand, and steadied himself by holding the back of Doug's right leg. Julian began to grow real hard. *this is too hot.* He turned around and swam away a little before surfacing. *I got a good look at Paul's that time, too… bigger than Danny, I think…*

No way could he last long enough down there to see it all. The snorkel was only a disguise; it didn't help him stay down any longer… but what he had seen was *amazing! I have to find a way to thank Sid for this little*

159

surprise. oh. wait. I can't do that, exactly. what am I going to say? better say nothing. Sid wouldn't know what to think; if he knew what those guys were doing? hoo! Julian put the mask up onto the top of his head. He was through snorkeling, for now at least. He looked around— *where is Sid? not over by the boardwalk... along the F dock? not there, either. I'll swim to the boardwalk...*

Sid popped up in front of him suddenly. "Lookin' for me?" he grinned wide.

Julian tried to stop before colliding, but he was too late. He didn't bump too hard. "Oop! Sorry!" He tested to see if he could touch bottom here. He could.

Sid treaded water instead; he smiled at Julian, a knowing twinkle in his eye.

Julian sensed something was up. This was one of Sid's famous gotcha grins he used when he's pulled one on you "What?!"

"Enjoy the show?" He smirked.

Julian got it. His eyes went wide, "How did…"

"I saw them yesterday." Sid giggled. "That's why I brought my snorkel! How well could you see?" He'd ended up behind Julian by accident. He was thrilled when he discovered where Julian was.

Julian wanted to stand on solid ground to talk about this. He nodded toward the shore, and began a slow walk... *what am I going to say about it?*

The Buddy Whistle blew. They stopped and held their arms up high.

Julian's mind raced. The Buddy whistle was lucky; it gave him a chance to think for a second. No one was close by. He took off the snorkel and handed it to Sid. His eyes were open wide. Sid was the last person he thought would be interested in something like this. *whoa... he must have been over here when Nick and I were on the dock!*

The all-clear whistle blew. They moved toward the shore again. "Well?" Sid had a pretty good idea what Julian had seen. What he was interested in more than anything was what Julian thought about it.

"I could see good enough, I guess." Julian could see **perfectly!** "The trouble is I had to go back up for air all the time. I was afraid they'd see me, so I gave up." He giggled nervously.

"I think it's a contest or something."

160

They reached the waist high part of the lake—walking was easier. Julian's stiffy had gone down. They leaned on the railing. This is where he had stood with Nick during the Lifesaver qualifying. They had a fair view of Paul and Doug.

"Contest? I don't get it."

"To see which one cums first, I guess. Or the other way around. They seem to time it carefully enough with that stopwatch." Sid clicked his thumb down on an imaginary stopwatch.

They watched the two for a while.

Sid glanced furtively at Julian. "I wonder what it feels like."

Julian blushed. He wondered the exact same thing. He glanced at Sid, then looked back out at Paul and Doug. "Yeah."

Sid was happy with that, though it was ambiguous.

The very idea that Sid had said the word 'cum' was mind blowing. Julian had never considered that Sid and sex would ever be acquainted. He realized suddenly how stupid he was to think that. Still, it would take a while to get used to. *Sid probably thinks the same about me, come to think about it.* The subject had never come up.

Sid was getting horny. He decided to take a huge risk. "You ever... um, you ever think about trying it out?"

Julian's mind was buzzing. He was still trying to get his mind around this. All of a sudden Danny's comment started to make sense. That first day in the supply tent, he said that lots of guys did stuff with each other. Does he know about this too? He could see that Sid was waiting for an answer. What to say? *I never even knew about it before—but it did look very hot. I'll be honest, sort of.* "I dunno... yeah, I s'pose, kinda." *I wonder what Sid thinks.*

"Me too. Those guys seem to really like it, from the way they look." Sid didn't want to come right out and ask Julian. But boy had he decided to wangle it somehow.

"Yeah. I could tell that when I was up close. Doug was **really** liking it." Julian remembered the look on Doug's face. That was hot. He felt a tingle again.

"I wonder if it tastes very bad or anything."

Julian didn't suspect what Sid was up to. He responded automatically, as if it were an objective inquiry. "It must not; they sure don't mind, anyway." Watching the two out in the lake was causing him more trouble, too. *whoa!* He grabbed Sid's arm and leaned close to him. "Look: I think someone's about to win out there. He looked at Sid with a big wide grin, then back out at Paul.

Sid put his free hand around Julian's arm and squeezed. *Julian's right! I didn't see this yesterday!*

They crouched down automatically, as if they might get caught. There wasn't any place to hide. They watched carefully... Paul's head shook erratically.

Julian just knew he was shooting—*why else would he grimace like that... this is so hot!* He looked at Sid with a big grin. He looked back out as Doug came back above the surface. Doug spit out a stream in an arc that landed right in front of Paul.

Sid and Julian looked at each other and laughed with glee. It was very comical. But it was also very hot. They were both raging hard now.

"Ummm," Sid looked at Julian.

Julian looked back, and knew. He nodded his head. He reached over and touched Sid. "Me too. I couldn't help it. That was really hot!"

Sid reached over and felt Julian's. *hmm. not bad, not bad.* "So...." *I'm such a coward... how should I ask this?*

Julian grabbed him again. "Look! Doug's going next!"

Sid reached around Julian's waist and hugged tight.

They watched Doug, facing almost head on, enjoy an obviously excellent orgasm. His head shook much more wildly than Paul's had.

Julian noticed that Sid was silent now, still focused on what had just happened. He's still hugging hard, sort of in a trance. *whoa! Sid wants to get sucked! whattayaknow! well. I'd just love to do that, in fact. I wanted to try that with Danny yesterday.*

"Well, why not?" He looked at Sid. *boy, Sid is roaring horny. this will be fun.* "Do we hafta do it in the lake?"

Sid didn't expect this. He released Julian and took a step back, aware suddenly how he might look. He gulped. "Maybe not, the first time... looks too advanced, don't you think?"

"Yeah. I can only hold my breath for so long. I got up to thirty seconds yesterday." *those guys were under twice that, at least.*

They were silent for a minute, each trying to figure how to set this up. Julian was enthused. He recalled touching Sid; it would be interesting to compare him to Danny. *he isn't quite as big.*

"Have you got a watch?"

"Yeah, but it's over there." Sid pointed to the cubbyholes.

"How long 'til the whistle, d'ya think?"

"Let's ask." Sid led their slow walk over to the lifeguard tower.

Twenty-five minutes. Not enough time to go anywhere, really. They drifted back to where they had been standing.

"So let's figure it out at lunch. We have to get rid of you know what you know where." Sid pointed down. Too bad they had to wait; he was ready now.

"Good idea." Julian looked out to the lake. "Where'd they go?"

They both looked. "Ah! There on the platform," Sid pointed.

They watched for a minute—two guys, obviously friends, obviously pleased with themselves. Who wouldn't want to look like that?

"Cold water works pretty good." Julian started out to the deep water. He had started to go limp already. He could go out to the platform and back. *wait. can't do that!* He chuckled. He didn't think he could look those guys in the face and keep from breaking up.

Sid went along. He wasn't sure cold water would be enough—he was plenty hard down there. He couldn't believe he had gotten Julian to go along with this. wow. He was having some trouble associating Julian with sex... he always seemed to be such a complete purity... never talked about it; never even told jokes or anything. Sid donned the snorkel again... *easier to swim with both hands free.*

16   *Geoff and Danny*

"Anyone at home?" Geoff peeked into the entrance of the supply tent.

"Oh… hi…" Danny's was so relieved! His mind had drifted far away. He wasn't worried, but he had been waiting a long time.

Geoff smiled and sat on his heels right in front of Danny. "I'm sorry I had to make you wait. I promise to make up for it." He was short of breath from jogging all the way up from HQ. He was pleased with what he saw waiting. *quite pleased. congratulations are in order.*

"That's okay." Danny was fascinated. Geoff was even sexier than he remembered. sweating some—Danny reached over to hand him the towel.

"Thank you! How thoughtful." *I'm not sweating too hard, thankfully.* Geoff tilted his head to the left slightly, and took a fresh look— *Danny looks irresistible in this light. this is going to be fun!* "Tell me: how many times have you been seduced?"

That broke Danny up. He had not expected a question like that! He got back in control and held up one finger. He didn't count the times he and Frankie had done some sucking. Frankie couldn't come to camp, so other than Julian, he was going without—until now. He could hardly wait.

Geoff bet he knew by whom, too. *I'll find out soon enough. this kid is gorgeous! this has to be done nicely. I want to be welcome any time.* He reached forward and stroked Danny's left shin.

"Danny. I'm sorry, I forgot your last name."

"Laskey."

"Oh, yes. Mine is Staley. Geoff with a G Staley."

Danny gave Geoff a puzzled look.

"You see, my father is English; they spell it G E O F F instead of J E F F." He's a TV bigwig in Atlanta. My mother is Cambodian. That's why I look so different."

"Well, I think you look pretty hot, if you want to know the truth." *different, yes. hot, double yes.*

Geoff was not used to direct flattery. He loved it… it made his scalp prickle. He fiddled with the top of Danny's socks. "Your folks?"

"Oh. My dad works in the Post Office. My mom is a secretary at Jackson School." *nothing fancy like Geoff's.*

"Well, Danny Laskey, I sure am glad to meet you." He smiled wide. He looked down at Danny's socks. "What do you say we take off our shoes and socks?"

"Good idea." Danny's shoes were already off.

Geoff took off his shoes and socks.

Danny pulled off his socks; *should I just go on from here? no…* Geoff hadn't. He sat back down.

"Once, eh?" Geoff admired the feet that had just been bared and crossed in front of him. He formed a plan.

Danny nodded.

"Was it fun?"

Danny nodded yes again. *only half true, but…*

"Well, that's good." He ran his right forefinger along Danny's shin, over his knee, and up his thigh. He opened his palm there, and gently stroked the fabric. *Danny won't mind if I tease for a while.*

Geoff's hand was wonderful. Danny looked at his incredibly pretty face. He had never seen such dark eyes. From a distance, they looked black. This close, he could see that they were deep brown, with blackish spokes radiating out from a black pupil. *Geoff can do whatever he wants.* Nobody since Tom had handled him, and that was a mixed pleasure. *this is sexy.*

"When's your birthday?" Geoff went up the other leg this time. *I'll stop at the cuffs, for now.*

"September 7th. I'll be sixteen. You?"

"January 12th. Seventeen," he fibbed. He would be eighteen. He saw no point in alarming this lovely. He worked both hands now, stroking Danny's thighs, along the edge of the cuffs. He could see the result pulsing in the center... *very nice.* He extended the tease just a bit. He looked at Danny's left foot. Gently, he picked it up and began to play with it... he traced his finger around the anklebone, down the heel, and along the edge of the sole to the toes. He played the toes like they were piano keys. He bent down and took the big toe into his mouth. He sucked on it and ran his tongue around it.

Danny gave an involuntary moan of delight.

Geoff returned the foot to the blanket. He looked Danny in the face. *those black curls fall so lightly over the forehead! look like they're made of silk.*

"May I take off your shirt, Danny?" He was delighted that Danny had worn his troop's T-shirt this morning.

Danny's eyes went wide. He sat up on his knees. His hard-on poked straight out and was very uncomfortable. He put up with it; the shorts were about to go, anyway.

what fun. Geoff had never done it this way before. Having a complicit and aware subject enhanced things nicely. He reached out to Danny's belt line and loosened the shirttail. He ran his hands around all the way to his spine, and then retraced the sweep, a hand width at a time, working the shirt upward as slowly as he could. He felt every inch of Danny's torso as he slid the shirt up.

"How's the sunburn today?" He could feel a trace of sun lotion.

"Better; the very tops of my shoulders are still tender." The small of his back and behind his knees were worse—but he wouldn't complain. Geoff was being gentle. Danny raised his arms as Geoff reached them with the shirt. *this is such a turn on. I need to fix my cock!* He squatted back to help Geoff remove the shirt—*what a relief!* He looked at Geoff expectantly. *why is he smirking?* It came to him suddenly. *I can be so dense at times!*

"May I take off your shirt?"

"Why, yes... thank you. It is getting warm in here, isn't it?" Geoff removed his kerchief and placed it to his right.

He couldn't do exactly what Geoff did—*I have to unbutton instead. I'll try to come as close as I can to those body strokes—they felt fabulous... man...* Geoff's body felt wonderful... He smelled super sexy, too.

"How long ago, Danny?"

Danny did not understand the question. His eyebrows crimped, confused.

"Your first time."

"Oh! Last summer." *wasn't far from here, in an empty tent where the Zebras are now. Tom tricked me into going in there with him.* He shook his head. *I was so stupid then.*

"Mmm! You amaze me. You must be a pro, by now!" *the opposite is probably true.*

"I wish!" Danny paused. "I... well, I'm sorta chicken about it, really." He blushed. It was sad, but true. His sex life was mostly a fantasy, except for Frankie... and getting to play a little with Julian yesterday. He carefully folded Geoff's shirt.

Geoff formed his plan; *this is going to be as much fun as it will be hot. I'm going to practice what I learned yesterday from Tom...* Usually he preferred being on the bottom. *maybe today I can do it both ways. we do have over an hour left... and there's always tomorrow.*

"Danny, I have to admit something to you, okay?"

Danny looked at him open eyed. He nodded his head.

"Well, I'm not chicken about it. I do it a lot. I like it a lot, too."

Danny was stunned. His mind raced. *oh, man, exactly what I have needed, for so long! somebody who knows what they're doing! and he's so hot, too!* He did not know what to say without looking stupid. So he just smiled, and flared his eyes, to show that the light was **green**.

Geoff looked around. *I don't see any.* "Do you have any K-Y?"

Danny was unsure about that at first. Then he realized what it was. He had heard about it. His eyes narrowed. "N-no. I think I know what that is. I've never had any."

That told Geoff a bunch. okay... *it's time to get moving here.*

gave away; he pulled off and looked up to see his face. The ecstasy he saw there was a real charge.

boy... Geoff sure does know what to do!

Geoff stood and faced him directly. "Fair's fair! You have to take off my pants, now." The expression on Danny's face was wonderful.

Danny dropped to his knees instantly. *I can't believe this!* He unbuttoned the pants; he moved the zipper down, and felt the pressure of the pulsing cock underneath. He did the leg nudge too. He would have chuckled, but this was too hot... down went the pants; he lifted the feet too. *now for the skivvies.* He started exactly as Geoff had—but stopped mid-way. A wet spot was appearing right at the point in front.

"Oopsie," he looked up with a grin. "Somebody's dripping."

Geoff nodded. "Guilty; I got too turned on."

Danny reached around to Geoff's buns and felt them tentatively. These were so firm and shapely... more muscular. *I like these! down with the shorts. now I can look at that cock: it's dripping all right!* He looked up at Geoff, and got a 'yes, you may' smile. He had to look for a minute, first: there was very little hair. *it's perfectly straight—no curlies and kinkies at all.* He looked close—the foreskin was halfway down the head. A droplet oozed out just then, and began to run down the shaft. Danny caught it with his fingertip. *boy. I've thought about this so often!* He licked it. *mmm.* He nodded: *this tastes just right. I'll get to taste some cock at last.*

He grasped Geoff's balls with his left hand. Tight! Almost hairless, too. He had to run his tongue across there! He ran his tongue on up to the top of the shaft and wiped it across the slippery area that had formed along the foreskin circle. "Mmm!" He kissed the tip, and pulled the foreskin down as Geoff had done to him. *man is this cock dark!* Twice as dark as any he had ever seen. He sucked it in, all the way down. He repeated Geoff's moves exactly. *whoops!* Geoff had trouble standing like he did when the bottom edge of the crown was hit. *man, does this taste good!*

Geoff pulled him up so that they stood face to face. *time for a kiss. look at those lips.* He embraced Danny and they kissed. It wasn't passionate, but it was nice. *I might be able to teach him a little here, too.* He pulled Danny down and put him on his back. His instant compliance was a part of the pleasure—as if they were performing a dance or a ceremony.

"I see you have a pillow. Put it behind your head... more comfy."

Danny pulled the pillow over.

Geoff kneeled between Danny's legs; he was ready, and Danny probably was too. He reached for the tube of K-Y... *time to follow Tom's routine. I'll do it right, too. this kid has become almost re-virginized by now...* He lubed three fingers and his cock. He wanted a seamless, non-stop action. He looked at Danny's face. He saw happiness. He saw trust.

He raised Danny's knees and spread his legs wide. He scooted close and put the tip of his forefinger right on the button. Danny puckered it for him. *excellent.* He touched the bud gently and coated it with a soft circular massage. He bent down to Danny's cock. With his left hand he slid the foreskin up and down, triggering the automatic sphincter pulse. He pushed his fingertip in as it puckered for him. He worked the finger in a little farther with each pulse. Danny seemed to like it so far.

Danny was amazed at how good this felt; he'd had no idea. His memory of this was completely different. Before, it had hurt like the dickens at first—and it was while he was bent over, on his feet. *this feels good!* He started to relax; he'd been tensed up, expecting to grit his teeth for a while. "Mmmm..."

Geoff felt Danny relax. He worked the finger in all the way; he loved the way Danny's sphincter grabbed. He inserted the second finger, and followed the same routine. He found the prostate at last. Danny bucked with pleasure as he nudged it. He knew just what Danny was feeling! It was wonderful being on the other side! He pulled down Danny's foreskin with his left hand and took him full length in the mouth. He sucked up and down, gently. *nice. very nice. I'll plan to do a good blowjob before camp is over...* As the rhythm allowed, he inserted the third finger. Danny responded with an approving moan. He could feel Danny's muscles adapt to this task—to enjoy it. He reamed a semi-circle with his fingers as he pulled them in and out. Danny began to squirm in sync with his manipulation. Geoff pulled his fingers out slowly and replaced them with his pulsing cock. There was no resistance. He moved up and kissed Danny as he started to push in and out. *ohhh...* Danny's sphincter grabbed very nicely... *have to be careful—that could send me over the edge before I want.*

Danny had never felt anything like this... so full, yet it felt so good. *Geoff is fantastic. when his cock hits that spot inside... I remember that from before. man! this just keeps getting better... didn't hurt for a second, even.*

They fucked for a long time. Geoff learned how to pause and delay, and extend. He had almost forgotten what it was like to be on top. *it's good too... might do it now and then, just for variety's sake...* He started to pay closer attention... *be nice if we come together. sometimes that isn't the best, but Danny will probably like it better. next time, I'll go off first...* He knew how to control that when he was on the bottom. He started the final run. His thrusts slowed, his cock swelled. He hit that inside button square on, each time. Danny writhed ecstatically. Geoff kissed him wet, and grabbed his cock with his greasy right hand. He felt Danny's shaft harden and stiffen—that's all he needed to tip him over, and they shot together. It was wonderful.

Danny was powerless for a while. He had no idea this was going to be so good. He had to lie here for a minute and let his heart slow down. He felt Geoff pull out and lay down beside him. He opened his eyes and saw the top of the tent. He didn't even remember closing them. At some point everything had become so intense he didn't know what was going on; all he could do was soak it up. He turned and looked over at Geoff. What a beautiful face. *like a statue... so smooth. even when he smiles, it looks almost too perfect. oriental eyelids are wonderful. wow... I have a lot to think about.*

"Danny, you were fabulous."

"You're the one who was fabulous. I've never had anything like that before."

"Well, I know what you mean. I like being on the bottom myself. In fact, that's what I almost always do."

"Wow. How come?"

"I don't know for sure. All I know is that's what I like. I wanted to do the top with you because Tom sort of filled me up yesterday."

Danny laughed. "I know about that, all right. I don't know if I'd want to take him again." *I don't want to, in fact. Geoff is as big as I want to go. he's perfect.*

"He had a special way that I liked. I wanted to see what it would be like to do it that way on top. It was good, too, I have to admit. But I'm still counting on you to do me, next."

"Wow... Really?" "Really."

Danny had not expected this either. He reached down and felt his cock. It's still half hard. That amazed him.

"You mean now? Twice in a row?" What a stunning idea.

"Sure." Geoff looked at his watch. "We've got half an hour before lunch." He looked over at Danny with a big, hungry grin. He reached over and took Danny's cock into his hand and stroked it. He felt it get hard again.

"Man, I've never done that. I usually have to wait a day." Danny was amazed. *I wonder if I can.*

"The nice thing about the second time," Geoff squeezed Danny harder, and looked him in the eye... "it takes longer."

Danny looked back. Geoff did mean it! *so be it.* He sat up.

Geoff assumed the position and grinned wide. He handed Danny the tube.

17   *after Archery*

Julian's arm wasn't nearly as tired this afternoon. He had pulled that bow back twice as much today. *well, almost twice.* Anyway, he felt virtuous for having done his best. He had used the smaller bow, that was true. But it was still plenty hard to pull. *Cory must think I'm a complete wimp. today I had more trouble with the string snapping my left forearm. they said I could buy one of those sleeve thingys in the Trading Post. hmm.* He wasn't sure if he should use any of the special money his mom had given him for that or not. So far, he hadn't spent any of it. *I'll think about it... will I spend a lot of time later in life "loosing" arrows? doubtful.*

He thought some about the plan Sid came up with at lunch. Sid was supposed to show up at free swimming as usual, be seen, even bring along his snorkel. He was supposed to talk to somebody—anybody. The idea was to be able to say that he was at free swimming this afternoon, and have someone who could say so. Julian was to do the same thing; it was his job to watch for Sid getting dressed; Sid was to go to the Flaming Arrow camp and wait at the table. Julian would wait a few minutes, then follow. They assumed that Doug and Paul wouldn't be there at the lake twice in one day; if they were, they'd try to watch again to get a few pointers before going to the cabin.

Julian wasn't clear on why this had to be such a secret and complicated operation. That was Sid's idea. *but it's kind of fun this way... I'm looking forward to it.* He'd been intrigued by the look-see he had under the water. He wasn't sure whether Danny wanted to do anything like this. He still wondered about the whole thing, really. Sid and sex seemed such an odd combination. Sid didn't turn him on at all. That's why maybe this could be fun. He thought of it more as fun and education, in fact. He was lucky to be doing this for the first time with Sid. Someday, he would need to know how. *I need to know about these things when it's time...* he remembered the smell of Mark's shirt. *when it's time to do it with Mark.* That was going to take longer than he had thought, unfortunately. *some day, Julian, some day.*

He had his sketchpad along, but no towel. He didn't think to bring it along after changing clothes. He didn't especially want to make another trip to camp... *I'll just have to hang things out to dry later. or, I could just sketch and not get in the water. Sid isn't here yet.* He sat down to wait in the same spot as yesterday. He opened his pad to the dock drawing. *I don't see how to improve it any... maybe add a cloud. yeah. right over the platform would look good...* he drew a small cotton ball type cloud. *hmm. too cartoony. I need to practice drawing clouds.*

Sid plopped down all of a sudden. "Still wanna play doctor?" he giggled.

"You bet! I'm countin' on you to find out what ails me."

"Good. I haven't been naughty for months. I was afraid I was going to get rusty, or something." He looked at Julian with mock seriousness. "This is naughty, isn't it?"

"Whah, Sidney, whatevah do you mean?" Julian teased. "You ah the very picture of Southern Virtue, ah you not? If you don't believe me, just ask yoah mothah!"

Sid broke up. He tapped Julian on the shoulder and handed him his Buddy Badge. "Here: saved you the trouble. Let's check in." He swung the snorkel as they approached the gate... he'd run clear back to the Wolf camp for it. *my alibi will be more complete with this along.*

Leonard was pleased. His new favorite was back—with Jack Spratt again!

Julian returned Leonard's smile. He didn't know what to say. "Hi, Leonard." He gave a small wave with his fingers and tagged along behind Sid to hang up his Badge.

Leonard's affection for this lovely just doubled. *so close, yet so far.* Leonard was harmless, sad to say. But he had fantasies that made up for that. He'd start a whole new series tonight, in fact. Julian reminded him of Glenn Huckaby, the only real crush he had when he was a scout. *Glenn had blue eyes though... ah well. if only.*

Julian watched Sid go to the cubbyholes and undress. It just occurred to him to assess Sid's buns. *might as well... yesterday I saw Bruce's.*

now I'll have a better idea of the S/B scale's other end...!! Sid twisted his hips and wagged his cock at him—then turned and ran to the water. *Sid is such fun all the time.* Julian glanced at the tablet... *I don't want to draw right now.* He stashed his clothes and tablet quickly and raced to the edge. *goody... lots of space for a good practice dive.* He jumped in. He swam out a ways, where it was deep, and stopped to tread. *where's Sid? ah. by the F dock. now then: who to talk to? I don't see Nick anywhere. Danny is still avoiding the sun... I don't see anyone I know.* He looked over by the boat and canoe dock: Paul and Doug weren't doing their thing, either. Trying to find someone out here was next to impossible, even when it wasn't jam-packed.

Sid swam across between the docks, just to show he was here. *maybe I'll bump into somebody soon.* He had to admit that the only person he knew here today so far was Julian... *oh there's a guy from Badgers. what's his name now? umm... Nelson. that's it, Chuck Nelson. I don't know him at all—I'll just swim by close and smile or something. I don't need to talk or anything.*

Julian was at a loss; he couldn't see anyone. *Bruce might be over in the F.* He swam over to the dock and climbed up. *yep. there he is, plugging away. might look odd if I go over there just to say hello. hmm. looking around is too boring. saying hello to Leonard will have to be enough. besides, I bet no one is going to ask, anyway. so how can I measure a few minutes without a watch? I know! swim out to the platform and back again. that's about right for time.* He walked out to the diving platform. He stood on the diving ledge. *focus... concentrate. do what Nick says... one; two; three: jump... great! no water up my nose...* The added speed helped him go farther under water. *I'll do that again on the way back. I haven't done any real practicing today... this is better than nothing. Nick will be pleased... it's a good idea to practice my crawl stroke.*

hah! I just figured out something: we should have used the first Buddy Whistle as a signal. oh well. Julian approached the ladder on the north side of the platform. *I'll climb up and jump off as far as I can. I'm a lot better now than I was the first day.* On top he paused briefly to catch his breath. He glanced at the guy lying in the sun over on the far side; he had his left arm over his eyes. *what's the deal—why do these guys want suntans, anyway?*

oh! look at that! he has a stiffy! is he asleep? what if it gets sunburned? I don't know who he is. why is he alone out here?!! The cock wagged. *ooo—how long should I look at it?* A tingle feeling started... he liked those tingles. There are times, like right now, when he wished he wasn't such a coward. He wanted to go over and touch it, actually. It was bigger than Danny, and circumcised. He made a mental photo of it. *ooo!* It just wagged again—four times! Was the guy doing that on purpose? *maybe I'm being invited over there.*

Julian paused to think. It was tempting… but a little scary. Besides: Sid was probly waiting by now. He turned and dove off.

nice picture to add to my gallery... does that guy's Buddy know? what if he isn't using sun cream? maybe I should tell Leonard. he'd know where the Buddy is, at least. should I tell Sid? hmm. better not. no telling how much Sid knows about this kind of thing. There sure seemed to be a lot happening around here lately.

He hurried onto the dock. *must be five minutes by now.* He trotted over to the cubbyhole to get dressed—I forgot! No towel. Dressing while wet was strange… not a good idea. He hurried to the Buddy Board to fetch his badge… *what?!* Sid was right there, standing by the table, swinging his snorkel. *oh-oh. something isn't right. he's supposed to be gone already.*

"See?" Sid looked at Leonard self-righteously. He grabbed his badge and darted out the gateway as Julian came up to the table.

"I hope you boys aren't having a disagreement about something. You barely had time to get wet." Leonard was confused. It was rare for scouts to leave so soon after checking in… *they seem to be okay, though.*

Julian blushed. "No, we're fine." He shrugged. "See you later…" there was no way to explain this to Leonard. *oh well.* He hurried after Sid.

later today? that would be nice. Leonard savored the view of Julian trotting up the trail. *I liked the morning T-shirt outfit much better.*

Sid tromped up the trail. His great plot had been destroyed by that… he didn't have the word he needed.

Julian caught up. "What happened?"

"Well, it seems that you have to check out together as well as check in. That guy wouldn't let me leave until he saw you come up for your clothes." Sid had forgotten that little detail when he planned this operation. He felt a little stupid instead of a little smart.

Julian could see that Sid was embarrassed. He kept quiet. Just for kicks he looked around to see if their trip up to camp was being observed by anyone. *nope.*

Sid thought a little about what was coming up as they walked. He was still amazed at how easy it was to talk Julian into this. He had been thinking of it for a long time, off and on. He'd heard about it, and was curious. And when he saw those guys in the water, it gave him this crazy urge to see what it felt like, finally. He appreciated that it was not exactly approved scout activity; but it was overhearing a couple of the big guys at a troop meeting that made him think about it in the first place. Not with Julian in mind, of course. He never thought Julian was interested in sex. *he's such a poster perfect kid. always looked like he just stepped off a magazine page or something. truly amazing that someone as good looking as Julian isn't just a spoiled conceited brat. nope. one of the nicest kids I know. I sure wish some of his good looks could rub off...* He expected his prospects for romance would not be so great when the time came. Blind dates, probably. That kind of stuff could wait a while, though. *doesn't bother me like it does some of the guys.*

Sid thought a bit about the glimpse he got yesterday of Paul and Doug under the water. He didn't know why, but he got a stiff one when he thought about it. *it must be something basic.* He'd been beating off for a couple of years now, in secret. That sure felt good. It's all he knew about, so far.

Julian nudged Sid as they came to the Farting Post; he pointed to it with a big grin.

Sid broke up. "So that's the famous post!"

"Yep."

Sid stopped to look… then backed up to it and bent over. "Are you supposed to lift a leg or anything?" He bumped the post lightly. "Eee!" A jagged branch stub had poked him.

They had a good laugh. The impending activity was growing a little ominous in Sid's mind. He didn't know how they were going to get started.

Sid spread his towel out on the Flaming Arrow table to dry in the sun. He looked around. He had not been here before. "Pret-ty rit-zy! Look at that stove!" *this is the smallest patrol and it has the classiest stove? Julian told me about that. only two tents.* The checkerboard pattern on the camp tablecloth drew his eye. *this oilcloth is nice.*

"Okay Doc, that's your exam room, over there." Julian pointed at the supply tent.

Sid looked puzzled. He had not thought this through. "Is there space in there?"

"Yeah. I think it would be sorta stupid out here in the open, don't you?"

"Oh, yeah. You're right. Lead the way. I'm new here, y'know."

Julian led him to the space behind the crates. He gestured grandly.

Sid put his hands on his hips. "So what do we do?"

"I dunno, for sure. I s'pose we should take off some clothes, for openers."

"Oh… yeah." They took off their pants and skivvies. Sid unbuttoned his shirt and opened it wide.

Julian took off his shirt completely. He did a "ta-daa!" and opened his arms wide. He was glad to get his clothes off; they were damp. *from now on I'll always have a towel along. just keep it with my tablet.*

Sid laughed and did the same thing. His confidence was back. He grinned and— *oh look: we're both starting to get hard.* He looked at Julian's cock close up for the first time. *gosh…* He expected to see some hair, at least.

Julian noticed Sid's interest. He shared it. He stood forward. "Let's compare." *should I call it Little S?*

oh. what an idea… Sid was intrigued.

They stood close together, tip to tip. Delighted, they both watched each other get completely hard.

"I think yours is longer." Julian put his alongside of Sid's.

"Yeah, a little." They bent down closer. "A quarter inch, maybe?"

Julian tilted his head. "Yeah, at least. But I'm a little wider."

"Think so?" Sid backed up and held his cock head right next to Julian's. They touched briefly, and pulsed. They both looked at each other and blushed. They had felt something new. They liked it.

180

Sid nodded, "yeah, yours is a lot wider. Especially around the edge; see?" He traced his fingertip around his crown, then Julian's. *ooo... nice.* Both cocks flipped up in response.

They looked at each other again and broke up laughing.

Julian put his hand to his mouth. "Oh gosh. I just realized something. We don't have a stopwatch!"

"I never thought of that."

"Well. Maybe there's no need, really, unless you want to run a contest, or something." *contests aren't that interesting;   who wants to hurry to end having fun?*

Sid shook his head no.

"So all we have to do is decide who goes first."

"Okay. Odd man it." Sid held out his left palm and swung. "I go first if it's even, you're first if it's odd."

They pounded a fist into the other palm three times. Julian had three fingers flipped out and Sid had two. Five.

"Okay." Julian was just as happy to go first. *now I'll find out what it tastes like.* Ever since that time in here with Danny, he'd wondered about that. He kneeled down in front of Sid. "You want Paul or Doug?"

"Huh?"

"They did it different, didn't you see?" He was about to show how Paul did it, but he hadn't looked at Sid's cock up real close, like he had Danny's. He did so now.

"No, I didn't really see any difference." Sid didn't have his glasses on yesterday, so he was going on a general idea instead of a clear picture. *I didn't stay down there long enough to see both do it...* In fact, he wasn't sure which one of the two was down there.

Julian studied Sid's cock. He moved his head around and looked on both sides. Sid had a real good start on growing his hair. He looked closely at the follicles at the base. Sid was circumcised. *just like me... a good quarter inch longer... very white... completely hard.* It bounced up again. Julian loved to watch that happen. He had not even touched it yet, either. He looked up at Sid.

"You have a nice one, Sid. I never looked at it before."

181

Sid blushed. His cock pulsed. "Thanks, Julian," Being complimented was always nice. This compliment was very nice.

"It's not that often you get to look at one of these up close. Do you mind?"

"N-no, not at all." Sid felt a strange rush all of a sudden. He looked down and watched Julian examine. *Julian lifted my balls! how come that felt so good?*

Julian pressed down on the shaft and watched it spring back up. He smiled wide and looked at Sid. He moved it from side to side. *boy, it's really hard!* He tested the skin on the shaft. He pulled it up a little, then down a little. He twisted it from left to right and back. *pretty tight, just like mine.* He bent down to look at the wrinkles in the scrotum... *those are so cool. they'll hang down loose* after a while. Swimming always made them get so compact. He touched it briefly again... *yep. just like my sack when I get out of the lake.*

Sid was undergoing something new... his heart was beating a little faster, and he wanted to breathe differently. *Julian can do this all day...* He had no idea it was going to be wonderful like this.

"Thanks, Sid." Julian was quite intrigued—being allowed to examine the base, and look at the hairs coming in down there was a bonus. "I'm jealous of all your hairs. I don't know **when** I'm ever gonna have some." He rubbed the hairs on top gently. Not near as many as Danny—or as long.

"Okay. This is what Doug was doing to Paul, as far as I could tell." Julian held Sid's buns in his hands, and took Sid's cock into his mouth. He kneaded Sid's buns with his fingertips, and slowly went up and down on the cock.

Sid's jaw dropped open— *!!!* His hands opened wide and jumped up beside his head... what a sensation! He looked down, amazed... seeing Julian's lips closed over his cock was so... and the **feeling!**

mmm! this is interesting. Julian didn't know what to expect, but this was all right. *very mild, really... maybe the aroma was more interesting, actually.* Julian decided on the spur of the moment to go all the way down to the very base—that's what Doug had done. It was a little awkward here, because his forehead kept bumping on Sid's tummy. Sid's knees bent when Julian connected with the head. He did this about six times, and pulled off. His lips smacked as it came free into the air.

"How was that?"

Sid was stunned. He looked down at Julian in utter amazement. "Wow!! Julian, that's incredible! No wonder those guys do this!" He smiled wide. He wanted more.

"Good. Okay… Here's what Paul was doing to Doug." Julian put his right hand behind Sid's left thigh, and took Sid's balls into his left hand. He took Sid's cock into his mouth again; he pulled gently on Sid's balls as he rapidly sucked back and forth on the upper part of Sid's shaft. He didn't go all the way down, and he crossed over the head with every pull out.

"Ohm oh…" Sid could hardly keep standing… his knees buckled every time Julian's tongue swept up over the back of his cock's head.

This was enjoyable; Julian looked forward to Sid working on him, of course, but doing this was fun all by itself. He experimented a little—he applied some tongue movement and suction levels. After ten passes, he pulled off again and looked up with a big grin.

"Was that better, or something?"

"Man! Julian, you have no idea! Now I see why they do this in the water! I can hardly keep standing."

"Yeah, I noticed that." He looked around. The ground didn't look very inviting to lie down on. *no furniture here… I don't want to sit outside at the table.* He hit his forehead. "Stupid!"

"What?!" Sid was startled.

"The **cabin**, of course. I don't know why I didn't think of that at first."

Sid looked at Julian in disbelief. "You mean **Mark's** cabin?"

"Yeah. There's even a clock… you know, just in case." Julian grabbed his clothes and stood up. "C'mon!" He headed for the opening.

"Wait!" Sid cried out.

Julian stopped and looked at him, puzzled.

"How can we do that? What would Mark say?" Sid felt himself going limp. He was verging on panic.

"Don't be silly. It's my cabin too, y'know. There's a bathroom and everything. C'mon, grab your stuff!" He went to the opening; better see if the coast is clear.

how can it be Julian's cabin?   ask later—he's leaving! Sid grabbed his clothes into a bunch and hurried after—he bumped into Julian at the tent opening. "Should we get dressed?"

"I guess so. I don't think anybody's around, but y'never know." Julian put his skivvies on his head temporarily and slipped on his scout shorts... *no point in putting on my shirt.* He reclaimed his skivvies and trotted out of the tent with his shirt and kerchief tucked under his right arm. "Don't forget your snorkel and towel."

Sid giggled and followed suit. "They're on the table. I'll snag 'em on the way." Julian seemed to know this was okay... his enthusiasm returned.

They made a dash for the cabin, skivvies in hand. They were there in a flash.

18   *Sid's cabin adventure*

Julian closed the door behind them. "See?"

Sid saw Julian's cot against the wall. He scanned the room. *there's the famous scrapbook!* He looked at Julian with a big grin. "Are you **ever** a luck out! I didn't know you stayed here!"

"Yeah! I use that table for drawing and stuff. C'mere, this is the best part!" He led him to the bathroom. "I don't hafta run down the hill any more!"

Sid was awestruck. He slugged Julian on the shoulder. "Trade ya an air mattress!" He was only kidding; but having a bathroom— *man.*

"Sorry." He grinned. Julian turned off the light and led Sid back into the main room. He removed his shorts again.

"What do you think?" Julian pointed. "There's the table. You could sit on the edge and I could sit in the chair." They thought about this. "There's the floor..."

They looked at each other and shook their heads no. "There's my cot, and there's Mark's bed." Julian was having fun. He'd already figured out what to do. *this time I'll use the bed. the floor is too hard on the knees.* He remembered the downside of administering Danny's sun cream. Besides, he was really curious to see if those featherbeds were any good.

"Mark's bed?!" Sid was scandalized.

"Sure, why not? I can spread my blanket out over it. He'll never know." Julian did just that.

Stunned, Sid just watched.

Julian stood back with his hands on his hips. "There. What's the matter with that?" He bent over slightly, looking at his feet. "Oh. We better take off these." He sat on the edge of the bed and removed his shoes and socks.

That sold it! Sid jumped to; over to the bed he scooted, and sat next to Julian. He took off his shoes and socks. He sat back up; had no ideas about what to do next.

"So how do we do this, anyway?" Julian scratched his head. "We never figured out things. We know it's not a contest, in our case, at least. How long should each turn be? Is it in minutes, or what?"

"I don't know… you're right. I didn't think about that."

"Or should one go all the way, then let the other one?"

"That doesn't seem fair, does it." Sid remembered back to a few minutes ago… he sure didn't want Julian to stop.

"By the way: which one was best, anyway? Paul or Doug?"

Sid looked at him in amazement. "Are you kidding! How can I decide that?! They're both wonderful!"

"Hmm. Probably have to alternate, then. Best of both worlds, eh?" He nudged Sid in the side.

That did it. Sid's cock began an instant rise. They both watched, fascinated. Julian's followed suit. They looked at each other and smiled wide.

"Now that we're ready again, is it still my turn? Or do you want to try out those things on me first?" Julian was eager to see what it felt like.

Sid thought a minute. *I want to be fair, here.* "I think you should have a test first. That's only right."

"Okay." Julian hopped up and stood on the bed. It still sagged in the middle… *not very springy.* He spread his legs apart for stability.

Sid kneeled in front of Julian. He looked up and saw Julian smile back. *gosh he's beautiful. I'll try to do exactly what Julian did…* He'd never thought about looking at anybody's cock up close before, but it seemed to be a good idea right now. He examined Julian closely. He held the balls the same way. *oh—they're soft!* He looked close… the fine nearly invisible blond hairs… *this is different from mine.* He tested the skin the same way. He tried to pull it out. Then he tried to pull down, but it was tight already. *touching somebody else's cock! what a thing to do! so warm…*

no idea this would be so interesting!   He looked at the eye at the tip. He pinched it open tenderly. wow.

"Say, Julian!" He leaned closer. "Did you know you had some little dark hairs starting in down here?"

"Whoa! No! Let me see!" he bent down so fast he bumped Sid's head. "Where?"

Sid pulled Julian's cock to the side and put his finger at the base of the shaft. "See?" Their heads were touching. Sid liked that. He held Julian's cock with his right hand, and counted them one by one with his left forefinger. "Seven." He changed hands and looked at the other side. They looked closely again. "Nine!" He pushed the cock up flat against the torso, and pulled the scrotum down. "Eleven!"

"Look on top!"

Sid pulled the shaft down as far as it would go.

"Ohmygosh! Look!" He cupped Julian's cock in his left hand to hold it secure. *why is it so warm?*   It pulsed for him, too. He looked close. "Scads, Julian! They're real little, but there are lots and lots."

"Oh, thanks, Sid! I have been waiting so long for this. I was afraid I was going to be bald down there forever!" *I'm glad they're dark...*   blond hair down there didn't seem like a very good idea.

"Well, it looks like it won't be long now." Sid let go of Julian's cock for a second. *it's plenty big enough to have hair.   I haven't had mine for very long.*

"Let's see… Doug, then Paul." *I need to concentrate on this.*

He put his hands on Julian's buns. He tried to knead them briefly… he looked up to see if this was right. Julian nodded yes. *good.   here goes!* He put his head down and sucked Julian's cock into his mouth. It took a second to notice the taste. *whoo!   how interesting.* He moved his head up and down a couple of times. *oops: forgot to knead.* Sid started to knead and suck at the same time. He went all the way down to the balls. He tried varying the suction like Julian had. He played with his tongue, too. He pulled almost all the way off, and Julian's knees buckled just like his had. *aha!   that's what caused it.   this is nice...* He forgot to keep count. *how many did Julian do?   he didn't say...   I'll do five more,   just to be fair.   I can tell Julian likes this,   too.*   After the fifth, he pulled off, licking the back of the head like Julian had. His lips made the same slurpy pop. He looked up to see how he had done.

Julian looked back with a mellow smile. "Sid, you are right. That is incredible. You cheated, though. You did more than I did. But I forgive you." He giggled. *Sid is talented though, no doubt about that.*

Sid couldn't **believe** what he was doing! But making Julian happy made him happy too. That amazed him. He had never thought of such a thing. "Okay. Here goes the other one." *Julian might like it best...* he put his right hand behind Julian's thigh, and took those downy balls in his left. Back in the mouth for another taste! He sucked back and forth more rapidly. He went the full length... mostly because Julian was small enough. He massaged the balls gently, and pressed his tongue against the head as he pulled back. Sure enough, Julian buckled when he did that. *o darn... I forgot to count again. I'll start now, and do another five. Man, Julian is shaking the whole bed!* He pulled off and sat back with a big grin.

Julian was delighted! "Sid, Sid! Why didn't we find out about this sooner?" He sat down on his heels and faced Sid. "Thanks for cheating again, too." He paused to catch his breath. "Wow." *a lot better than I expected.* Still, it did seem odd to be kneeling across from Sid, of all people.

They looked at each other for a moment. Things had gone differently from what either had imagined. Had they discovered a new favorite pastime?

"Well, we've each had a turn now. Do we do that again, or should one go all the way, and then the other?"

Sid didn't know. He didn't care. *Julian can decide... either way, this is the best day of my life.*

"Wait! I have another idea... let's try it lying down instead of standing up!" *that way I won't keep bumping into his tummy with my forehead.* He looked eagerly at Sid for approval.

It was infectious. Sid nodded his head eagerly. Julian pushed Sid down onto his back. He straightened his legs and spread them apart. He kneeled between them. He looked down briefly. "I can't do the buns this way. What do you think?"

Sid had no clue.

Julian tilted his head. "I know. I'll try this instead. Tell me if it's any good."

Sid nodded yes.

Julian knelt down and took Sid's balls with his left hand, and the shaft with his right. He did the long up and down suck. *I can do it so much better from this position. I don't keep bumping my forehead.* He went up and down several times. He didn't bother to count. *I like Sid's taste. I'll go until he tells me to stop.*

Sid moaned; he had never experienced anything like this! He lost contact with his rational mind. He focused on his pleasure centers; concern about taking his turn had vaporized: he paid full attention to what Julian was doing with his mouth and lips and tongue. *ohh... mmm...*

Julian decided to alternate the two methods; doing this well was important—he wanted to give Sid a good time. He figured he'd get one in return. He sensed that the second method was a speedy way to cause Sid to come. He did it that way very briefly. It was pretty obvious now that Sid would like to go all the way. He looked forward to tasting Sid's cum, too. He'd been wondering about that ever since he tried to taste Danny's that time in the tent.

He didn't pay attention to the time... he enjoyed doing this. He was learning some new things... how to sense what Sid's twitches and hums meant. He learned how to vary his pressure, tongue movement, and hand coordination. He tried a sequence, then a series. *I can do lots more detail. wups... a change in the taste... ooo-ee! does that mean he's getting close?* He increased the pressure with his right hand gradually. Sid's balls tightened. *oh boy!* The shaft swelled bigger in back... the head got harder... *here it comes!* Sid shot at last. Julian milked every drop. *gosh... I kind of like this stuff!* He swallowed a couple of times so that he wouldn't gag.

Julian just noticed something: Sid didn't pump—he bucked and twitched, but no thrust! *that's something I'll have to sneak in when it's my turn. Sid needs to know about that for the next time.* That's one thing he had learned from Danny—Danny really pumped away when he was at it. It did make it better, somehow.

At last Sid relaxed… Julian kept the cock in his mouth. *I'll keep it there until it stops pulsing. when I pull off I want to give him that intense last minute intense feeling. here goes…* he pulled off, dragging his tongue mischievously.

"Uhnnh!" Sid bucked hard.

Julian sat back on his heels. He looked at Sid—what a wonderful expression on his face.

Sid opened his eyes at last. He looked at Julian in utter disbelief.

"What?! Wasn't it okay?"

Sid grinned. "Are you kidding?" He didn't know how to describe what he felt. It was a quantum leap from anything he had thought of. "I gotta rest for a sec, okay? Then it's my turn. Julian, you are not going to believe it. It's the best thing ever." His faced was flushed, and he flopped back onto the bed.

Julian swung around and stretched out beside him. He gazed over at Sid's face. *looks different now. oh, of course: he took off his glasses. huh. looks better without them… still awful skinny, though.* Julian looked back up and studied the ceiling. He had not looked at it before. *knotty pine, just like the walls… all the way up to the point; must be twenty feet to the top. they could put in a loft if they wanted.*

"I swallowed it."

Sid sat up at once. "You did?!" He looked at Julian with concern. "Why'd you do that?" *I didn't think about that at all… maybe Julian shouldn't have.*

"Well, we're not out in the lake, y'know. I couldn't very well do what Doug did." He chuckled. "If I did, I'd probably have dribbled all over your stomach. He must have mixed it with lake water. Otherwise he wouldn't have made that great arc." He chuckled again. "That was funny!"

"We forgot to think about that." Sid didn't know what he should do. "Was it real uggy?" *Maybe Julian felt like he had to, or something.*

Julian smacked his lips, pondering… there was an aftertaste in his mouth. "No, it isn't bad. It's different. Not like anything else that I can think of. Kinda sweet and salty both. But that's not it either. It's okay." He wiped his tongue around his lips. "It's mostly gone, 'cause I swallowed it right away." *probly just as well for Sid not to know I liked the taste, actually.*

"Huhm." Sid was impressed. Julian was so incredibly thoughtful. *I shouldn't be surprised. I've never known anybody less selfish than Julian. he always looks out for the other guy. that's one reason we miss him over at Wolf.* He felt a little guilty all of a sudden. He wasn't sure if he would have done that. Not automatically, like Julian did.

"Well, when I knew you were there, y'know, about to go, I didn't think about what it would taste like or anything. I thought it would be bad to stop, y'know? Do you think I should have? Stopped, I mean? Maybe you wanted to finish with your hand, or something."

"No way!" Sid said firmly. "I couldn't do **that** with my hand!"

Julian just remembered... he scootched a little to test how the featherbeds felt. *huh. it is a lot softer...* He could still feel that lumpy stuff underneath though. *I forgot to ask Mark what he thought. maybe tonight... yeah. maybe he has a new name for the bed.*

They rested some more. Sid had made a decision. "Well, then. I'll swallow, too." He was a little curious about the taste, anyway. He sat up and looked at Julian, all stretched out. *he's so handsome. I never thought much about that before.* He turned around and spread Julian's legs apart and kneeled between. He was determined to do everything exactly as Julian did. There was absolutely no revision needed. Julian deserved this.

"Oops... You've gone all limp."

Julian looked down. "Hmm. I bet you can fix that soon enough." He grinned and raised his eyebrows a few times.

Sid giggled. "Yeah." He looked down at Julian's cock. *looks a lot different when it's soft... amazing how much it expands!* He took the balls into his left hand. Julian's cock twitched. *neato!* He massaged the sack gently. wow! It started to grow; he put it in his mouth... he was curious about what it would be like limp. He ran his tongue under it, then held steady. *there's that interesting taste again...* he felt it swell inside his mouth. *man, this is something. it's making me start to get hard again, too... feeling Julian go hard is... woo!* Julian just pushed up a little with his hips: *he must want to get going.*

Okay. Sid put his right hand at the base, and started the up and down motion with his head. *I remember what he did; I'll do it the very same way. this is a new thing, so I need to be careful.* Methodically he went through the variations in suction, pressure, and tongue movements that he remembered Julian performing. It was important to do it right.

Sid was a little short of breath. He'd expected Julian to come by now; his mouth was getting tired. *I better stop for a minute and ask if something is the matter.* He kept his hand in place, but pulled off and sat back on his heels. He took a couple of deep breaths. He looked up at Julian's face.

"Sorry. I had to take a breath."

"That's okay... I'm sorry I'm taking so long."

"Am I doing it right, you think?"

"Well, it sure feels good... maybe if you squeeze a little harder when you pull your hand down, and hit the tip with your tongue some more—I notice those things are real nice. Maybe I'll start pumping a little, too. Would that be okay?"

"Pumping?"

"Yeah, you know, like this." Julian pumped up and down with his hips a couple of times. "I'll shoot pretty soon if I can do that."

"Oh!" *what an idea!* Sid returned his mouth to Julian's cock. He applied more pressure. This helped him discover a rhythm... it felt better to do. *I can tell he likes this much better. next time I'll try that myself.*

Julian gently pushed with his hips. He learned to anticipate where Sid would have his mouth and hands... *oh yes: this is it.* "Mmmm."

Sid sensed the progress, and kept precisely the same movements and pressures. He felt Julian push harder. *wow, this is getting intense! this is the way to do it... I figured it out!* He felt Julian's shaft harden. He felt his balls contract! Julian thrust very hard suddenly! Sid felt the head swell and shoot. He held on tight, and let Julian do all the moving. *man this is powerful!*

Julian shot five nice spurts. *boy,   that felt good.   Sid got it right, finally.* He laid back and rested. He had to take a few deep breaths.

Sid kept his mouth in place. He had felt the jet hit the back of his throat. Wow. He noticed the taste now. He moved his tongue around gently. He wanted to get a better idea of what it tasted like before he swallowed it. *it's all... smooth feeling,   no texture. taste is very mild... interesting.* It pulsed again. *time to pull off... I want to do that slowly.*

Julian liked what Sid was doing; *he's being careful,   which is good. oh! I have another shot!* He thrust once more. *boy, that's a new one!* Sid had pressed his lips just right. "Mmmm!" Sid licked that special spot as he pulled off. "Whooee!"

Sid sat back. He smiled happily. He knew what Julian was feeling. He still held the cum in his mouth. He washed his tongue back and forth in it. "Mmm-mm," he hummed. He wanted Julian to guess what he was up to.

Julian looked up and saw the odd smile on Sid's face. His eyes went wide. He realized what Sid was doing! *what does he think about the taste?*

Sid raised his hands from Julian and held them up on either side of his face. He watched Julian's expression as he swallowed one big swallow.

"Ah!" Sid exhaled. "Dee-licious!" He was so proud of himself.

Julian put his hands on Sid's thighs and smiled. He had no special words. He felt super mellow right now. *Sid did that just for me—just like a friend would.*

Sid looked down at his renewed hard-on. He looked up at Julian. "You don't suppose this is habit forming, do you?

They laughed.

"I sure hope so!"

They laughed even harder. Sid stretched out next to Julian. A little rest would be good. He had to calm down a little. He studied the ceiling for a while. He had a lot of figuring out to do. All of this was very different from what he imagined. He looked down at himself. *oh-oh.* He had a problem.

"Julian?"

"Uh-huh?"

"It won't go down."

"Hmm?"

"It got hard all over again, and it won't go down."

Julian sat up and looked. "Wow! Look at that!" He looked at Sid. "Does it hurt?" *mine would; Little J usually wants to rest half a day at least.*

"Nope. But it's harder than ever." Sid looked at it. He pulsed it. "It did that when you started to get close, you know, when you were pushing up and down?"

Julian was wide-eyed. He sat up and moved close. *wow.* A couple of blood vessels were pulsing like mad. He had no ideas.

"Should I beat off, or something?"

Julian went smiley faced and wide eyed at once. He looked at Sid and nodded his head eagerly. "Yeah! I want to watch. That will fix it for sure. I've never seen anybody jack off." He hunkered down to witness it up close.

Sid grasped himself in the way he knew so well. Having an audience was wild. He liked it. *won't take too long.* He closed his eyes and concentrated… he started a fast two fingered one.

Julian was barely a foot away the whole time. He witnessed every detail. *this is hot… this is in the memory! wow. it jetted up almost two feet!* "Cool, Sid." He lay back down. It wasn't as interesting to watch as he expected… Sid jacked too fast.

Sid held himself afterwards. It wasn't as good as the sucking, of course, but it took care of the problem. He could feel the drops on his stomach… *I'll wipe it up in a minute.*

They rested some more. "Julian?"

"Yeah?"

"It tasted kind of good."

"Yeah… I think so too."

Sid lifted his head and put on his glasses. He looked at the clock. "Julian?"

"Yeah?"

"We eat in an hour."

Julian sat up and looked at the clock. "We gotta scramble!

Everybody's gonna be coming back soon!"

"Oh boy! Gotta wipe up first..." Sid dashed to get some T.P.

They dressed in a flash and put everything straight. Julian carefully straightened the quilt on Mark's bed, just to be sure it looked okay. He looked out the door... coast is clear. They went back to the Flaming Arrow table. Julian put his tablet on the table and opened it to a blank page. He wasn't planning a sketch just yet; but it was good to have a page handy just in case he got an idea. In the distance he saw Stu and Norman crossing the meadow below the cabin. They were headed for the Wolf camp. "There go your cooks."

Sid looked around. "Well, I better head home." He stood up. "See ya." He wanted to say thanks, but that didn't fit. There wasn't a way to express what he felt. He wasn't through thinking about it. The day had changed so much. But this was **Julian**. He gave his customary wry grin. "Watch out for those bad habits, kid." He flipped the towel over his left shoulder and moseyed down toward the Wolf camp. He was hungry all of a sudden... *what are we having for supper tonight?*

Julian gave him a thumbs up... *good old Sid.* The Zebras were coming up the trail on the other side of the cabin. The Arrow cooks would be here soon, too. Julian watched Sid again—he was twirling the snorkel in his right hand. What a nice surprise the afternoon had been. boy. This morning he thought that Sid and sex would never... *what a stupid idea.* He could see that now. *everyone must have the same basic need, come to think about it... like eating and sleeping and... well, the basics. hmm.* There were some guys that were hard to imagine, though, when it came to sex. Bruce came to mind there. *oo-eee!* He shook his head.

I've seen two in action now, up close, in daylight. One thing he had experimented with this time—he pretended it was Mark part of the time. But that would be different. *way different. Mark isn't circumcised. I saw that—not well enough, but enough to tell. Mark is more like Danny.*

ooo… now that's a thought. maybe one day Danny might want to try this. good idea. after inspection one day.

What a surprise day. There was a lot to think about. Julian glanced at the blank page he had flipped to earlier… *not everything can be sketched.*

19 *after the campfire*

Nick sat on his haunches to wait... Tom wouldn't be much longer. He won the latrine footrace, of course. *I could never have won, but it meant a lot to Tom that I make the attempt.* That had always been true... what was new was Tom's need to share. That was very different from simply winning a race. Tom didn't want to race, really—no one else was involved tonight. *we waited until the rest of the troop was finished down here. He wanted to run, to let off steam... and to do it together.* Nick was delighted to accommodate him.

Nick inhaled deep... the evening air smelled fresh. Being this close to the lake probably helped that. The width of the moon had increased—about two thirds is showing—lots brighter than last night. *one of these days I should get straight in my head how to track all the moon phases. astronomy is always interesting; never have the time to study it. is it waxing when it grows larger? strange...*

The third skit was a total dud... *some nonsense about Hiawatha— Cub Scout stuff.* Nick shook his head in disbelief... *I might have expected something like that from the Zebras, but the Panthers? Tom and I will collect the ballots during the morning rounds. Mark insists on a secret ballot. I'm betting on Max's skit.*

The squeal of the door spring announced that Tom was on his way out.

doggone it. if it wasn't for that stupid door, I could have snuck up on him from behind... Nick's waiting for me, as always. I never paid any mind to that before... Now it was important. Tom couldn't imagine Nick not being there.

Nick stood and they walked leisurely from the latrine back up to the Flaming Arrow camp. Tom bumped Nick as they walked. Nick bumped back. He chuckled. This reminded him of Kitty Katt in the Badger skit, bumping Sheriff Dilly. Tom had started giving him these love bumps. Boy did they make him feel good. It was risky with the moon this bright— somebody might notice. *the one he did when we were fixing supper caught me off guard... I couldn't tell if anybody noticed or not...* He didn't want Mark to get any suspicions.

we haven't had a chance yet to talk about the card game. I'm just as glad, in a way... I haven't completely sorted it out myself. I'm embarrassed to admit that I enjoyed it. really enjoyed it. I could never do such a thing again, of course. Tom wouldn't permit it, to begin with. But that was okay, too. Nick never wanted anybody else anyway. But it was fun to get a peek at the rest of the world, once at least.

"Nick?"

"Yeah?"

"I'm gonna talk to Danny." Tom had decided that he and Nick would sleep together until further notice. That would require Danny's help.

"What about?"

"Tonight... after Lights Out."

"Again? Tom, that's two night in a row! Do you think that's smart?" He couldn't see Tom's face well enough... *what's going on?* This would be the third Code Green night in a row! *and we had two rounds in the poker game this morning.* Nick doubted if he could produce much—if anything.

"What of it?" Tom didn't know how to talk about this stuff. He needed Nick to prop him up. It pissed him off that he couldn't say what was in his head. Nick could always help get him untangled. It was hard to admit that to himself, let alone Nick.

Well... no use in arguing, Nick knew that much. *not that I mind; it would be nice if we could come up with a padding program, though— especially if this is going to be all night again.* That must be what he has in mind. Otherwise there wouldn't be any need to talk to Danny. There was always an annoying lump or two; he had a couple of sore spots this morning. *if this is going to happen a lot I might not be too happy... it will take a month to catch up on sleep after we go home. hmm. I'd better talk to Danny myself, later. he's cool, but I need to make sure Julian is kept clear.* If Julian knew anything, he'd have to tell Mark about it, sooner or later. Mark would never put up with this; he might have his suspicions already.

"You want me to wait 'til you start the rounds, like last night?"

"Hmm. Dunno. What do you think?"

"Well, unless we both talk with him, or something. He'll be sitting right there."

"I didn't think about that." Tom had been thinking about something else. He had to be with Nick tonight, that's all. "You want to talk to him?" *boy, do I want that. last night all I could do was grunt a last minute command.*

"Yeah; probably be a good idea. You can back me up, okay?"

"Thanks, Nick." He hugged him by the shoulder. He had to. He figured if anybody saw it… well, too bad.

They walked into the Flaming Arrow. Danny had already lit the lantern and was sitting at the table writing in his notebook.

oh-oh… Julian was there, too. "Got to wait," Nick muttered out the side of his mouth. *forgot about the newsletter. Julian is always on the ball.*

"Yep."

"Hey, Julian." Nick sat next to him.

"Hi, Nick. I thought maybe you'd want to talk about the skit tonight, y'know." *be good to put down ideas for the newsletter and scrapbook while it's fresh.* He glanced at Tom. "Hi, Tom." He liked Tom now.

"Hi, Julian." *man, look at that smile.* Tom felt himself blush a little. *Julian seems to like me or something. that's a really friendly smile. not sexy, just nice.* He had a sudden flash of guilt over what he had planned to do a couple of days ago. *now I want to put a guard around him.*

"What have you got?" Nick sat down. *I have to spend a little time on this… otherwise, he'll wonder. I'll make it as quick as possible.* He checked his watch: *we still have twenty minutes; I'll try to polish this off in five.* "Danny, old pal, can you get my notebook? It's on my footlocker."

"Sure thing." Danny stood carefully—glad to have an excuse, actually. He fetched the notebook and took it over to Nick. He didn't want to sit back down—his butt was still humming nicely from this morning. It felt good to stand. He wasn't about to tell these guys, of course… not with

Julian here. *I don't need their laughs anyway—it's probably old news to them. I'll walk around... where? I don't need to go to the latrine.* He looked at Nick briefly. *amazing. how the devil can he take that thing of Tom's? Geoff said he liked it too.* He looked at Tom, the monster man. *Geoff was plenty enough, thanks. I'll wait a little while for that one again, too. a day, at least...* he smiled proudly.

Tom leaned against the stove. He didn't want to crowd Nick and Julian. His mind wandered. He glanced over past Danny; the Farting Post was illuminated by the moon—it looked like some kind of sentinel or totem. He had to smile. *Mark is a damn genius. luckily, I didn't have the splurts again this morning. maybe that was a one time thing... no way to tell. I got rid of a pretty good sized load today at the poker game. what a trip! I sure gave Brian a good reaming. pissed me, the way he played up to Nick.*

He looked over at Danny... *man.* Another conscience attack jabbed him good: he remembered well how he'd done Danny last summer. *mmm! he was really fine. how come I never went back for another?* He'd forgotten why... Danny still had a great set on him, anyway. *look at the way he shows it off... he stands there, one leg bent... must not have a clue about how hot that looks. why do I not want to go over there right now and grab that? a week ago nobody could have stopped me. I still enjoy the view; that's enough, now. weird.*

why don't they have anything besides those benches to sit on, anyway? I don't want to sit at the table, but there isn't anyplace else. He sat on the opposite end and watched Nick talk to Julian. *I just realized: I haven't spent that much time looking at Nick. I should do that. Nick... supposedly, he isn't a good looker. well, I'm not one myself, especially... my main qualification is below the belt.* He gazed at the back of Nick's head. *the hair comes to a point... it's aimed right at some kind of knob at the top of his back...* Tom wanted to scoot over and touch that. He'd seen that so many times but hadn't really seen it before... same with his Adam's apple. *so many fine details that are... well, they're sexy, that's all.*

Tom's eyes blurred as his thoughts turned inward. *what the devil has happened? it's like I've been drugged, or hypnotized: I don't want Nick out of my sight! not for one minute. I was able to jockey things part of the day... but Nick couldn't cut the merit badges. I went with him today, but it wouldn't be very smart to do that again. Nick has to help me figure this out. last night wasn't near enough.*

"What do you think, Tom?" Nick asked.

"What? Sorry, I wasn't listening."

"I was just telling Julian we should have the ballots counted before free swimming, easy."

"No sweat," Tom sat up straight. "We'll bring 'em right over. Probably before you finish the inspections, even."

"Okay... that should do it." Nick gave Julian a pat on the shoulder. "You do a sketch of Nathan at the fire, I'll do the story, and we'll be set. Thanks, Julian."

"Sure." Julian closed his tablet. "Thank you right back. Well, I'll take off then. I can maybe do a little before lights out." He looked down to the Wolf camp—Mark was still standing by the table talking to Norman. *good... that meant he had a little time.* He stood and looked at Tom again. "G'night." *Tom looks different. I noticed that before, when he and Nick were fixing supper. Tom's in love with Nick, all right.* Julian gave him a short wave and a smile. They were returned. He walked toward the cabin. He punched Danny on the arm as he passed by. "Pancakes?"

Danny looked up, his preoccupation shattered. "Uh, yeah. Links instead of patties, though. See ya in the early!" Funny: he just realized he had not been thinking about Julian at all. *that's odd.* He watched Julian's cute little butt walk down to the cabin. How could I forget about that? *hmm.* He looked at Julian again—suddenly he felt protective. *wow.* His feelings for Julian had changed somehow. *I couldn't think of anybody else the other day. he's still wonderful... now I'm not sure exactly what I feel. maybe after camp. that's a thought! that would be a good way to break in that clubhouse. yes. but Julian isn't ready yet, at all. not for what Geoff and I did today... no way!*

"Hey, Danny!" Nick called. "C'mon over and park a sec, okay?"

Danny walked to the table. He was about to sit down opposite, but Nick shook his head no and patted the bench right next to where he was sitting. *how strange... Tom's on the other side, at the far end.* Tom just shifted from one elbow to the other, in his typical slouch. *what the... he looked at Nick. *why is he smiling?* "What's up?"

"Danny. I didn't thank you for covering our butts this morning."

Danny blushed. "Glad to." He looked up and grinned. He glanced over at Tom. *wow…* It looked like Tom was blushing. "Any time."

"Danny… those words are music to my ears." He put his arm around Danny's shoulder. "Y'see, we need to have you help us again tonight."

Danny was surprised. He looked at Nick: *real sincere. something different is going on...* he looked over at Tom again. He was looking down at the table. Danny looked away quickly. "Sure. No sweat." *maybe Nick will say why… I'm too chicken to ask.* A silent moment. "No sweat. What are friends for? Any time." He smiled at Nick, and raised his eyebrows— *I'd like to know what's going on. maybe he'll fill me in.*

"Every night." Tom's voice from the end of the table startled them both.

Danny looked over at Tom in surprise. He hadn't moved; he was still looking down at the table. Danny looked back at Nick, who had taken his arm back. *wow.* Nick was blushing too. The expression on his face! Inside, Danny knew what was going on; he did not know exactly how to say it to himself, but he knew that Nick and Tom were in love. *they aren't fooling around.*

"Every night," Tom repeated.

Danny and Nick looked at him.

Tom looked up. He was looking at the two most important people in his life. This was one of those times he hated. He loved these guys. He wasn't supposed to, but he did. He did not know how to say it.

He didn't have to. His face told Danny and Nick everything. They both felt a rush. Danny looked at Nick and smiled. It was a friend's smile. He nodded. He was blushing now himself.

"Thanks a lot." Nick got up to begin setting up for the night. He put his hand on Danny's shoulder briefly. He was almost as amazed as Danny must be.

Danny watched Nick go to the tent and get his sleeping bag. *this is something.* Suddenly Tom gave him a big hug from behind. He had snuck around the table! *wow.* It was quite a hug!

"Thanks Danny," Tom said softly. "I owe ya." He stood back up and went to help Nick setup for the night. *man am I lucky to have Nick—he can do such a job at talking.*

Danny looked at his watch—twenty minutes until the Two Minutes. He watched Nick and Tom. He felt privileged suddenly. It was a good feeling. It was slightly awkward though, watching them move their sleeping bags. But there wasn't anything he could do. He looked at the tent. It looked funny now: the front two cots were bare. *maybe I should... nah. they have to move everything back in the morning. hmm... after lights out maybe I can try one of the other cots... just for the night. I'll think about it.* He checked his watch again. Nineteen minutes until the two minutes. What to do for Nineteen minutes? His eye drifted over to the Badger camp. *I miss being a Badger sometimes...*

—◦—

Julian sat at the table with his tablet open. He had started his nightly list, but found it hard to concentrate. The memory of Tom and Nick in each other's arms this morning kept intruding. He longed to be like them. He glanced at the bed. His goal was to be in that bed with Mark and look just like Tom and Nick. It seemed like an impossible dream—but he wanted it to happen more than anything he ever wanted in his life. *trouble is, everyone treats me like I'm a little kid. especially Mark.*

"Face it, you are a little kid," he said out loud. *but I don't feel like a little kid. little kids don't think about these things all the time like I do.* He tapped his pencil eraser on the table unconsciously. *how am I going to get anyone to talk about this stuff? I tried to talk with Nick, but he changed the subject as soon as he could. I could tell it was because he thinks I'm too young. I'm afraid to talk with Mark for fear that he'll get mad or something. what if he sent me back to the Wolf patrol? I couldn't stand that. what would I tell Sid and Jeremy?*

"You're just chicken. Little kids are always chicken; that's why you're a little kid." Julian frowned. Logic seemed to back up the accusation.

Julian talked to himself sometimes because it helped him sort things out. Calling himself chicken was useful because it had shown him what he needed to do—what he had to do—if he wanted anybody to think of him as no longer a little kid. Someone being Mark, first of all. He had to do something that a little kid wouldn't do, for a start. His Inside guy continued to speak aloud:

"Like what?" *good question. umm…* "How about not chickening out all the time like you did last night?"

He felt guilty about that. He'd sidetracked Mark into putting those featherbed thingys on top of Lumpy Louise. He was about to ask about buns. *well, maybe that would have been a stupid thing to ask.*

"Maybe; but the point is, you chickened out. It might have been just the right thing to ask. It would be honest, at least."

Julian laughed. *Lumpy Louise.* Mark was always saying or doing funny stuff like that. *I never think of funny things. I'm sort of boring, when you think about it. all I ever do is draw stuff. yeah. why would Mark ever…*

"Cut that out." *okay, okay.* His mom told him once about doing that, and she was right. 'If you think bad stuff it will only make bad things happen. If you can't think of something good,' she said, 'at least think of something else for a while. Then maybe the answer will come along when you aren't expecting it.' That was good advice— *it's never gone wrong yet. Think about good stuff for a while.*

Why don't you make a list of good things… Inside guy preferred operating in silent mode. Talking to himself out loud was weird and kind of stupid.

Mark left the Wolf camp pleased; Norman was proving to be an excellent mentor for Billy, the new boy. *it never ceases to amaze me how abilities like that emerge.* The other boys seemed to have everything in hand very nicely. *Stuart is ready to move on… but he's still a good leader. when he's gone I'll probably pass the patrol job to Norman.*

Mark headed straight across the meadow for the cabin. He felt guilty about short changing Julian last night. *we barely got started; I took most of the time fussing with that infernal bed. not that I'm sorry about that. it made a huge difference. I sure owe Sarge.*

Mark paused at the open door. Julian was at the table as usual, but he looked preoccupied. He wasn't busily writing or drawing. *I still haven't seen his drawings. maybe there'll be time after our chat.* Mark

indulged himself briefly. Looking at Julian gave him a special feeling of—
*what... a mix of things... pride, responsibility... nostalgia... a sense of
witnessing what a truly bright and talented and happy boy could be.* He felt
privileged. He felt that about all the boys in a way, but Julian was special.
let's have a good talk tonight, Mark. He stepped in and closed the door.

The sound made Julian start—his mind was miles away. He turned
around. *Mark is here!* He broke into a wide smile. *he's here at last.*

"How did everything go today?" He gestured for Julian to drag his
chair over for the nightly conference. *what a great smile. Julian has
a way of cheering you up with a single glance.* He grabbed the folding
chair—it had ended up by the fireplace.

Julian hopped out of the chair at once and pulled it over to the middle
of the room. *Mark was brilliant to think of this conference thing.* He
started right in: "Things went pretty good. It was real busy. I did better
at Archery." *maybe I should let him sit in the big chair... too late.*

"What do you mean?" Mark knew about Julian's arm because Cory
had filled him in. He wanted to hear about it directly. He trusted that kind
of information more.

"I maybe should have waited a year for that. I picked the small bow
today, but it's still hard, y'know? I'm always sore for a while. Nick says
I should get some weights and practice my arm muscles." Julian kneaded
his right bicep.

"You and Nick getting along?"

"Oh, yeah. He's really great. Did you know he's a lifeguard now?
Boy, he is a good swim coach, too." Julian figured a detailed account of
his swim lessons would be too boring, so he didn't go into detail.

They talked about Forestry briefly. *hmm... lots of short answers.*
Julian wasn't as chatty and bubbly as usual. Mark sensed that he wanted to
talk about something else. *I need to open the door for him.*

"What's really on your mind, Julian?" Moonlight spilled in the
window on the west wall; the shaft of light fell directly on Julian,
enhancing the overhead light. It took Mark a minute to figure out where
the effect was coming from. *remarkable.* He was grateful the curtains
were still open.

Julian's internal scold was on duty: *Well, Chicken Little? Are you gonna tell the man, or not?!*

all right, all right. here goes: "Lotsa stuff." He didn't know where to begin. He looked at Mark directly for a second, but didn't hold eye contact. He knew better than to risk that. He glanced back again—*wow*. The Moonlight was shining on the back of Mark's head. It sort of glowed silver-ish around the edges. He looked down again... that song melody just whacked him again.

Quit that! Pay attention, dum-dum.

Mark smiled patiently. "Lotsa stuff." That was boy code for 'I don't know where to begin,' a frequently encountered response in the scoutmaster trade.

Julian mustered the courage. "Why..." *this is hard.* "Why does everybody treat me like a little kid?" *there.* It felt good to spit it out, but he was scared to death right now. *what if I went too far?*

whoa. This surprised Mark. He was delighted that Julian had the guts to verbalize that much, though. "I guess I don't know what you mean, exactly." Mark paused; he didn't want to put words into Julian's mouth. *everybody includes me.*

"Okay." *talk about Nick first.* "Every time I want to ask about something, they hurry to change the subject or something. How am I supposed to find out stuff if they won't talk about it?"

Mark could see that Julian was genuinely frustrated by this. Mark held his tongue... he was sure Julian was on the verge of giving a specific.

"There were these guys today at the waterfront. They were racing down the F dock. They jumped off and swam out to the platform." Now that he had started, it wasn't so bad. "Nick was teaching me how to dive and stuff. Then Tom and these other guys go running by." He looked at Mark with a shrug. "Tom won, of course."

"Of course." Mark grinned.

Julian decided to go for the easy one first. "What's a Beefcake?"

"Beefcake! Where in the world did you hear that?" Julian always surprised him.

"Nick said this guy was a Beefcake. He was one of the guys with Tom. I was gonna ask what it meant, but I got that look again." Julian exhaled in frustration. "He always does that. I'm not supposed to know, or something, I guess. What can be so bad?"

"Did you ask?"

"No. I was chicken." Julian fiddled with the edge of his tablet. "I don't want to be a pest or anything."

This seemed harmless enough. *why would Nick be worried about that word? how to go about this? might as well be direct.* Mark never thought it wise to waltz around and be vague. "Well, it's a word, a slang word, used to describe muscular types who like to show off how big and strong they are—like the Mister America contests, or pro wrestling. It's kinda like pinup girls, only it's big **guys**.

"What's a pinup girl?"

"Real sexy girls, like in Playboy."

Julian felt so stupid. *how can I tell Mark these things? here's another word to deal with.* He didn't know Playboy. He took a deep sigh. "Mark?"

Mark was concerned... *he sounds so plaintive.* "What is it, Julian? You know you can trust me."

"I'm so **dumb** about things!" He said, petulant. "What's Playboy?!"

oh my gosh... Mark had a lot more to cover than he thought. He began to see what Julian was talking about. Of course he wouldn't know about Playboy.

"I'm sorry, Julian. I forget, sometimes that you're... you're... well, you're new at life, I guess. Please don't think you are dumb or stupid. You are not that. There's nothing wrong about being the new kid in town." He leaned forward and took Julian by the shoulders. "You have **nothing** to be ashamed of, okay?"

Julian was silent. *Mark is so wonderful.* He didn't know exactly what to say.

"Julian, Julian," Mark wanted to hug him, but resisted; he sat back waited for him to relax and respond. "You have to be patient with me, Julian. I'm the one who is stupid here. You have to help me know what you need, what you don't know. It's my fault for assuming you know things. Never feel bad about asking anything. From now on, please, ask away. Knowing that you trust me means more to me than anything. Please don't be afraid. Let me do my part, okay?"

Julian was thrilled in a bunch of ways all at the same time. It took a minute to get a grip. He needed to say something before that inner crabby guy started up again. He looked at Mark gratefully and nodded.

"We left off at Playboy."

"Oh. That's a magazine. It specializes in big pictures of sexy women. Some men tear them out and pin them up on the wall. That's why they call them pinup girls."

"Wow! That makes sense, now. And a Beefcake is the same thing? Only for... why don't they call them pinup boys?"

"Hmm... probably because they're so muscular. Beef means real hunky types. The slang word for pinup girls is cheesecake—I don't know why." He shrugged and opened his hands to show they were empty. He had a very limited knowledge in this area, and even less interest.

cheesecake? that's pretty goofy too... at least Mark doesn't know about some stuff himself... that was comforting, in a way.

"A pinup boy, if there are any... hmm." Mark got a newsflash: *this is why Nick didn't want to talk about it.* Mark had a sudden appreciation of Nick's dilemma.

Mark shrugged. "I don't know. There might be pinup boys, someplace. I've just never seen any, I guess." Mark hated to tell a white lie like that, but it would have to do for now.

Julian screwed up his face, curious.

"What's the matter?"

"Why would anybody pin a picture of one of those Beefcakes on the wall?" *or a sexy girl, for that matter.*

Mark laughed heartily. He agreed with the underlying declaration of taste. "Good question." He looked at Julian's wide open expression. He was struck suddenly by the special responsibility he had right this minute. "Really, Julian, that is a good question. And there is an answer."

Julian's eyes popped open. This he did not expect.

"There are lots of different people in the world, Julian. They like to look at different kinds of things. Some people like pictures of cats or dogs, some like flowers, some like mountains and lakes." Mark shrugged. "Some people like pinups. Some people like Beefcakes." Mark avoided the obvious slang assist of 'different strokes'. *Julian is bright enough to make the connection.* He leaned forward and tapped Julian on the knee. "Some people I know like model airplanes." He winked.

Julian felt himself blush... in a flash, a wave of some kind radiated out from below to every outer tip of his body... he glowed all over. Mark had just connected in a major way. *boy oh boy does Mark know how to do that!*

"What else won't Nick talk about?" Mark was amused and pleased at how well this was going.

Julian looked directly at Mark. He was impelled to ask. "Mark, what are Choice Buns?"

Mark laughed. "You are too much, sometimes." *what a question.*

"Nick says I have Choice Buns."

"He is absolutely right about that!" Mark said, without thinking. *Nick, again. hmm.*

Julian's eyes nearly popped out. Had Mark actually said that? His heart had nearly stopped. what will he say next?

Mark took a second. Nick's discretion was laudable, but he now understood why Julian was so frustrated. *everyone in his life, me included, has been so busy protecting him that they forget that he is a real boy with real questions. here's where I have to earn my wages.*

"Okay. I see what's needed here, Julian. You have some catching up to do. I'm going to try to help you out there. Just understand, if you can, that I might not be able to answer all your questions. I'll try, but you have to be patient about things. If you are honest with me, I'll be honest with you. Deal?"

Julian nodded. He was mesmerized.

"Choice Buns is a term to describe the butt of a particularly good looking sexy guy. You do indeed have Choice Buns. Many features of the human anatomy are pleasing to the eye—or can be. Some people have pretty faces, some have wonderful hair, arms, chests—legs, and **buns**. One of the blessings of being young is that you have most of these things all at once for a while. As you grow older, they start to look older too. You get fat or skinny, your hair falls out…

Julian's attention began to lag... He had locked onto a particular statement: 'you do indeed have Choice Buns.' *Mark said that. he actually said that.*

Mark stopped his commentary… it was going past Julian suddenly.

"I don't get it." Julian's brow was wrinkled in confusion. "Why are they called **Choice**? I've been studying them for days, and I still don't see what that means." He looked up at Mark open eyed. "I mean, I s'pose it's nice to have them and all, but what difference does it make?" He just thought of Danny's pink buns, on the way to being tan. "What's the big deal?" *once they're in a pair of pants they're out of sight anyway.* "All you do is sit on them, after all."

Mark was taken by surprise by this. Here he had been presented with a totally honest question. That didn't happen very often—especially when the subject verged on sex, as this one clearly did. *got to speak with care, here, Mark.*

"Thank you for being honest with me, Julian. You are a brave and honest person." He stepped carefully. "They are considered Choice because of two reasons. One, the person who sees them as choice is maybe a little envious—and, because the person wants to… touch them."

Julian's eyes widened.

"Have you ever wanted to pet a puppy, or a kitten?"

Julian nodded.

"Why?"

"I dunno **why**, exactly." Julian considered that briefly. "I guess because I like them; they feel nice and soft… they make me feel good. And they like being petted." He remembered back to the time when Larry got his puppy. "They always try to lick my face."

"Well?" Mark waited for Julian to make the connection.

The light turned on in Julian's mind. He blushed with happiness and embarrassment. He felt really stupid, and he felt very flattered.

Mark saw the moment. *what a thrill to see that.* "As time goes on, Julian, you may have to be on guard. There are some people who can't keep their hands off those. You might get a few pats back there." *I resist doing that myself.*

"Huh." Julian remembered now that he'd gotten a couple of those. yeah… both Danny and Nick had patted him there on the Boardwalk. *it felt nice, actually.*

Mark did not want to pursue the topic any further—he had no idea how to handle it, for one thing. For another, Julian probably needed to think some more about what had just opened in his mind. This was a good place to change the subject.

"How's the Scrapbook coming along? I haven't seen that since we arrived." Mark was curious about that. Julian's work is always a pleasure to look at.

"Oh, wow!" Julian jumped up and ran back to the table to get his sketch tablet. He could hardly wait to show Mark the swimming race one. He was so glad Mark asked. *his comments always help me find things to fix.* Going over his drawings with Mark was his favorite thing to do.

20   late night

Nick had found a relatively smooth space, finally. *I for darn sure want to find something soft tomorrow. being here every night is a very exciting prospect, but does it have to be a punishment too?* He relaxed. Tom had given him such an incredible kiss just now. He still didn't know what, exactly, had caused this. He really wanted to know. *this is one thing I have not read about.*

"Nick?" Tom asked, softly. He stroked Nick's shoulder. Looking at him in this dim light was fascinating; he looked different... *so soft... smooth.*

"'At's me."

"I really hate the mushy stuff."

Nick knew that well enough. *I won't make the obvious wisecrack, though.*

"Why do I feel all mushy?"

Nick frowned. *is his mushy the same as my mushy?* "Well, I'm not sure." He let his fingers play with the back of Tom's right hand.

"Nick, what did you think about today?"

It was a long day. *I thought about a lot of things.* "Well..."

"When you were doing it. In that tent... you know."

This startled Nick. He had not been thinking about that poker game at all. "What did I think?" Nick didn't know he had thought anything. "I don't know; I was pretty busy. It was all so different from what we always do. It was like I was in a movie, or something." *Jack sort of helped me along, actually.*

"I thought about you." *there. I said it. what a relief!*

"Me? Whatever for?" *is Tom angry because I was messing with Jack? I was just doing what the game required. it was hot and I really liked it, but I wasn't thinking about it. I don't care about Jack at all.*

"I had to pretend it was you, instead of Brian."

It was starting to make sense, somehow. Nick flushed. He was aware suddenly that Tom was incredibly vulnerable. Tom had lost all his macho defenses. *he has to learn the vocabulary of love—we both do, come to think about it.* Nick's heart went out to him. *oh, please don't let me foul this up!* He turned on his side and embraced Tom solidly. He kissed tenderly, lovingly.

Yes! 'Thank you,' Tom said silently. He wanted to know, to be sure that Nick loved him. How could he say that?

"I hereby give you permission to feel mushy," Nick said, softly. "You can mush with me all you want. I promise not to tell."

Tom laughed. Nick had said just the right thing! "Nick… I love you." What a load removed. He collapsed on his back with a sigh.

Nick leaned over him again and put his lips just above Tom's. "I'm really glad." He kissed him tenderly, and briefly. "I love you right back!" Enough moonlight filtered through the tent roof tonight—they were able to look at each other. They gazed at each other in a new way—as if they were meeting someone for the first time. In a way, they were. The low light was fortunate… it limited the impact sufficiently to allow them to look at each other directly for almost a full minute. Nick kissed him again, lightly, and lay back down. His head was spinning and his heart racing.

They found a way to embrace while they rested quietly for several minutes. They had said all that was needed for a while. They had to adjust to this new reality they had just entered. They were not at all sleepy. They were not at all horny, either.

"I was a real butt hole, wasn't I?" Tom honestly didn't know how many cute little rear ends he had broken in. *those days are over.*

Nick was silent for a while. Then he chuckled. It turned into a laugh.

"What!?"

"Oh, Tom! I know what you mean… but maybe you should use a different word. You, of all people, can see that." He giggled a bit more.

Tom thought for a minute... then he saw the irony. "Oh!" He laughed. He sat up and attacked Nick with tickles and kisses. "You! You're such a smart ass, too!"

They laughed for a long time.

Nick felt privileged... witnessing Tom drifting off to sleep in his arms was beyond anything he had ever dreamed. *I'm so darn happy. Tom is back on his feet, too. well, then: he can jolly well rustle up some padding tomorrow.*

—m—

Sid waited as long as he could. He didn't know if Jeremy was asleep yet or not. *I'll be real careful... can't wait any longer. the air mattress usually masks the squeak this darn cot makes. at least the moon is behind the tent. Another raging boner...* He was afraid he had become a sex fiend or something: *I have to beat off again... the third time today. that will be a new record. I can't help it* Ever since this afternoon, all he could think about was what Julian and he had done in the cabin.

He stroked for a while and imagined the feeling he got when Julian sucked. *boy that was nice.* He jacked for a long time. He replayed every detail... the Paul style, then the Doug style. He switched hands. He thought now about how Julian tasted. He remembered doing the Paul. He remembered doing the Doug. He liked doing the Paul best. His tongue was good at that. He remembered Julian shooting. *o boy... oh—oh!* Bam! He'd just done his third. He stopped finally, and held himself for a while. *I'm a sex fiend all right. oop... forgot to tuck in a towel. I'll have a cold spot somewhere when I turn over. so be it.* He tucked himself back into his skivvies... *now maybe I can go to sleep. somehow, I have to find something else to think about.*

—m—

The tent shadow created an interesting line across the middle of Danny's sleeping bag. He was trying out Nick's cot, just for fun. *it's different from being in that dark cocoon in the back of the tent. maybe I should put my head on the outside... hmm. I might switch around later. yeah... come to think about it, I can try Tom's tomorrow night if I want.* He had lots to think about tonight—which cot to use was the least important—but being free to do whatever he wanted after lights out was fantastic. He needed to run the day through his mind again. It was so wild and wonderful.

wow... listen to them laughing over there. hum. what a thing all that is! That talk with Nick and Tom! Boy, that made him feel good. He didn't understand the how or the why at all... But the what was capital letter clear. For the first time he understand those guys. *I had it backwards before! Nick is the strong one, not Tom. what a good thing, too. I've gotten to like Tom, but it took a little work. now, I really do like him. I'll do what I can to help those guys.*

my butt feels almost back to normal now... The memory of what it felt like this morning was super vivid. *I have to play it back one more time.* From the first pat back there yesterday up to this morning, Danny had never met anyone like Geoff; he seemed to know about everything. There was no doubt, no fear, no hesitation, no guilty feelings. *hmm. a pro. that's what he is, a pro. now I understand what that means.* It didn't have anything to do with money at all—it had to do with knowing what to do. Like at the golf course... the pro knows what you need to improve your game. *Geoff sure knows all right... boy oh boy does he ever.*

what's so special is Geoff taught me how to do it too. he wasn't there just to jump on me and get off his hornies, like Tom was last summer. Geoff wanted me, Danny, to have just as good a time as he did. he would stop and show me things. little things, like angle, speed, muscle control. it was really complicated, if you think about it. I'm not sure I actually got it all, either. but he promised we would do it again some time before camp is over. working with him every day is sure lucky. maybe we can do it more than once. I'd like to be good at it without any coaching...

This was perfect, with Nick and Tom in the other tent. He flung off the top cover... *too warm out right now.* He started to beat off slowly, remembering what it felt like to enter Geoff. The fantasy was ruined suddenly... *stupid waistband...* he pulled off his skivvies. *there. hmm... something isn't working...* he tried several hand positions. None of them were quite right. The palm up with fingers curled around under wasn't bad. yeah... pretty darn good. The trouble was he couldn't keep it wet... *I need some of that stuff from Tom's tube that Geoff found. that's magic, that stuff. wait a minute... maybe it's still there! I didn't pay attention when they moved their things. should I take a chance?* He listened... *no way to tell if they're asleep or not. probably not. but I can be quiet!* He got up.

Luckily the moon was bright tonight—a third full, almost. He could see quite well. He walked over to the supply tent to see if he could hear anything. It felt brave to be walking out in the moonlight, stark naked. He stood up straight and looked down at his hard cock. He wagged it back and forth. *that feels so great! I'm being daring tonight! I better take it easy—somebody from Wolf camp might be up and look up here.* He tiptoed over to the opening and listened: total silence. *hmm.* They could be asleep. He'd never heard either one of them snore... They stopped laughing a while ago. He was tempted to peek in, but that would be stupid: *it's dark in there; I wouldn't be able to see a thing. well, I saw them this morning. it would be the same, probably... sure looked nice.*

He went back to the crew tent and opened Tom's footlocker slowly. He felt down around in there... lots of socks. *why does he need so many socks?* A toilet kit... ah! A **tube**. He pulled it out carefully and held it up to the moonlight: K-Y *that's it! I remember now. oooo-oo, here we go!* He scurried back to his cot. He paused a second. Right or left hand? *I usually jack with my right. but I'm not doing the same old thing.* He squeezed some goo into his left palm. He was still nice and hard. *ohh... wow... I have to get some of this! mmmm.*

This is choice. He could buck and fuck all he wanted, because no one was around. He did a re-run in his mind of his morning with Geoff. He flipped back and forth. At times, it was Geoff going into him. At times, it was him going into Geoff. *they're both good. uhm. uhmm. I don't want this to go too quick.*

He finished "on top." When it was over, he found himself on his knees, having squirted right through his left hand. *a puddle right in the middle of my new sleeping bag! what a doofus.* He cleaned up as well as he could, and snuck the tube back to Tom's locker.

He was at peace, now. 'Think about pancakes, Danny,' he told himself.

"Okay."

—m—

Mark dried himself off in an unusually graceful, almost pensive manner. He was still playing back the extraordinary conversation with Julian. It was unique in his experience. It was startling how clumsily, how sloppily he had prepared for it. His assumptions about Julian had been so off center. It was alarming to realize that he had been drifting onto the same stalebrained adult mental plane that had always outraged him when he was young. *I am becoming one of them. maybe, thanks to Julian, I have been saved in time.* He was appalled at how arrogant he'd become, how **patronizing**. All the things that he **despised**. *well. I'm paying attention now, that's for sure. the next conference is likely to be a bigger challenge—and I've already promised to answer any and all. way to go, Mark.*

I've fudged on the time a little. I'm used to taking long showers at home—especially when my mind is buzzing with some challenge or other. tonight qualifies there. A long hot shower helped relax and calm him so that he didn't toss and turn for an hour before he could fall asleep. *I indulged myself tonight; but I earned it.*

He glanced at himself in the mirror—*drat!* He grabbed the towel back and gave his hair a good rough up. He hated waking up on a damp pillow. *hmm. I'd better shave in the morning. it's late and I don't want to keep Julian awake. he worked hard tonight; he is made of tougher stuff than I thought. he still looks like a cuddle puppy, but he has backbone and intelligence. some day, he will be in charge.*

The second he crawled into bed, the blessings bestowed under him by Sarge took effect. The goose down featherbed was wonderful. *this is my reward for having done a good job today*... no loose ends to sort out or worry about. Mark fell asleep faster than he had in a long, long time.

In fact, there were a few loose ends in the unconscious realm, ones that Mark had lost track of lately. They often provided him with wonderful dreams, happy dreams, wish-fulfillment dreams—drawn from memories of his brief time with Erik…

…right now, he was being patted on his rear end affectionately. "hey there, hot cheeks..." Erik says. he's

caught up with me at last... I was afraid I'd get all the way to the end of the beach. "c'mon, let's get wet..." he pulls me toward the surf. "tide's coming in..." we play around and make sure we splash each other good... "hey, far out..." staring down at our feet... the water running back out to sea makes it look like we're moving... almost makes me dizzy. The wind picks up and we run back toward the hotel end of the beach... we stop to look at this driftwood stump... it curls around in a unique twist... must have been on a windswept cliff that fell into the sea... it looks strangely familiar, but how can that be... maybe I saw a photograph...

Mark dreamed intermittently during the night. He awoke from time to time when the intensity of the scene insisted on being recognized... but they faded away as usual. Mark would awaken without recalling any of them specifically; he will be rested, pleased to have had a full night's sleep.

Julian's entry into dreamland was very different on this night. When he crawled into his sleeping bag, he forgot his usual routine entirely. Standing vigil for fresh glimpses of Mark's private parts didn't even occur to him. He was resting on his back instead of on his side. His brain was on full time duty processing the conference. It would be a different brain in the morning; he wasn't aware of that, but he wouldn't have been shocked if he were told. He had achieved a milestone and he knew it. He had a brand new definition for exciting.

His hands were folded, resting quietly atop his tummy; his eyes were closed. He was unaware of his physical position... it had been assumed without purpose or conscious thought. It was not a position he was generally inclined to use. His mental sorting system was in charge for the time being, and it required a stable unobtrusive platform, as distraction free as possible.

The sounds of Mark taking his shower and crawling into bed went unnoticed entirely. An image of Mark talking appeared... the sound was turned off. Julian analyzed it as if it were a portrait. The glowing fringe of lunar backlight lent the image an enabling quality... *Mark is so much more than I ever thought about. he makes me feel an inch high in some ways, and he makes me feel ten feet tall in others. it is so weird and wonderful. I don't understand why I fell in love with him, now. I didn't even know him. I'm just beginning to know him... boy oh boy is that ever true. I think I love him even more, if that's possible.*

so much to learn... a bigger job than I ever imagined. makes me want Mark even more—it's going to be worth more, too.

His mind shifted to the first time he met Mark. He remembered it so vividly—it was a couple of years ago. *he was looking through my scrapbook. I studied his face as if it was under a microscope. he was looking at the Bear drawings. my favorite year in Cubs. we had lots of fun playing on the beach. I remember running into the waves with Larry—the water knocked us down. that was such fun. I remember the little criss-cross teeny waves coming in with all their little bubbles. It felt good when the water rushed back though our toes. Then we played tag around this driftwood stump. It twisted around in crazy ways so you could peek through it. I thought it was so interesting I went back and drew a picture of it for the scrapbook.*

huh. I just thought of something... I feel like I'm waving goodbye to that little kid. why aren't I scared? it was fun to be a Cub. it's fun to remember it was fun. Julian had just understood something. *that's who I'm waving goodbye to, isn't it?*

He had to think about that for a minute. *should I be sad about that? happy? both? maybe that's closer... or maybe it's neither one.* He just thought of Lucy's cat. It was so cute and fun when it was a kitten. When it had grown up it was still okay, but... *hmm. why did I think of that, of all things?!*

Well, figure it out: everything has to grow up. It isn't something to be sad or happy about. It just is. Inside guy was tuned in, as usual.

oh yeah, I know: Mark was talking about how people like to pet kittens and puppies—and I said it feels good, and they like it when you do that. Julian smiled. *Choice Buns. one of these days I am going to feel a certain set of those... and he is going to feel mine, too.* He giggled softly.

ooo. Julian sat up and looked across the room. *did I wake him up with my laugh? no way to tell for sure... it looks like he's asleep. he's been there a while.* He lay back again; *what was I thinking about? oh yeah... buns.* It just dawned on him: *the big difference tonight is I never got a stiffy once.* He ran his hand downward. *I don't have one now.* He frowned. *what does that mean?*

Without thinking, he turned onto his side. He had started to feel uncomfortable. He yawned. *maybe I should go to sleep. I can figure out the rest tomorrow.* He yawned again. *yeah… good idea.*

He had been granted permission to end the data processing. He fell asleep at once.

Thursday

Fifth Day

Water Polo teams are formed. **Mark** is selected to be one of the coaches. He asks **Tom** to serve as his captain.

Geoff decides he should get to know **Nick**. He is surprised by what he discovers.

A new story emerges: **Robin** Simmons from Troop Nine, and **Jack** Haley from Troop 152. They were put together in the second "layer" of yesterday's Poker game. Robin is one of Tom's "initiates;" Jack is one of the original Poker Club members from Atlanta. Some special unexpected magic follows from that second game.

Troop Nine has the third annual troop barbecue at Camp Walker. Mark ordered that the supplies provided for this one meal be centralized. Preparing and eating this meal together as a whole troop is a part of his ongoing program of building morale. He sought always to offset the negative tendencies of intra patrol competition. He wanted them to intermingle and mix it up as much as possible. If too many members of a patrol clustered together, he forced them to separate and get to know someone new. He has succeeded in fostering friendly competition as an alternative to intense patrol rivalry.

21   *breakfast news*

Julian heard a faint click. He sat up at once. *my gosh! that's the clock.* The alarm was about to go off. He flung open his sleeping bag and raced across the room. He grabbed it just in time. All that escaped the dark brown shell was a dull clink.

"Mmmm…" came a muffled appreciation. Mark's head was mostly covered in an attempt to block out the sound of the birds. But that metallic click and what was supposed to follow it was programmed into his wakeup regimen so securely that he nearly always beat the alarm sound. Today would have been one of those awful exceptions. He heard the click, but he would never have reached the table in time. He was way over on the opposite side of the bed.

Julian looked over…he had never seen a groggy rumpled Mark. A wave of affection passed through him. He looked for as long as he dared. He turned to go into the bathroom.

"Coffee…" came another muffled utterance.

Julian giggled and closed the door. *potty time.*

Mark uncovered his eyes and ears… *wake up Mark.* He looked at the knob on the bottom dresser drawer because that's where his head was aimed. *why am I still sleepy?* He shook his head and threw off the blanket. *I had dreams all night long. what did I eat last night that caused that?* He sat on the edge of the bed—*ahh, the cold floor is on my side. that always wakes me up.* He reached for his socks.

Julian opened the bathroom door and raced across the room to finish dressing.

"Ten bonus points for getting the clock." Mark held up a thank you thumb. He stepped over to the window and pulled the curtains open wide. The view was to the north, but it was plenty bright enough to erase any hope of a second shot at getting more sleep. He headed for the bathroom. His first task this morning was the usual; *got to empty the tank.*

Julian was zipping up as Mark passed by... he glanced up to give a good morning smile; as luck would have it, Mark was yawning wide and his eyes were closed. This allowed Julian to look directly at his favorite object of speculation. It was still performing its nighttime function of keeping the bladder valve closed—it wasn't hard, but very puffed up. In motion like this, swaying inside Mark's skivvies, estimating its size was difficult... Julian didn't mind. His imagination would have a fine time making estimates... his eyes followed Mark all the way to the closing of the door. *wow.*

He was tempted to hang around for another visual treat, but he had to get the coffee started. *oh well.* He finished dressing and headed out.

He paused on the porch landing and took a deep breath. The air was terrific this morning. He started up the trail; *there's so much to think about now, after last night's talk.*

And this morning's parade.

Julian giggled softly. Even the inside critic was impressed.

As Julian approached the Flaming Arrow he could see that no one was up yet. *odd... I'm not early—maybe a couple of minutes or so. Maybe Danny is at the latrine. sure glad I don't have to use that any more.* That was the one thing on the first day that was unpleasant. *might as well start the coffee.* He headed toward the stove. *huh?* He noticed a bare leg out of the corner of his eye. *is Nick uncovered this morning? might as well have a look-see...*

hey, wait a minute... it's Danny! he's in the wrong cot—this is where Nick... wow: The other cots were empty again! Julian felt an instant surge of joy... he was so **happy** all of a sudden. The scene he saw yesterday flashed into his mind. *sure wish I could talk to Nick about it. someday, maybe. so... what should I do?* He wanted to go peek into the supply tent... *hmm. maybe I should wake up Danny first.*

let's do a look-see. He walked over to the crew tent quietly. *ooo...* The sleeping bag was flipped open... *wow!* He was completely naked... only his left leg was covered. *does everyone in this patrol sleep in the nude?* A couple of days ago it was Tom. *boy, Stu would never let the Wolf patrol do that!*

Danny was beautiful, lying still like that. *isn't he cold? maybe I should cover him up or something... nah. a good look-see, then I'll go make the coffee.* Danny wasn't hard—maybe a little puffy. Julian got down on his knees for a close look. He remembered the hard one perfectly. Seeing it now with only the tippy-tip of the head peeking out of the foreskin was interesting. He studied the hairs. *hmm. he does have a lot of hair... I'll have some one of these days... or years.* Danny was more developed all around—nice chest muscles. *I love the way the pelvis bone makes the space between the belly button and the cock look so... touchable.* The belly button: an innie. He looked up at Danny's face. *lips are a little puffy; they're nice to kiss.* His soft black curls seemed to spill over his forehead—his hair **never** looked messed up.

how long should I look? I need to get the coffee going for Mark. but this is just too good a chance not to do something! He felt mischievous... *let's see if I can give Danny a stiffy!* He grinned and reached forward... *don't tickle him, Julian... don't make him scratch...* he touched the top, just behind the head. *I'm the least sensitive there... with all this extra skin... ooo—it's warm.* Julian increased the pressure on his fingertip very gradually... he felt some resistance... he held steady. He felt a slight stirring... *oooo! it's starting!* He remembered the way it looked when the head came out. It started to do that; he kept his finger steady. *good morning, Little D!*

Julian didn't have to increase the pressure... Little D did that by himself. It grew in pulses—it got harder with each heartbeat... Soon it would begin to stand. *what to do... if I let go, it will spring up and slap his tummy. nope: let it get as hard as it can—then I can slowly take my finger away it so he wakes up by himself... I want to see the expression on his face. boy, it's getting hard!* Julian grinned wide. It was out almost all the way... pulses were strong... *he has to wake up, any second.* He glanced at Danny's face: *yes!* His eyes moved a little behind the lids—he pressed his pelvis forward just as they opened.

Danny saw Julian's impish grin. It took a second to wake up... he remembered where he was. *something weird is going on*—the grin told him that. He felt his cock pulse—it was being restrained by something. He looked down and saw Julian's finger pressing on the top. He looked back at Julian's wide grin. He grinned back.

"I must have slept in."

"Yep. You were fun to wake up." He pulled his hand away—sure enough, it slapped the tummy. He laughed, and stood up. He grinned and pointed to the supply tent. "Again?"

"Ohmygosh!" Danny leapt out of the cot. "You're not supposed to know! Can you do what you did yesterday?" His cock bounced happily up and down in the bright morning sun.

"Okay, but I gotta get Mark's coffee started." It was hard not to stare at Danny's beautiful morning salute.

"I'll do that… We hafta hurry!" He looked down at himself… *yow*.

"Can I peek in first?" Julian wanted to see them together in there again. He remembered last night how Tom behaved so differently toward Nick. He wasn't surprised they had spent the night together again. But it was a little daring.

"Be **super** careful. I **promised**! As soon as I'm dressed, you have to scat!" *cripes… forgot to put my skivvies back on last night. lucky Julian was the first one here. boy oh boy, Danny—if those guys are awake you are in big trouble. Julian isn't supposed to know! what if he tells Mark?*

Julian stepped quietly over to the supply tent and inched in. He wanted to see their bodies wrapped together again. They made him think of himself and Mark. *I always wonder what that will look like…* He inched around the corner. Nick was holding Tom in his arms. *gosh they're beautiful.* Tom's head was on Nick's chest—his left hand rested on Nick's right shoulder. The cover was down to about the elbow. Nick's arm was outside. It looked pretty much the same as yesterday. *this is like a painting… maybe someday…*

Danny poked him from behind. He backed out slowly. He mouthed a silent "thank you," and hustled off toward the cabin.

He ducked down just in the nick of time: Nick and Tom dashed from one tent to the other. *hee-hee!* Cocks bounced up and down like mad; they both had hard ones. They each had a sleeping bag wadded up in their arms. He counted: *one thousand one, one thousand two…* he stopped at twenty and stood. Danny was at the stove; he hurried over.

"Sorry, I sort of slept late today." Julian pretended to be short of breath as he trotted toward the stove. He didn't glance at the tent, even though he wanted to. He went right up next to Danny, who was bending over the drawer: he couldn't resist. He patted him lightly. "Coffee on?"

Danny wagged his butt back and forth. "Yep." He stood and smiled conspiratorially. "Forget to set the alarm?"

"Nah. Mark never forgets that. I was just pokey." They smirked at each other and proceeded to fix breakfast.

During breakfast Julian was impressed by how well Nick and Tom pretended. When Tom started to sit down by him, Nick made him sit across the table. Julian was proud of them. They were good actors—especially Nick. He took care to act as if he didn't know a thing. He snuck a glance or two was all. Danny was a good actor too. For now, Nick and Tom's secret was safe. Julian didn't look at Mark—*that might make him wonder why. best just to pretend everything is the same as always.*

After breakfast Mark started the morning meeting. He didn't get formal about it today. Julian was just as glad. Doing that was silly, since this was such a small group.

"Gents, I have some interesting news. Tom, you especially will be interested. They have asked me to coach a water polo team this year."

Tom sat up, eager... *that is my game.*

"I want you to announce this to the patrols when you pick up the ballots this morning: they're going to begin a water polo intramural today, during the morning free swimming period."

"You're a coach? Man, that's **great!** How will it be run? Like last year, or the one before?"

"Sort of in the middle. This time, each person earns individual points for playing, and those are transferred at the end to their troop. That's in addition to the scores they make. So we can get a lot more than before."

"We got it made!" Tom lined up the troop talent in his mind...

"Not so fast. This year there is a big change in the way the players are selected. Each **coach** picks his players instead of the captains. And, they have to **alternate** and draw from a different troop on each pick. Then the coach picks a captain from his lineup.

"Whose hot idea was that!" Tom was disgusted. His advantage just flew out the window. Last summer he was able to load up his team with

Troop Nine swimmers. It had helped them get a lot of points. "So I won't be able to pick a team beforehand."

"Nope... I think a small group of scoutmasters has decided it's time for us to come in second place, or worse. This year, we have to work for it."

"So how many guys will get to play?" Nick jotted down this information for the official minutes.

"That could be a problem. If every troop sends someone, we might only get four, or five, depending. There are too many troops here. We could get eight if there is a low turnout. I wouldn't count on that, though."

Nick had figured it out. "So only fourteen scouts can play, total?"

Mark shook his head. "There's a good change. This time they are going to double it so that twice as many can participate. Squads will alternate playing, and use the full ninety minutes of free swim time. That means there are actually four teams. That's why they want me to be a coach this year. The squad that plays first tomorrow will play second the next day, and so forth. Then the last two days will be a playoff tournament."

"Wow! We could actually have more players than last year... but they'd be divided between all the teams." *so I still need to line up the best swimmers. I have four in mind right away—Jay and Casey for sure.*

"Exactly. It was smart of them, when you think about it. We can't snag an easy win by stacking a team like last year. But we can still get as many points as anyone else, if we have as many of our guys playing as any other troop. It's more fair, all the way around. Besides, I don't like an easy win, anyway. So you need to scare up as much talent as you can."

Nick saw the implication of this development at once: no more morning poker games for Tom. *good. I'll get a little free time back too.* His chances of getting on one of the teams weren't that hot. He barely understood the game—he'd never played it. *I'll try anyway, just for Tom... but there's no reason to think I'd ever be picked.* He was glad Tom would get the chance to stand out. Tom needed that kind of thing. *I'd just as soon fetch and carry, anyway.* He looked across the table—he loved it when Tom was enthused like this.

After Mark adjourned, Danny and Julian went to get a tub of water to do the dishes. Nick finished writing his notes of the meeting. Mark took Tom off to the side and put his hand on his shoulder.

"How's it goin?"

Tom looked at him in the face. *if only you knew!* "A whole lot better. Yeah."

Mark saw the relaxed confidence in his eyes. "Good." *things are working out. Nick is the right one to tame this beast.* He hugged him slightly with one arm, like a coach would. "We still haven't had that talk. They've kept me busy most of the time. Maybe we can catch a minute after polo one day. You know, I've never coached a team of my own before. I'm counting on you to be my captain, of course!"

"For sure!" Tom looked into Mark's eyes. It was a look of trust and admiration.

Mark pinched him on the shoulder and winked. "See you at the lake!" He left for HQ, satisfied for now. *looks like they're in control at least. as long as Julian doesn't get suspicious or snoopy... if he sees anything, I hope he'll sit on it. Julian can be trusted, and he's bright. I need to talk with Nick about helping Julian in the growing up department.*

Tom watched him walk away. *man, am I lucky to have Mark.*

"Y'know," Nick came alongside. "He's almost as hot as you are." He gave Tom a bump. He looked at Mark's butt as it grew smaller in the distance.

"Geez! Listen to you! I'm s'posed to be the horny one." He looked at Mark. "Whoa... you're right. I never really noticed those before." It almost looked like he wasn't wearing any skivvies. "Anyway, you can't have any. Those belong to Julian!" He bumped back.

They broke up laughing.

"What's so funny?" Danny and Julian arrived with the big pot of water.

Nick and Tom looked at them, and stopped. These were probably the two best looking kids in the world. Julian, especially.

"Inside joke; sorry." *Julian, playing with Mark's buns? that would be the day.* Nick punched Tom's arm. "C'mon, we have an election to run!"

They headed off to the Zebra camp at the upper end of the string.

22   *office on the platform*

Nick watched the practice begin from the edge of the F dock. Tom was the captain of the team that had the east end. The other coach picked Casey Snyder to play—having two guys from the troop on opposing teams was going to be interesting. He chuckled quietly: *another poker player out of service.* Mark had been able to pick Jay Porter, too. The second set of teams had one each, so there were five from Troop 9 altogether. Nick was biased, but with the combination of Mark and Tom, their troop would still get more points than the others. *it's good to not be so lopsided like last year, anyway.* He'd never been a water polo fan. *I should learn about it, at least; it sure means a lot to Tom. looks like the second teams are impatient to start...* They were hollering up a storm.

It was hard to see what was going on; the playing area was in the zone where the deep water begins; roped off with buoys, it was well away from the possible spectator viewing areas. The shore side of the playing area was at six feet deep, the lake side at twenty feet—that's why they had to pick good swimmers. From either the boardwalk or the F dock, all anybody could see was heads and arms and splashes. It was rather boring after a while: not a spectator sport—at least not at Camp Walker. The coaches and players pretty well filled the boat and canoe dock. In fact, Nick couldn't be sure which head over there belonged to Tom.

Suddenly someone emerged from the water and pulled himself up onto the dock. It was Geoff; he plopped himself down at Nick's left.

"Hey, Man of Mystery!" He nudged with his thigh.

Nick, true to form, blushed.

"I **love** it when you do that!"

"What?"

Geoff reached over and tickled him under the arm. "Why, turn so nice and rosy in the face, silly. It makes you look so irresistible!" He banged against his thigh again.

Nick was embarrassed and delighted. The treatment Geoff gave him yesterday had become a delicious memory already. He didn't usually feel shy, but he didn't want to look at Geoff. He had no idea what to say.

"So, how did you make out at the little game in my tent yesterday?"

Nick smiled, in spite of himself. He didn't answer.

"Easy puns are a bad habit of mine." *wait for it, Geoff... wait for it... yes! Nick just got it; another blush...* he chuckled. Geoff realized that this was not the place for a chat. He looked over to the platform. *thought so! vacant. perfect!* "You're right, of course. This is not the proper place to talk about such things. Why don't you come over to my temporary office?"

Office? Nick looked at him, puzzled. Geoff pointed past his face to the platform. It was unoccupied, and about seventy feet away. He looked back at Geoff, who was smiling. Nick hesitated. He sort of wanted to... but he was apprehensive.

"C'mon. I really do want to have a chat with you."

Nick looked at him again. *looks harmless enough. besides, what could he do out there anyway, really? why not?*

"All right. But we have to get an okay from Leonard. I don't want to get on his blacklist."

"Good thinking," Geoff followed Nick over to the sign in table.

"Who did you come in with?"

Geoff pointed over to the crowded boat dock. "Rodney."

Nick smiled at Leonard. "Hi. We came in for the water polo sign up but weren't picked. If we sign in as Buddies for the rest of the time, can we move about as usual?"

"Good for you! Yes! I've been going nuts trying to track down others."

Leonard was most agitated. He hated not knowing just who was where at his waterfront. "Didn't they make an announcement? They didn't tell me how many of you there were. Show me your badges, please."

sometimes Ben Bradley could be so inconsiderate. he should spend a day down here!

Nick and Geoff went over to the east side Buddy Board after their badges. Normally, that was used for canoe and rowing. They put them in front of Leonard.

"I'm practically alone here today, thanks to this water polo thing. How they expect me to run down all these scouts is beyond me. I don't even know who they all are!" Leonard put them on his Buddy List.

"I think most if not all of them are still on the dock with the second teams." Nick saw no cause for concern. "I think you're fine, really."

"Oh. Well that's the first positive thought I've had this hour. Thanks for that too." Leonard looked over at the crowded boat dock. He had no way to tell who the players were. *why didn't they issue caps like last year?*

"Regular Whistle schedule?" Geoff was amused. He had Leonard's number. He was tempted to flirt a little, but not just now.

"Yes. The game has special whistles. You can tell easily. It's at a higher pitch." Leonard felt somewhat reassured now. He looked at Nick gratefully.

Nick took the badges over to a hook, then walked out to the end of the F dock. On the way he noticed that the rowboat guards had moved into place, one on each side. Each one had a referee standing up, trying to keep his balance and watch the game at the same time. The game took up nearly half of the deep water swimming area. Geoff was waiting at the end of the F. He gave Nick an "after you" gesture.

Nick jumped in— *I'll race, and get there first.*

Geoff waited five seconds, then jumped in. He wanted Nick to get there well ahead; he planned to approach the open side, not the ladder.

Nick reached the platform; he grabbed the steel ladder rail and pulled himself up. He looked back to see how far ahead he was... no contest. *why is he heading for the lake side, not the ladder?* Nick went over to the edge to wait; he stood with his hands on his knees and caught his breath.

When Geoff reached the edge he put his feet against the platform and raised a hand in the air. "Give me a hand."

Nick pulled him up. He kept his balance, but only just. It was awkward and they collided. *maybe I should work on my biceps.* He rubbed his right arm.

"Thanks," Geoff assumed the hands on knees stance catching his breath.

"Why didn't you use the ladder?"

"I thought you knew!" Geoff looked at him in the face, and waited until there was solid eye contact. "I **always** prefer the back door," he winked suggestively. *yes! the blush, the wonderful blush.* Geoff sat down with his legs pointed parallel to the shore. He patted the space next to him. *let's see… that was number three? I'll keep count today. Nick was such fun yesterday.*

Nick sat where Geoff had indicated. "Are you always this naughty?"

"I try… I always try," he said in a singsong. "Seriously, now. I want to know all about Tom. You're the one who knows, I can just tell."

"How can you tell?"

"Trust me, sweetheart," he patted Nick's thigh. "I always know these things. It's a born talent of mine."

Nick was amused; *no way to not be.* He had never met anyone like Geoff.

"Raise your left knee a minute."

Nick raised his left knee… *no reason not to.* "Why did you want me to do that?"

"I'm so glad you asked. There are three reasons: first, I want to admire the inside of that handsome leg while we talk..." he paused.

"The other two?" Nick blushed at the undeserved compliment.

"Well, they're related, really. One of them is that I don't want anyone to notice when my comments arouse your interest," he chuckled, mischievously.

"And?" Nick knew he was blushing, but couldn't stop. He realized now that he was sitting on the shore side, and the lifted knee effectively masked his lap.

"Well… you know," Geoff slid a finger along the side of Nick's right leg, from the knee toward his waist. "I wouldn't want anyone to think I was being too naughty."

Nick felt his cock begin to betray him. He had to head this off, somehow. "So what do you want to know about Tom, especially?"

"Ah. How long have you known him, for openers." He took his hand back. *let's do a slow tease.* He didn't want to spook Nick… it was a half hour before lunch, and he wanted to play every minute of that. *besides, I'm up to six blushes.* That's what he wanted to achieve most of all: a personal record for blushes caused during a single occasion. *I have to give Nick a chance to get off guard again. I'll level off for a while.*

"Three years—close to four, I guess."

"Where did you meet him?"

"Scouts."

"You were a Tenderfoot, and he was…"

"Second Class."

The Buddy Whistle sounded. They raised their arms automatically and continued the conversation.

Geoff had missed by a year. *so Nick is only a year younger.* That made sense. He paused. "Was he always so well endowed?"

"Oh, yes! Sometimes I think he was born with it." Nick chuckled. "But the last couple of years it has gotten bigger." He shook his head. "I hope it has stopped." Nick realized he had just made himself blush that time.

"Ooo! Really? Tell me more!"

Nick's brow wrinkled as he thought about it. "Well, it's at least a quarter inch longer than last summer." He felt sure about that, though he hadn't actually measured it. It was almost nine inches now, if not that already… that's the main reason he'd been trying to keep Tom away from the little butts.

interesting; Tom is still growing? That did amaze. *maybe there are more like him!* "Is Tom an only child?"

235

"Nope." He looked at Geoff, pointedly. "He's the baby of the family. Three older brothers!"

"I don't suppose the others…." Geoff was curious about size and inclination.

"No idea. I've only met two of them. Tom's the only one left at home."

Geoff had to digest this information. It was not at all what he had expected. Tom seemed more like an only child. *interesting.*

"Why do you want to know so much about Tom, anyway?"

Geoff looked at Nick directly. *jealous? maybe, a tad. be light about it, just in case.* "I'm often curious about the men who have taken me." He looked slyly at Nick and smiled out of one side of his mouth. "Especially if they are as énorme as Tom." He didn't want to bring up the subject of technique yet—his original objective. *Nick has to know about that.*

Nick ventured a retort. "He wasn't too much for you, though?"

"Silly boy. My nickname is Cleopatra to my intimate friends."

Nick did not get this one.

Nick's puzzled expression was a nice surprise. "She was famous for taking men of **all** sizes. She was reputed to have serviced an entire company of Caesar's army in one evening." *I love to report that one.*

Nick was genuinely surprised. "Really?"

"Well, she had an advantage, didn't she?" He waited for the puzzled expression to return. "She had **two** entrances!" He giggled naughtily.

"You are impossible!" Nick blushed anew. He laughed. He'd never heard anything so outrageous.

"Thanks, awfully." Geoff used his father's best East Midlands accent.

"It's the **front** door!" Nick feigned being cheated.

Geoff was surprised this time. He looked at Nick to explain.

"**That's** the back door." Nick pointed to the ladder.

"Excellent!" Geoff laughed. "You've caught me on one. Congratulations! Not many are as clever as you are, you know." He patted Nick's thigh.

damn! he got me to blush again. Nick scolded himself; this is fun, though. the guy's a genius.

Geoff decided to have a teeny bit of naughty fun. "I want a secret story. Tell me about the first time." Geoff spoke low and soft. "You know, with Tom: did he jump you like a wild man, or did you lure him into your lair?"

What a question! He looked at Geoff, stunned. He had never told **anyone** about that. He and Tom never talked about it, either, for some reason.

Geoff looked at him sweetly... his very best non-threatening look— no eyelash batting. He had a hunch this would be fun.

Nick paused for a moment. It was a special memory. He had not thought about it for a long time. He and Tom had been together, sort of, for so long, that there were many other stories as well. He looked at Geoff. *why not?* He had a sense of security now. He was confident in a new way. He looked at Geoff again, longer. Geoff had helped him realize this. *what a nice thing, even if it wasn't intentional.*

"I had a crush on him from the first." Nick thought back. "I had been in the troop for only a month. I was put in the same patrol: the Panther." He sighed. "During the meetings I always admired the way he behaved. He seemed as smart and able as the older guys. Even though he was only a Second Class, he seemed more like a First Class or Star. He helped me out a lot." Nick paused and refreshed his memory. "Two weeks after I joined, the patrol went on a campout. The older guys sort of tricked us into a game of strip poker. It was the little league version, of course. All we did was jack off. But it was a big deal to me!" Nick paused. "It was all by flashlight in a six man tent, and it was raining cats and dogs." That seemed so long ago now. "Then, a few weeks later, we came here, to this camp. It was Tom's second year here, so he knew a lot about everything. I used to follow him around every chance I got, of course. But it was the first day that did it to me."

"What did he do?"

"He didn't do anything. We just went to the Swimming Certification. That was when I saw him—it—for the first time." Nick was so innocent then. Tom was so experienced. And huge. Nick could see that that Geoff's curiosity was engaged. "Even then it was almost four inches limp!"

Geoff noticed a slight stirring between Nick's legs. *lovely. I'll wait a while before providing assistance.* He listened with interest.

"I thought at first he must be older, or something, because he was so much better developed everywhere, not just **there**. He looked at least a year older than he was."

"And had the experience, too, you think?"

"Well, yes, to a degree." Nick stopped for a second... he didn't want to mess up the sequence. "You see, at that time, all I knew about was beating off. I had a friend, Russ, who taught me how."

"Ooo!"

"We used to go to his bedroom after school and have contests to see who could come first. But they moved away, and for a year—more, really—I was on my own."

Geoff noticed that Nick's head had begun to appear. *hmm... I can see something else: probably an inch and a half more length, down toward those nice tight balls. very nice.*

"Well, with Tom, it was an accident, at first. That first day we had free swimming in the afternoon, just like now. I looked everywhere, but I couldn't find him. Then I just happened to see him come to the lake from that path over there, the one that comes from the Merit Badges? I thought at first that he was working late on a badge. But I found out that he wasn't."

"The plot thickens!" Geoff traced a line down Nick's thigh.

"The next morning it was the same thing: Tom came in late, all by himself. I had to know why. I followed him the next day."

"Ooo! You naughty boy!" Geoff was delighted. He patted Nick's thigh again.

"He went past all the places where the badge classes are held, nearly to the swamp. There was a little clearing hidden there in the trees. Tom went in. I followed carefully, so he couldn't see or hear me, and I watched."

Geoff breathed in a deep gasp. He grabbed Nick's thigh, but not too tight.

"That was the first time I saw it hard." Nick's eyes flashed. "It was Tom's private beating off place. I watched him from start to finish. It was so hot! Of course, by the time he was through, I was raging hard myself, and I had begun to do it as I watched." *what a dunce I was back then.*

Hmm… Geoff observed Nick's yummy growth: *you're getting there now.* Geoff removed his hand. *I don't need to help.* Nick was doing just fine all by himself.

"When he was done, he took off almost at once for the lake..." Nick blushed and chuckled. He looked at Geoff's intense, expectant grin. "He caught me, red handed."

Geoff rolled back with laughter. *this is wonderful.* He sat up quickly. He was ready for what had to be coming next. He sat cross-legged. The story was everything right now. His other game could wait.

Nick was into it... it was fun to tell this. Geoff was just the right person to hear it. *I'm no longer embarrassed about it.*

"'Well, if it isn't Little Angel!'" Nick quoted Tom. "That's what he used to call me: Little Angel." Nick shrugged. "Tom was delighted, and took me right into his secret hideaway, and insisted that I finish. It was a very hard thing to do, too. But he made me. He watched the entire time. That was my punishment."

"This is fabulous, Nick! He wasn't angry, or anything?"

"No! Just the opposite. I found out why, soon enough."

"Ooo-ooo!" Geoff could hardly wait.

"He did have a punishment in mind." Nick was having the fun, now. He had begun to feel more equal in this conversation—that was very nice. It was also a nostalgic delight; he had developed a hard-on just thinking about it, and it didn't bother him a bit. He looked at Geoff's rapt expression: this was a new sensation—a small buzz zipped up his spine.

Geoff, exasperated, nodded his head vigorously. He was getting aroused himself.

"He said I had to report there every day, to that very spot."

"Were you afraid?"

"A little," Nick nodded. "But he said not to worry. 'You will like it,' he said."

"And you did, of course."

"Oh yes. That was how both of us learned to do it. After two weeks, I was sore as hell and happy as could be. Tom was ready to attack, at will."

Geoff opened his eyes wide: "You've been a **team** all these years?"

huh. That question took Nick aback. "Wow. I never thought of it like that." He pondered. "No, not team. Definitely not a team." He smiled at Geoff. *I'm more of a guardian angel than anything else.* He wouldn't tell about those things.

Geoff was newly respectful; Nick wasn't a plaything any more.

Nick looked at Geoff with a wry grin. "And now..."

Geoff looked up. This face was new... *what's this?* "Hmm?"

"Now you have to tell me about your first time." Nick just realized that he had taken over. What a great feeling. A wide gotcha smile took over his face. He raised his eyebrows. No way could Geoff back out.

Geoff blushed. *wonderful.* He had met someone he could respect, at last. What a pleasant surprise. He looked Nick square in the eye. "That will be my pleasure. You will have the honor, Nick, of being the first person, ever, to be told that story." *it will be fun to see Nick hear this, actually.*

The whistle blew; that snapped them back into things. They had completely blanked the rest of the camp out, water polo shouts and all.

"During water polo, I presume?" Nick tilted his head.

"That will do perfectly." Geoff stood and helped Nick up as a courtesy.

They looked down at their current situation; they had gone down some already.

Geoff gestured an invitation to the lake. "A little cold water, before lunch?"

"I believe I will." Nick jumped in first. He didn't know if he'd win the race to the dock, but it didn't matter. He had come out even on the platform, at least. He was proud of that—and amazed at himself.

23   *Forestry discoveries*

Julian stooped to examine the teeny bud on a flowering grass—*is this a baby Blue Eye? that's one we don't have yet.* He and Justin were having a productive day. Their Forestry bag had nine different types of forest grass, and they still had a half hour left. They had worked out a good system: Julian would cut strands from the ground and put them into an envelope, while Justin found the variety in the book. If he could, he got the root system too—the ground was too hard, usually. He'd pried a few loose with his knife, but he didn't want to dull it too much. They labeled the envelope and checked it off on the list. They had worked their way over near the swampy wetland area, where they assumed other kinds would be. *we only need three more.*

"Julian…" Justin spoke softly and nudged his elbow. "Look over there." He pointed into the woods. Just barely visible between the trees, something was moving.

They stepped toward it to get a better look.

Julian's eyes went wide. He looked at Justin and put his finger to his lips. "Shh!" He crouched and pulled Justin down. He looked some more. Two scouts—their backs were turned, so they couldn't see Julian and Justin—they were very busy. What were they… "Wow!" Julian covered his mouth.

"What are they doing?"

Julian looked at him, amazed. "I don't know…" he squinted slightly… didn't help. "I bet it's something us little kids aren't s'posed to know about, though."

They inched forward a little. One guy was sitting on his heels… his shorts were down around his shoes. The other was bouncing up and down on his lap, his back also turned. The shirttails flopped and waved, emphasizing the up and down movement.

Julian looked at Justin. He was blushing—he had figured it out too. They watched a while. Those guys were sure busy having a real good time; Julian couldn't see it very well at all. He wanted to move around in front of them somehow. Seeing that guy squish his shirttail on his heels wasn't that interesting. He signaled Justin to follow him. They backed out of sight silently.

Julian whispered low: "I want to see them better… how about you?"

Justin grinned wide. "Yeah! How can we do that?"

"I have an idea." He scanned the area. "Ha! Just the thing! C'mon!" He led Justin over to a small mountain ash. "Be Prepared!" he whispered gleefully, and took out his scout knife. He cut off two branches that had a few nice wide fernlike fans of leaves; he handed one to Justin.

"We go over to the right, where it's just a little more open. We go up close on our hands and knees, real quiet. We hold this up in front of our face and peek through the leaves. I saw it in a movie once!"

"Oh yeah, I saw that one," Justin giggled. "Okay. You hafta go first."

They snuck back. They got within twenty feet. Julian was afraid that they'd be spotted if they went any closer. A large clump of swamp grass provided good cover below the head—all they had to do was peek over that through their branches. The view was much better: it was a three quarter frontal one, so the bouncing boys were facing at about a forty-five degree angle off to their right.

I thought so! we can see a lot better here. Julian looked closely… *they must be Tom's age…* the top guy had a lot of hair down there. So did the bottom guy. It looked like the top guy had to do all the work. His leg muscles flexed… his cock bobbed up and down so fast it was almost a blur. He grimaced real hard. It didn't look like it was that much fun. *the guy on the bottom is sure happy, though… it's his cock that's going in and out. I never heard about anybody doing this.*

Julian was reminded suddenly that he was very ignorant. *do lots of guys do this?*

oh-oh. They stopped for a minute.

"Do the dog," one said.

242

"Right!" the other one agreed.

Julian and Justin looked at each other, puzzled. They watched again... the top guy stood up, bent over, and put his hands on his knees. The other one got right up behind him. They had turned a little, so Justin and Julian had a side view.

The guy flipped his shirttail back out of the way: whoa! Julian gasped. *what a huge cock that guy has!* He pulled down his foreskin and put it right at the other guy's butt hole—slowly, he pushed it in.

Justin's jaw fell open; he looked at Julian in astonishment.

Julian grimaced. *that had to hurt.* They watched again.

The back guy had put his hands on the front guy's sides to hold on. He pushed in and out hard and fast. *man! look at those leg muscles work...* Julian could hear it! He could hear a slippery kind of noise. But the two started to grunt and moan too much, so the sound got covered up.

What Julian saw didn't seem to agree with what he heard. *to listen, you'd think these guys were having the best one of their life... but it looks terrible.* The front guy was writhing and shaking his head and groaning something awful. The back guy was working the hardest now. His head was thrown back—he strained as he pumped. He grabbed the other guy so tight it had to hurt: he gritted his teeth and groaned.

"Aaaa!" Suddenly the rear guy pulled back: "I'm cumming!" He stood to the side and started to jack off right there. He squirted out into the clearing, jacking and bucking real hard. He grunted and squealed.

where did all that come from!? Julian was amazed... *there's so much. he must have shot four or five feet out!*

"Whoo! Good one, Chris. I needed that." He panted some more. "Gimme a sec, okay?" He put his hands on his knees and caught his breath.

Justin and Julian looked at each other; they were in awe. They looked back: the guy who was bent over sat down.

"Yeah, sure."

The other one sat down too.

ug. Julian was surprised: both guys sat their bare butts right on the ground! The second guy's cock started to go soft—it lowered fast. Julian stifled a giggle: the guy looked funny; his pants were still around his feet—he forgot to take them off.

Julian and Justin looked at each other again. Justin smiled wide. He said a silent "WOW!" Julian held his finger to his lips—they watched again.

The guy who had shot scooted up next to the other one and took the cock into his left hand. *it's one of those bend down ones!* He pulled back the foreskin with his left hand and smeared saliva into his right palm; he started a spiral jacking up and down. The guy named Chris got hard again quick. He moaned a little and leaned back on his hands.

now that looks like it feels good. Julian started to get a stiffy. *this is hot!* He stared, mouth hanging open. This one he understood. It reminded him of Danny and the sun cream. It looked really good... he had to adjust himself. He forgot that Justin was right there.

Justin had gotten real hard; he had never seen anything like this. He knew how to jack off, but he kept that a top secret. He saw Julian adjust himself. *what a relief!* He did the same. It was starting to hurt, because it was pointed wrong.

Julian saw Justin fix his stiffy out of the corner of his eye. He looked at him and smiled. Justin grinned back and shrugged. Julian raised his eyebrows up and down several times. They watched some more.

Now the guy who had shot sucked on Chris, the bent down guy... he closed his eyes and tipped his head back. He licked his lips and hummed. *boy, this just gets hotter all the time!* The guy worked on him fast and furious. He sucked a little to get it all wet and slippery, and then did the spiral thing. Chris started to buck up and down in sync with the spiral hand work. He made a high pitched moan... the other guy licked him real quick and pressed harder. Chris bucked real hard and froze for a second. Then a huge wad came spurting out. Because his cock bent down, it didn't go very far.

Julian couldn't tell for sure where it went... between his legs somewhere. He bucked a few more times, and each time he shot some, but not as much. His finish wasn't nearly as spectacular.

Chris sat back, relaxed. He looked at his friend and smiled. "You've sure got a good hand, Ted. Thanks." He breathed hard.

Ted slowly squeezed Chris's cock. It produced a last drop; Ted caught it on his finger. He looked at it for a sec... then flicked it away. It struck a stiff reed-like strand of grass and clung tightly, forcing the stalk to sway back and forth a few times before bending down toward the ground. Ted watched, expecting to see it fall off. No such luck—the large drop hung there, defiant. "Well... better jet." He stood and brushed off his butt. He flicked the needles and crud off his shorts.

Chris got up and fetched his pants; they were draped on a scrub pine. They walked toward the trees on the far side. Chris slugged Ted on the arm: "Tomorrow, **you** will have the privilege."

"Promises, promises." Ted led the way out of their little hiding spot. They stopped briefly by a pine tree and looked both ways before walking out of sight.

Julian and Justin put the branches down. They both had to jack off, after seeing that. They looked at each other and knew that instantly. Julian looked around to see if there was anybody... didn't seem to be.

Justin pointed: "Maybe we should go in there."

Julian nodded. They hopped over the tuft of grass and trotted into the clearing. They sat and unzipped... by accident, they sat opposite one another. They started: *oh yeah... this will help.* They alternated taking furtive glances. Each was curious about what the other had down there. It did not occur to either of them to imitate what they had seen. They were simply in need of releasing some pressure. It was fun, all the same.

Justin sat up suddenly: "OOO-oo! Here I go..."

Julian watched, of course. Justin was a little bigger, but just as hairless.

He shot a respectable quantity. It made an arc of about a foot or so, in four squirts. He grinned proudly.

"My turn!" Julian pressed harder... he stuck his tongue out of the corner of his mouth... an old habit. He pumped a little, too—he had learned lately that it all got out easier that way. He got up on his knees for the final strokes. It increased the distance by about half a foot over Justin's. He got off five shots, the drops weren't all that big.

"There!" Julian smiled at Justin. *what a surprise day! I'd never thought about seeing Justin's. it's nice.*

They zipped up.

"How long you been doin' it?" Justin had never done anything like this with anyone before; he always thought it was probably wrong to do it at all.

"Couple a years," Julian was sort of proud of that fact.

Wow... Justin felt a lot better now. "Yeah, me too!"

Julian was impressed by that: Justin had started a year younger. wow. "Hey!" Julian just thought of something. "I want to see how far that guy shot!"

"Yeah, me too! That was something!"

They walked carefully over to the area where it must have landed.

Julian stopped to examine a strand of grass—it was bowed down, but didn't touch the ground. Amazing. The wad of cum was still clinging tight. The guy named Ted had flicked it over here like it was a lump of nose candy. *it isn't as big as I thought; why didn't it slide down the blade or fall off?*

Justin spotted something. "Here!"

Julian stepped over to look. Sure enough, there was a big glob, right there on top of the ground. It hadn't started to sink into the dirt. A bunch of pine needles were under it. It was more glassy and clear than the wad on the grass blade.

"Wow, is that ever **big**!" *well, after all: the gun that shot it had a pretty big barrel!* He drew a line on the ground next to it with his shoe. "Go stand where he was." He looked close... maybe it wouldn't dissolve. Maybe it would just shrink up. He pictured a pale raisin... *eew.*

Justin went over and studied the ground. He pointed to a spot. "It looks like about here." A faint scuffmark marked the spot.

"Put your foot there; I'll pace it off." He put one foot in front of the other all the way. "Six and a half of my shoes. When we get back, we can measure my shoe, and get the distance." *we used to do that in Cubs.*

Justin looked at the span. "Wow. I could never do that." He probably wouldn't try, actually. He shrugged and turned to step over the clump of grass.

"Me either. How we doin' for time? I don't want to be late for Archery again."

Justin glanced at his watch: "five minutes left."

They were back where they had left the pouch. Justin looked inside and counted. "Only nine. Guess we're a little behind."

"We can get caught up tomorrow." They headed back. "As long as we don't come across another sideshow or something!"

They cracked up laughing, and jogged toward the Forestry clearing.

24 *Jack and his basket*

Jack was in a rather sad state today. Luckily, he had chosen basket weaving for a merit badge this summer. It was a fairly brainless activity… it didn't matter **that** much if he was preoccupied by other things… so much of this was a rote operation… *once you start the pattern…*

Robin, Robin, Robin… he couldn't get Robin out of his head. He couldn't sleep worth a darn last night because of Robin. Ever since the card game yesterday morning—*no, that isn't right, either…* Ever since they met on the platform the day before, even. He was attracted to Robin from the start.

Jack wasn't interested in Tom any more, even if it was his "turn" at bat in the poker club—*I understand Geoff's fixation on him, natch. I like 'em big too, once in a great while… but it isn't that important.* He laughed out loud briefly: the way Tom handled Brian was something… *now that was interesting.* He hadn't seen that side of Brian before. Brian enjoyed being manhandled! The rougher Tom got, the more Brian loved it. Once, after Brian was on his back, Tom grabbed him by the shoulders, pulled him close and lifted him clear off the blanket and flopped him down again, as if he was a huge gunnysack full of potatoes! *Tom is two inches taller. he's a little bigger across the chest, and a lot bigger between the legs. first time I've ever seen Brian with another big stud; usually he has someone smaller, like me, good old party boy Jack. I wanted to stop and watch, it was so wild. but Nick moved around the other side and needed my attention. he may be Tom's regular, but he's obviously inexperienced. so, I lost track of what Tom was doing; the last thing I remember is the whump sound Brian made landing on his back the second time. gotta ask him about it first chance…*

Jack didn't recognize himself today, frankly. He always prided himself in the ability to have 'em and then leave 'em smiling. He wasn't as accomplished as Geoff, but he had adopted the same attitude toward sex partners. For a year now, he had sought to widen his range; generally he avoided repeat encounters and involvements. Refining techniques and seeing what new things there were to learn was his game. He was usually an observer as well as a participant. That had helped him show Robin a good time yesterday. He liked to think of himself as a party animal, mostly. Brian was a regular only when a poker game came along. *Brian knows how to suck, that's for sure.*

Jack wasn't exactly afraid of getting personally involved—it just never seemed important. He had friends who were always upset about this or that in a relationship—eventually it seemed to be a hassle for them all the time. Who needed that? *but now, along comes Robin: upset my apple cart. swept me out of my comfort zone entirely. Robin, Robin...*

"May I ask a question, or are you unavailable at this time?"

The sudden sarcasm shook Jack out of his reverie. "Huh?"

"Are you trying an experiment here, or—dare I think it—have you got your mind on something other than this Cherokee Double Wall?"

Jack looked down at his hands. *cripes.* His face turned red. He looked at Scoutmaster Fuller. "I guess my mind wandered some." He was using the dyed oval reed where the bleached round reed is required.

"Ah. I wondered. Well, if you're careful, you can undo it without losing your tension." He looked at Jack with some amusement. This was not typical. *everyone has one of those days.* Jack could recover if he paid better attention tomorrow. "You have just enough time today to undo the mistake. You'll have to concentrate a little better tomorrow." Fuller winked, and moved to the next weaver. There was no need to rub it in.

*man, Jack, what a **klutz**.* He glanced over at Ryan, his nominal partner in basketry. He was busy tucking in a tied end join... ***too busy.***

Ryan was being diplomatic, pretending to be oblivious. It was hard to keep a straight face. He hadn't been following Jack's work or he might have said something.

hmm. why didn't he say anything? thanks a lot, Ryan... maybe I can return the favor some day. He looked at Ryan's Cherokee basket. It's perfect, naturally. *thanks again, Rye-uhnn!*

Jack looked at the basket he had been working on for two days. *I honestly can't remember doing any of this! He held it up close. hmm. it's pretty good work, actually. just the wrong material is all. I reached for the wrong coil of reed stock. blast. well, I'll do it over tomorrow. I have to get out of here pronto, too, the second I have this torn down. I have to see if I can Buddy with Robin for the afternoon swim.* He had a plan in mind.

—⟋⟍—

Robin was in a quandary: *should I talk to Casey about this, like I usually do, or not?* Now that Casey was a water polo player, Robin was unattached in the mornings—he now had a new "activity" in mind for those mornings. *it isn't as if we're steadies, or anything, Casey and me. it's just that I'm so used to being with him and talking about everything. I almost feel obligated to mention it at least.* But for some reason, he was reluctant... this was a new thing. He had never felt like this. His stomach felt up in the air or something. *I'm not sick or anything—it's like when an elevator drops real fast and leaves your stomach behind on the floor above for a second.* That's the way he'd felt most of the day. *I need to see Jack... Jack will get me back onto the ground.*

"Brake a little more, we're coming in too fast..." Calvin was at the bow, ready to cushion their arrival at the dock.

Robin put more drag on the oars. *sure glad we've come in at last. I'll position myself by the fence. if Jack is coming to swim, I'll see him right away.*

"Nicely done." Phil Jensen made a notation on his clipboard. These boys had this well in hand. The Simmons boy was as good as any he'd ever seen.

"What do we work on next?" Robin shipped the oars.

"Distance, I believe." Calvin uncoiled the bow painter. "We start with a quarter mile, and get up to a full mile out and back by the end of the course."

Robin wasn't worried. *I can row half a mile now, by myself.* "Great." He climbed onto the dock while Calvin tied up to the mooring cleat.

"Well, see you tomorrow, then." He headed for the Buddy Board to get his badge.

Calvin was surprised somewhat by Robin's hasty exit. *huh... he seemed a little distant today.* Calvin knew they didn't have a problem, so it must be something else... *maybe he needs to make a latrine stop.* He didn't know Robin well enough to be nosy. *well. I'm off to buy some cartridges at the Trading Post. I have some major target practicing to do.*

Robin didn't know what badge Jack was working on—but more than likely he had to come down the west trail. *I'm fairly sure he won't go to his camp first—it's way to the north.* Unless Jack was in Archery or Marksmanship, or going back to his camp, it was almost guaranteed he'd come here. Robin leaned on the fence just to the right of the boat Buddy Board. He was still checked in... he kept his badge in hand, expecting to put it back on the board along side Jack's... *all I can do is wait.* He took a deep breath. He had scoped out the shore this afternoon and had a place in mind. Surely Jack will be interested. *what will I do if he doesn't show up?* He wasn't used to having doubts, uncertainties... *Jack is so polished and cool about things. makes me feel like an amateur. I've learned to bluff fairly well... I'll rely on that... I have to.*

A surge of energy unlike anything he had ever known: suddenly he was light and buoyant, as if he was in danger of floating away: Jack had just come into view, jogging down the trail. *excellent!* Robin could feel his skin prickling in anticipation—his stomach just went up another floor. *he has to be looking for me.* He'd placed himself prominently, between the Boat Buddy Board and Leonard's table. *Jack, Jack... over here!* He stared with concentration... he sent out his best telepathic rays, resisting the urge to shout and wave his arms.

Jack worried that he might not get to the lake soon enough... *yeah! There, standing at the fence. perfect. look at him! just like I remembered.* He slowed to a walk. He felt both relief and confirmation. It was as if he had grown taller, stronger. His eyes fixed on Robin's and locked.

"Hiya." Jack's artifice had flown. He wasn't playing... *Robin is a keeper.*

"Hey. I hoped you'd come here this afternoon." Robin couldn't keep the eye contact. It was too strong. It made him burn inside. He wanted to jump the fence and roll around on the ground and wrestle and kiss and grab ass and kiss more and you name it until sundown.

Jack saw at once they were on the same beam. His spirit soared. "Yeah. I hoped that's what you'd hope." Jack waited for Robin to look at him again.

Robin looked up. He saw himself reflected in Jack's eyes. It was intense. "I spotted a perfect place half an hour ago. Check in and put your badge over here on the rowboat board." He knew, somehow, that it would be inexcusably clumsy to frame that as a request. He saw how correct he was in the way Jack glowed. He put his badge back on the hook and walked slowly over to the rowboat he and Calvin had just moored. man... He was so **thrilled** right now. *why aren't I nervous?*

"Good afternoon, Leonard." Jack flashed his badge. "I'm out for a little boat ride with Robin." Being cool about it was the hard part.

"Good plan. The pond is going to be very busy afternoons, now— water polo, you know." Leonard wasn't happy about water polo hogging all that space in the morning. Besides, team sport was an annoyance generally, land or lake.

Jack put his badge on the boat board next to Robin's. *we have the first boat out today... nice.* He ran out on the dock and... *there he is, oars in hand, ready to leave.* "Well, well." He looked at Robin with intense, fascinated interest. *I'm not going to have any real work to do today: Robin is roaring to go!* Jack held onto the gunwale and climbed into the boat; he sat on the stern bench. He watched Robin's eyes as he backed the boat away from the dock. *this is exciting. I didn't expect to be taken for a joyride! pun intended!* Robin suddenly plied his oars deep. Wow. Jack grabbed the sides to steady himself... he realized suddenly that he was in very skilled and powerful hands. Rowing was one thing he had not studied.

Robin was a driven person—he had no time to waste. He set his feet on the stretcher and pulled hard. His arms and legs were not tired from the merit badge session just completed—if anything, he was warmed up and ready for this. He aimed the boat and they were off to the inlet he had discovered east of the dock.

Jack held on to the edge of the bench with a grin... *Robin is a dynamo!* He'd never thought about the work involved in rowing. *the view of his rippling shirt is sure a tease. I'll have trouble keeping my hands off him if this takes very long...* An idea formed.

"How far to where we're going, Captain?"

Robin laughed. *maybe I'll let Jack row back afterward.* "Not too far, maybe five minutes." *Jack is so much nicer to look at than Calvin.*

"In that case, I have a favor to ask. Stop rowing for a minute, if you don't mind." Playing with Geoff had given him an idea.

Robin stopped rowing and let the oars seat in the oarlocks. What could Jack want? *we don't have far to go.*

"Thanks. Umm..." He looked back toward the dock. It was almost out of sight.

"So?" Robin liked what he was looking at, but he wanted to romp sooner than later. Presumably this wouldn't delay things too much. The drift was in the right direction. Jack's face was still an unknown... *what's he up to?*

"It's fun being in suspense and all, but watching the stresses on your shirt is too tantalizing." Jack grinned slyly. "I was hoping I could talk you into taking it off. Studying your muscles at work would be a lot more rewarding. Five minutes of that is just about right, I think."

Robin was delighted. "Just about right?"

"Yes. I'll be in such a frenzy that you won't be able to stop me from... well..."

Robin chuckled. "But is disrobing in the boat allowed?" he asked coyly.

"I hope not! That would spoil the fun part." Jack wasn't usually a rule breaker. But being around Geoff had lent him an appreciation of making a tweak here and there.

"I know... I'll leave the kerchief on." Robin pulled out his shirttails and began unbuttoning. "No music for this?"

Jack laughed. "We'll imagine that part—my singing would ruin things, believe me. I can sour a whole choir." He was tempted to take off his shirt too.

"I read your mind: leave it on." Robin was inspired. "I can't remain a serious operator of this craft if I have undressed and irresistible passengers. We'd take in water because of all the thrashing around... my frantic leaps and grabs at your body can only be allowed on land." Technically, they were in violation of the basic rule to put on life jackets before pushing off. Robin had been in a hurry—because they weren't going very far it had slipped his mind. Fortunately, the lifeguard was looking the other way. He removed his shirt and folded it carefully. He handed it to Jack. "You are charged to keep this safe and dry." He looked at Jack hungrily. His presence was magnetic. *I need to start rowing again, now.*

Jack almost swooned. He had underestimated Robin entirely. *I am being taken for a ride!* What a wonderful surprise. *look at those biceps— and pecs!* He had no idea his prank was such a good idea.

Robin looked around to check on how far they had to go.

Jack raised the folded shirt to his face. *mmm.* He did that again. *mmm!*

Robin worked the oars hard—*I want to be there already.* He was amazed at himself. He had never been this witty or clever! Ever! Jack seemed to prompt him—make him bloom. *I'm right about keeping my head—I don't want to spoil the afternoon by having to sort out a swamped boat. man, I feel good today.* He just realized something: his stomach felt fine—never better.

Jack watched Robin's pectoral muscles at work... as fine a set of chest muscles as he could imagine. *soon, I'll be pawing them mercilessly. those delicate tufts springing from his armpits... oh boy...*

Robin marveled... the request to take off his shirt! Flattering and comic. *this is going to be great, that's all... we should be there by now.* He looked over his right shoulder and scanned the shore... there!

The inlet, nearly a mile east of the dock was invisible from every angle except directly on. Robin had mastered the skill of steering, and turned precisely where it was required. "Tell me when we're about fifteen feet from the bank."

"We're close... now!" Jack was impressed by Robin's skill. It was hard to believe he was still working on his badge. He watched the bank loom close. The boat slowed perfectly and kissed the bank gently. "Beautiful."

"Thanks. I learned a bunch from my grandfather. This lake is a picnic compared to the river where he takes me fishing." Robin shipped the right oar. "I haven't been ashore here. But the woods hereabout are fairly open. I figure we can find a spot easy enough." Robin looked down— the bank dropped off without a beach for landing. He plied the left oar, bringing the boat parallel to the bank. He sculled the oar to achieve optimum contact with the bank. "Climb out carefully and help hold the boat side to the bank. We'll lift the bow out when I'm ashore."

Jack climbed out and put Robin's shirt on the grassy bank. He reached out and steadied the boat. He held the bow painter while Robin scooted across the thwart and climbed onto the bank.

"I don't see anything to tie to." Robin frowned. "They don't have anchors onboard yet, either. We'll have to beach her, I guess." He joined Jack at the bow, and they pulled the boat out of the water.

Jack felt like a Tenderfoot. "I suppose you're Daniel Boone, too?"

"Well, I've done my share of trail blazing, I suppose… but I'm willing to place the land side of the operation into your hands." Robin picked up his shirt.

nice… that made Jack feel better. "I was handy at mapmaking and compass reading in my First Class days." Jack would do his bit now. He moistened a finger and stuck it into the air, as if he were checking the wind direction. "This way should do." He headed inland.

The woods near the shore were heavy with undergrowth. Inland ten yards, the taller red oaks opened things up considerably. They came to an open area at the base of a ridge: room for an entire campsite.

"Here we are. Reserved for you and me today."

"Excellent. I knew you could get us here." Robin looked around. "You could hold a poker **tournament** here." There was room for half a dozen games, at least. "What do you call this wonderland?"

Jack improvised: "Whispering Pines." That sounded exotic.

"Oh!" *why not?* That had a poetic ring to it. Robin looked around. *oop.* No pine trees in sight. Lots of oak trees… a birch and a poplar. He squinted, peering between a distant pair of oaks: *is that a pine? hmm.* He bent down and picked up an acorn. He showed it to Jack.

"Okay, so it's Whispering Oaks then." He cupped his left ear and aimed it upward. "Hear that?" The breeze was audible, barely.

Robin smirked and cupped his ear. "Ah, yes." He could hear the leaves rustling above. He smiled wide. "A welcoming committee!"

Jack examined the ground. He wanted a place free of branches and lumps. Next to a wide patch of bluebells he tested an area by swinging a foot back and forth. No debris... a fine grained ground cover, lightly sprinkled with remnants of what had been shed from the oak and poplar trees last fall. "Here? You be the judge." He smiled at Robin.

Robin came over to Jack's side. He didn't even glance at the ground. He reached over and put his right hand on Jack's left bun. They both felt the jolt. The banter was at an end. Their eyes met. They embraced at once and kissed. It started gently, but grew intense. They lowered themselves to their knees. Their eyes remained open. They pawed at each other's shoulders, they combed each other's hair with their fingers. They had to stop kissing and catch their breath. They stared at each other briefly. This was a new place for them both. They entered eagerly.

Jack took Robin's kerchief ends into his left hand and removed the slide with his right. Robin did the same. Jack started to unbutton his shirt, and Robin pulled out the shirttail. He unfastened Jack's scout belt buckle, and waited while Jack took off his shirt. Jack unfastened Robin's belt. They pulled down each other's shorts and briefs by touch, each unable to look away from the other's eyes.

"Umm... how are we going to do this, anyway?" If Robin reached for Jack he would be unstoppable. Their pants were only down to their knees... he wanted them all the way off.

"In as many ways as we can, of course." Jack licked his chops. "We have almost an hour now, and then... well tomorrow, we start again at 10:30, don't we?"

Robin felt his face flush. He took a deep breath. "Man, you sure smell good!" He reached for Jack's cock with his right hand as he pulled Jack's head to his lips.

Jack responded in kind. They massaged each other's cocks gently, lovingly, as they kissed. He tugged at Robin to lie down... his knees were complaining.

They enjoyed each other's kisses so much they didn't want to stop. Brian had assigned them a sixty-nine at the card game, and as the second layer, they didn't have time for much else. They had an overwhelming farewell kiss—that's where they both wanted to start. They paused.

"Where did you learn..." they both asked at the same time. That broke them up.

"Okay," Jack propped up on his left elbow. "I can see that we need to figure this out here. We have to take turns, or something. We seem to be evenly matched."

"I was just thinking that!" Robin looked at Jack in wonder. He did not remember ever having anything go as perfectly as this.

"Well," Jack sat up. "I was planning to wrestle you to the ground, pin you good and insist that you submit. I see now that that would be a lot of fun, but pretty silly."

"I was thinking more along the lines of flipping a coin." Robin sat up and ran his fingers up along Jack's bicep. "But wrestling sounds very good, too. I'd get subjected to a lot more aromatic parts that way."

"You're big on smells, aren't you?" Jack checked under his arm with a sniff. He didn't detect anything offensive, at least.

"I'm very big on your smells!" It was true. Jack's body chemistry made him go crazy. Robin rolled onto his back and pulled off his shorts... *that's better!* "Do you spray yourself all over with some kind of magic stuff, or what?"

"No. I just naturally stink, what can I say?" Jack was enormously flattered. He enjoyed Robin's smell too, in fact. He felt like he had cheated a little by sniffing the shirt in the boat. He sat back and removed his shorts. He tossed them with a flourish—they landed directly on Robin's. He lay back down and faced Robin.

"Well, you should go out and patent yourself or something." Robin thought about that a minute. "On second thought, don't you dare do that. The entire camp will come sniffing. I'd just as soon keep you a secret." He nuzzled behind Jack's ear and took an exaggerated sniff followed by a very wet swipe of the tongue.

Jack shivered. Man that was a turn on—as if he needed one. "Do you want to do the same as yesterday?"

"If you insist. But I like sucking on your face a lot better."

"There you go again, stealing my exact thoughts!" Jack was amazed. He reached over to take Robin's cock in his hand.

"Later on, I might lick you from head to toe. You happen to taste almost as good as you smell." Robin filled his palm with saliva and took Jack in hand. He waited for Jack to follow suit.

No more words were spoken for a long time. They kissed and stroked each other with care and fascination.

Jack had some KY in his back pocket, but he left it there. This was more honest, somehow. He liked having to refill his palm. Licking it tasted so good—it had traces of Robin that he enjoyed so much yesterday. He was learning to focus on those smells— *Robin's scent is just as wonderful as mine could ever be!*

Robin paid attention to the contours of the object in his right hand. Jack was slightly smaller, maybe by half an inch. That made it possible to completely surround his cock with all his fingers. He moved his left arm from behind Jack's shoulder and put it down at the base. He pulled the foreskin down while he pulled his right hand back. Each fingertip crossed over the cleft at the tip, drawing some pre-cum along as it passed by. The effect was instantaneous.

Jack moaned. "Wait a while for that one! Two or three of those, and I fire!" He panted briefly, smiling. "Let me try that on you!" He moved his right hand down.

As luck would have it, Jack was left handed, which made this position ideal. He refreshed the saliva in his palm, returned to the lip lock, and repeated Robin's move.

"Mmmm!" Robin pulled back. "Wow. Jack, Jack, Jack! You do that so much better than I do!" Robin was amazed. He'd done this one solo for a long time. Why was it so superior here?

"I've played around quite a bit, but this is a new one. I plan to learn it well, O great teacher." Jack looked at Robin. That in itself was a thrill.

"Oh good. Today, let's practice doing it lightly, saving the tippy top for the glorious finish. Let's see how long we can go before we have to come."

Jack was delighted. "I like that. Should we try to come together?"

"Hmm..." Robin spiraled Jack. "The first time, yes. Later we can go individually. Sometimes that's better because you can control things so much better."

"Exactly." Jack marveled again at how they saw things so alike! "If I back up suddenly it means stop now unless you're there too and want to go for broke."

"Perfect. Back to work now..." Robin slicked his palm again and puckered his lips, daring Jack to meet him half way.

Jack did just that, after filling his palm.

The nuances of integrating careful pumping of the hips with the manipulations of their hands, kissing all the while were learned, perfected. Kissing took precedence for both of them—it was the **basso continuo**, the foundation, the generating force that energized everything. The delights being felt below were sublime and exciting, but were also an excruciating interruption. They had to do both, but they hated to do both at the same time. Yet if one was paused or neglected, the other seemed lessened. The challenge was to focus on them both at once. That was a new skill. They welcomed the opportunity. They didn't stop to analyze this, of course. Now, they learned, they practiced, they enjoyed, they shared.

The first signs of the impending climax grabbed Robin: he moaned softly. Jack moaned a response—he was ready too. They opened their eyes and watched each other as their thrusts grew slow and deliberate. They squeezed their hands tighter by subtle degrees, and it began. Their moans merged into a high, constrained peal... soft, muted "uhms" accompanied each shot. It was wondrous. It was exhausting.

They removed their hands and embraced as hard as they could. They rolled over and over to the far side of the clearing and stopped. They broke out laughing and lay on their backs. They rested. Jack's left hand moved over to Robin's right. They held them together until their heart rate and breathing returned to normal.

"That was the best..." they said in unison. They laughed, embraced, and laughed some more.

25   *musical fruit*

"Who is your patrol's advance chef?" Nick felt witty this afternoon.

"That would be me," Doug Tucker stood up. Supper was his regular duty at the Panther camp.

"Grab your beans," Nick, the assistant to the Assistant, pointed to the cans on the table. "We'll drop them off at the Flaming Arrow." He was delivering last minute instructions to the patrols before they came over to the campfire. Each patrol provided one person to be a barbecue cook, and that's what Nick was doing, rounding up the eastern three; Danny was gathering up the western half. They had to report to the campfire first, and get their super-sized frankfurters over the fire.

"When do I bring the lemonade?" Nathan was the Panther Patrol leader.

"Fifteen minutes or so, maybe twenty." Nick checked his list. "If anything changes, we'll send a runner." He waved Doug forward.

They stopped off next at the Lynx. Some kind of a meeting was in progress. "Hey, Gary," Nick hailed the Patrol Leader.

"It's the bean collectors!" Gary West jested. "Thought you'd never get here."

"Do you have a really good can opener, I hope?"

"Yeah, I think so."

"You'd better bring it along. I don't know if ours can handle fourteen cans."

Gary ran over to get the Lynx can opener. He was assigned to be the chief bean cook, but he had to use the big stove over at Flaming Arrow.

"I have a P-38." Robin pulled out his scout knife; the army surplus can opener dangled on the chain attached to his Cub Scout three-blade. He smiled demurely.

Nick smiled demurely in return. "Thanks… we'll send a runner if we get into a bind. Who's your wiener guy?"

"Here I am!" Paul jumped up from the table. He rather liked that title.

"Outstanding!" Nick spoke to Gary again. "We have to get Tiger's beans next." Gary was still rummaging in the sideboard drawer.

Alex had a four-blade with a can opener. He was about to offer it when Gary ran back to the table with what looked like a sturdy new can opener.

"Perfect." Nick gave the 'Onward,' arm gesture.

As they entered the Tiger camp Brad was chopping up onions. Two large onions per patrol were going into his mountain of quarter inch thick chunks; Jay Porter had drafted Shawn to help him slice up the dill pickles. They occupied the other end of the table.

"Man, how can you stand to do that?" Nick's eyes would be swollen shut.

"You have to stand upwind, and wipe off your blade pretty often," Brad shrugged. "I did some time at Hamburger Harry's last winter. They have a big tub of lemon water to dip the blade in—that works good." Onions were one of Brad's favorite things… one of the best "afterburner" fuels he had found. Besides, these were Vidalia sweets, first harvest of the season. *they aren't that bad—they don't need to be thinly sliced, even.*

"How come so much?" Nick was amazed at the size of the pile.

"Hey, we may not have enough." He had already instructed his patrol to sprinkle everything they ate tonight with a big handful. *I wish I had an extra one to add to the pile.* "Sprinkle some on your hot dog, some on your potato salad, and some on your beans, too. They make **everything** taste better!" You could never get enough of these things. Brad loved the way they crunched when they were raw like this. You could eat these like an apple. A tangy apple. He tossed a freshly chopped cube into his mouth and chewed happily as he chopped away.

"Lead the way." Jay Porter held up his cans.

Nick watched Brad munch the raw onion. *hmm. I'll wait for supper, myself.* He led the line of bearers over to the Flaming Arrow where they put the beans on the table. "Okay, wiener roasters, go on down to the campfire—Tom's waiting for you there." He stepped over to the stove and reached under the apron for the big pot. *I'll help Gary open the cans and get the beans going.* He looked at the table… *that's a lot of beans!* "Start opening cans; I'll get the big wooden spoon."

Each patrol had been assigned its part in the one and only Troop 9 barbecue of the summer. The Flaming Arrow patrol was in charge of setting and cleaning up, as well as the meat and buns.

Mark had been able to get the disposables from HQ as a favor. That meant that cleanup would be a matter of tossing things into the fire, for the most part. Chef Pièrre had lent him the cooking tongs for the night too, which helped greatly. It would be the troop's only open flame meal this summer; Mark was supervising everything himself.

"Grab the other end." He handed one end of the tarp to Julian, who was at the campfire site helping out. "We'll have all the ingredients set out on this. We don't have anything we can set up to make a serving counter." He put a chunk of firewood on each corner in case a late afternoon breeze came up.

Tom stood by the open chest waiting to pass out the frankfurters. These were the deluxe oversized kind that came in a linked string. They had to be snipped apart; the skin casing split wide open when it was cooked over the fire. They were one of Tom's favorites. *these tongs are perfect.* He had preloaded them with six franks each—which was a squeeze, with extra fat ones like these. The tongs were hinged at the fire end, and held the franks tight so they couldn't fall into the fire—always a risk if they were just poked onto sticks. He watched the line of cooks approach. *excellent. we need to get these things going.* The fire coals were just right.

"Step right up," Tom held up a tong in each hand. "When you have these done, you put them into the big pan over there." He pointed to the large Flaming Arrow dishpan, parked near the edge of the coals. "Then refill your holders with a second load from the cooler here."

"How d'ya know when they're done?" Chuck from the Badger patrol had never done this before. He'd only roasted hot dogs on a stick.

263

"When they split open is usually the sign that they're halfway done."
Tom watched them locate themselves around the fire. "They'll stop
dripping fat, and they'll look done, really." He performed a sample flip.
"Keep 'em a foot or so above the coals. Turn 'em over pretty often. If one
won't split on its own, give it a poke with your pocketknife. You don't
want them burned on the outside and undercooked inside."

Doug got down on his haunches next to Paul and watched the franks
in his holder begin to swell and turn shiny. "It's hard not to have nasty
thoughts when you look at these fellas trapped in their cages."

"Trying to ruin my appetite?" Paul smirked. "It won't work... in fact,
I'll pretend, when I take my first giant bite, that I am feasting on an old
friend."

"Cannibal!" Doug pulled his left hand in front of his crotch.

"Don't flatter yourself," Paul smiled. "I was thinking more about..."
he nodded in Tom's direction. His gross basket bulged as usual; no way to
hide that.

Doug chuckled. "Speaking of," he spoke low... "I don't see him going
up the trail this year on his "special training" trips." He glanced over at
Tom. He had to admire the bulge. Even limp it evoked a certain memory...
hmm. it is almost the same size as these things.

"Robin says he's been tamed." Paul watched Tom join the circle
with a tong full of franks. He hated to admit that he envied Tom's
masterpiece. *I'm nearly eight inches.*

"Baloney. Who could do that?" Tom outsized everyone in the troop
in every department. *no one is going to hold him down.*

"Robin says Nick has him corralled."

Doug looked over to the tarp where Nick was talking to Mark. Then
he looked over to the other side of the fire, where Tom was watching his
own set of tongs over the fire. "Hmm." He wasn't convinced.

It didn't take long for the aroma of the roasting franks to spread. The
breeze was variable and light, and it soon seemed to be everywhere in the

Meadow. As the first set of cooked franks were being emptied into the pan, the rest of the scouts began to arrive.

Nathan was first, a pitcher of lemonade in each hand. "Where do these go?"

"Right here, at the end." Danny was there to guide the placement of items in the self-serve line. He was tempted to have some of that right now. *the Zebras haven't brought the cups yet...* He waved the rest of the Panthers, with the milk cartons and water canteens, over to the same end of the tarp.

Julian brought over his first load of hoagie buns from the Flaming Arrow. Four dozen of these was all he could manage at once. These were twice the size of a regular hot dog bun. One would be all he could handle. Danny had him place them in the second slot in the line. As he bent down to put them in place, something very cold poked him from behind.

"Better not back up too fast," Sid lifted up the ketchup bottle with a big grin.

"Wrong buns," Julian quipped. He was tempted to do something in return, but there were too many guys around. He was content to aim the ketchup bottle to the right. "Danny's the one to see about that. Hi Jeremy."

"Boy, Julian! Those sure smell good!" Jeremy had the mayo jars. He was super hungry. "How long 'til we eat?"

"Any time now, I think." Julian hurried after the rest of the buns.

The Zebras arrived with all the tools. Cory was in front with the cups. Danny showed them to the first place in the line. "Take the cups over to the lemonade and milk." Jim West had the plates and Kurt had the plastic tableware. Tad had the napkins.

"Onions, anyone?" Brad marched in proudly with his big kettle mounded above the brim.

"Next to the ketchup." Danny did a double take at the mountain of chopped onions.

"Beans, beans, the musical fruit," sang Max as he helped Gary carry the big pot from the Flaming Arrow stove.

Danny directed them to be put in the third spot; the potato salad was next in the lineup. *here it comes.*

The smile on Bruce's face—as well as a telltale residue at the corners of his mouth—betrayed the fact that he had performed an unauthorized taste test. *I had to approve the addition of those chopped onions the Tiger guy brought over, didn't I? I like the way they crunch. it made this even better... this stuff isn't store bought; Chef Pièrre made it right here at camp!*

Everything was just about ready. Mark had determined the in line priority: by individual rank instead of patrol. They wouldn't expect that. He'd checked with each patrol leader—everyone was present. Falling in would be too formal... *I want things to be loose tonight.* As the second batch of franks was being emptied into the tub, he clapped his hands and announced: "Eagles, you get in line first, then Lifes, then Stars. You know the rest. Let's chow down!" He clapped his hands again. "Everybody gets two dogs, but just take one per trip. I want everyone to have some beans and potatoes to balance your meal. I don't want a bunch of leftovers to worry about, either." He got in line last, behind Freddy Scott, the smallest of the Tenderfoot scouts.

Reluctantly, Tom waited for Nick to fill his cup with lemonade—he was hungry. He led Nick over to the right of the fire. He'd scooped out a nice place to sit near the pan of franks. Soon everyone had found a place to sit and begin to deal with their massive hot dog. No ceremony was needed..

"Hi." Julian sat down by Bruce. He hadn't seen him in a while.

"Mbgfp!" Bruce's mouth was very full.

Julian took his first bite of hot dog. "Mmm! This is good! I've never had this kind of hot dog before." The frankfurter skin snapping under his bite was different... regular hot dogs didn't have that.

Bruce swallowed. "Bgyeahb." He swallowed some more. "We have 'em at home lots; they're the only kind my dad allows in the house!" He looked at Julian's plate. It looked sort of skimpy. "Not hungry t'day?"

"Sure." He shrugged. "I can only put so much down. This bun is practically as big as my whole stomach." Julian didn't see where these guys put all the food he saw piled on the plates. He had been taught to clean his plate... he'd learned to go easy around here when he loaded up.

Bruce leaned close in confidence: "You oughta skip the bun, then. This other stuff is what's really good, anyway."

Julian saw the wisdom in that advice. He looked at the frank. *how can I hold it without a bun? hmm. aha!* He tore off the top half. *I'll eat it like a slice of pizza.*

Justin joined them. "Man, these are gigantic!" He made a small depression in the ground for his cup of lemonade. *I need both hands to deal with this.* He watched Bruce take a bite. *wow.*

Julian glanced at Justin. He felt a little mischievous. He waited until Justin was looking straight ahead, and then nudged him with his elbow. He held the top of the bun he had torn off right at the edge of his plate. With his other hand he pulled down the other end so that it drooped over the edge. It was about the same size as the bent down guy they had seen during Forestry.

Justin almost choked.

"Here: you need some more." Brad sprinkled some chopped onions on Andy's potato salad and beans. He had brought along a measuring cup to use as a dipper. He was making sure, personally, that all the Tigers were fueled to the max.

"Geez, take it easy, will ya?" Andy liked onions well enough, but Brad was a little weird about them.

"Yeah," Tony agreed. He looked at Brad's plate. "Y'know, you really ought to try some salad and beans with your onions some time." He squinted at the stub that remained of Brad's first hot dog. "Say: there's room for another spoonful there, if you have any extra." He held his fingertip near the vacant spot.

Brad looked at his plate. "You're right!" He sprinkled some on.

Tony looked at Andy. They broke up laughing.

Brad was unfazed. He moved on. He still hadn't inspected Jay's plate. He had to make sure all the Tigers were prepped. *man! this is the best meal all camp! I'm going for seconds of everything. hmm... too many onions left; I'll sneak some into the bean kettle. better check on Shawn first...*

When it was clear that only a few were still eating, Mark nodded to Max, who had finished. Max stood and walked away from the troop unobtrusively, as if he was on a trip to the latrine. In a few minutes he returned with his guitar. As he approached, Mark stood in front of the fire. He didn't have to give a command—the troop automatically gave him their attention.

"Let's have a big hand for the cooks!" Mark led a vigorous applause. "I see there's some food left. I hope to see it all disappear tonight. If you want more later on, be sure to keep hold of your plates. After we finish the assembly, there are marshmallows to roast. Those are first come first served, and you have to roast your own. Tom has a pile of sticks ready, but he'll hold off passing them out until that time comes." He gestured to Danny to come forward with the announcements.

"Not much today, except that the Trading Post has decided to stay open during lunch. That way you don't have to wait for supplies until after Badges. They got a new delivery of stuff today, so you might want to stop by just to check things out.

"There's an overnight hike sign up sheet at HQ. That's open to anybody who wants to chalk up some miles for his merit badge. Remember to okay it with your counselors, because it means missing a class. Your patrol leaders need to know, too." Danny nodded at Mark; he was finished.

Mark returned to the front. "I'm pleased to announce the results of your vote this morning." He motioned to Max to come on up beside him. He paused while the troop cheered and applauded. "Instead of rehearsing tonight, we're going to do something different. Max has agreed to lead us in a good old fashioned songfest. After that we'll hang around and roast marshmallows." Mark produced his folding stool for Max, and went to the back of the semi circle of scouts.

Max stood in front of the stool and strummed a familiar chord. He started a rousing rendition of **You Ain't Nothin' but a Hound Dog.**

The songfest was underway. The troop loved this. Many joined in and sang along if they knew the song. Favorites were **Sixteen Tons, Poor Little Fool,** and **Day-O.** There was a request for **Davy Crockett, He's Got the Whole World in His Hands,** and **Yellow Rose of Texas.** They loved doing the old fashioned round, **Row, Row, Row Your Boat.**

268

A good forty minutes of singing had been enough, though, and Max knew when to wrap things up. He had a surprise prepared. "Okay, guys. Now the Lynx Patrol has a finale all ready." He gestured for his fellow Lynxes to join him up front. "Now: we'll run through it first. Then we'll divide up and everybody can do the second verse, like we did for Row, Row." He turned to the Lynx and raised his arms. They did a full run through before demonstrating how to perform it as a round:

Beans, beans—the musical fruit;
The more you eat, the more you toot!
>> *Raspberry. Raspberry. Raspberry!* <<

The more you toot, the better you feel;
So let's have beans for every meal!
>> *Raspberry. Raspberry. Raspberry!* <<

The troop broke into laughter; when they had calmed down, Max divided his patrol into thirds, and performed it as a round:

Beans, beans—the musical fruit;
  Beans, beans—the musical fruit;
    Beans, beans—the musical fruit;

The more you eat, the more you toot!
  The more you eat, the more you toot!
    The more you eat, the more you toot!

>> *Raspberry. Raspberry. Raspberry!* <<
  >> *Raspberry. Raspberry. Raspberry!* <<
    >> *Raspberry. Raspberry. Raspberry!* <<

The roar of approval was even louder. Max placed his patrol duos so that each stood in front of about a third of the circle, and faced them directly. Max gave each third the beginning downbeat, and his patrol members led their third. It went as smoothly as if it had been rehearsed, even though they weren't in a patrol formation.

It took a while for the laughter to subside. The raspberries in the second verse were a little ragged and mixed with laughs and "echoed" repeats.

Mark was tempted to join the last group, but thought better of it just in time. He didn't need any reports about being too chummy. Allowing the song was okay, but participating wouldn't be too smart. He returned to the front. "Excellent!" he gave Max a good pat on the back. "A big hand for the one and only Max, everyone!"

The applause and cheers waned and Mark continued. "Now to wrap up—Tom has the sticks, and Julian has charge of the marshmallows. I see four leftover hot dogs. See what you can do to get rid of them. There will be no formal dismiss, so you're free to go back to your camps when you want. The Flaming Arrow will clean up and return things tomorrow. Put your empty plates and cups in the pile before you take off." Mark pointed to the start of the disposal pile at one side of the stone ring. "Anything for the good of the order?"

Tom stood: "Let's have three cheers for Mark!" He led the troop in an enthusiastic "Rah! Rah! Rah!" and applause.

Mark smiled and blushed in spite of himself. He tried without success to shush them. Finally he sat on his stool and waited for it to quiet down.

Julian was bursting with pride. It was all he could do to stop from running over to hug Mark. He wiped the tears away. He glanced around— no one had noticed. He went over to Tom and got the marshmallow bag. Boy was he glad he had something to do right now. *what a great night! what could be better than scouts? it's neat to be next to Tom, passing these out.*

The Tiger patrol was the first to finish their marshmallows. One by one, Brad gave each member a nudge: the time had come. The Tiger Patrol was set to have its own party. For two days now, Brad had been talking it up—Shawn, the Tenderfoot, especially was eager to see the magic.

Andy got the lantern going. He was looking forward to this. *Brad is sort of comical, but he's an expert, no doubt about that.* Overnights with Brad were always guaranteed to entertain. He slid the lamp over to the west end of the table. The "arena" was ready and waiting.

Jay arrived last—his visit to the latrine took a little longer than usual tonight. He wasn't sure about Brad's program... *I'll go along with the majority.*

Brad rubbed his hands together... *it's time to get started at last—* He'd been looking forward to this all day. Experience had taught him that Vidalia sweets delivered a payload faster than just about anything. They'd had nearly two hours for the magic to work down in the pipes—and he'd seen to it that everyone was prepped. *mmm... I can feel a little pressure building.* He twisted his torso to help things along. One of his specialties was the blue sparkler. The trouble was, that required pepperoni pizza. Beans and hotdogs usually meant orange blossoms.

Andy was the first to cut one. It was modest. There was no special reaction, since this was expected.

"Hey, try to hold 'em, you guys!" Brad scolded. *I have to get this organized.* "Who hasn't done this before?"

Shawn McGee and Chris Smith raised their hands. Jay and Dale were chicken to admit that they had only heard about it.

"Okay. I'll show you how it's done first. Does everyone have a book of matches?" He saw four hands rise. "Okay, you'll have to share, then." He sat down on the ground and raised both knees up as he spread his legs apart. "What you do is reach around underneath like this..." Brad reached around his left side with an open book of matches. He reached his right hand around under the right side, tore out a match and struck it. "You hold it real close. If you don't, it won't catch." He demonstrated, touching the tip of the flame at the point in the seam that was directly above his anus. "Timing is real important, too. The match has to be lit first. Otherwise, it will escape. It happens real fast."

"This place is gonna smell pretty ripe before long," Jay observed.

"Not true." Tony had done this before. "The flame burns up the smell completely. You smell the burnt matches instead."

Brad was pleased that he had a knowledgeable accomplice. Andy was an old hand at this too. "Be sure to let everyone know you've got one coming, so we can all watch. Oh! I've got one..." he struck another match.

Everyone leaned forward to see.

> > *prrra-aat!* < <

Brad's first one caught perfectly. Just as he expected, it was orange. The flame was bright, and moved slowly like an amoeba. It lasted about three seconds, and covered an area about six inches across, just tickling the contour of his balls.

There was a mix of wonder and amusement.

"Wow!" Chris nudged Shawn.

"Hoo-oo!" Shawn laughed. He wanted to try one.

Tony twisted his torso. He was experienced at this. He had been holding one for a little while. He assumed the position. "Get ready, get set…" He had the match ready. He had been holding too long, so he had to strain a little to time it just right.

> > *praaatt — pfft!* < <

It burst forth with some force. The first part was orange colored like Brad's, but it didn't float out, it was more like a jet. The second part, however, was very different. Luckily, the match was still aflame, because it crept out softly. It was a greenish yellow, and it floated out, lasting longer than the sound.

"Whoa! I'm glad **that** one caught." Andy knew that kind… it would have been one of those dense ones that really stink. It inspired him to stand up and take off his shorts. He preferred to do this in his skivvies. He had one on the way. *Brad was sure right about the onions.*

"Doesn't it burn?" Jay felt a little pressure now, himself.

"It gets pretty hot all right," Brad nodded. "Don't try it naked."

Andy was ready. "Here goes!" He strained a little. It was almost silent.

> > *pwuu-uuub* < <

The bloom was a slow and bright iridescent orange… it clung and quivered across Andy's butt. "Hoo! **That** one was **hot!**" He pinched the seam of his skivvies and fluffed some cool air in.

It was the largest one yet… cheers and applause.

Shawn was ready! He lifted his knees. "Quick, somebody: I need the matches."

Brad handed him a matchbook.

Shawn got the match lit in time, but he held it too far away.

> > pooom! < <

It sounded like a slightly flat French horn. The force blew the match out, but didn't ignite. The cloth puffed out from the force of the wind.

"Oh, maaan!" Shawn was embarrassed and confused.

"You have to have the match real close. You were too high up and an inch out." Brad was disappointed. "Too bad—that would have been a good one."

"Nice tone, Shawn," Tony stood back.

The aroma of the untorched fart was detected, and hands began to fan the air.

"Nice smell, Shawn," Jay wrinkled his face.

"And make sure your pants are real tight: you want it to blow straight out and not get trapped in all the loose cloth." Andy had learned that from personal experience.

"Okay…" Jay raised his knees high and got his match poised. "Here goes." He struck the match and held it close. It seemed to take forever, but at last:

*> > **prrrrit!** < <*

It was more trumpet than horn, and it was wonderful. It was yellowish white, and it was more of a detached cloud. Jay was amazed.

There was a cheer with applause. Brad was happiest of all. His biggest critic had been converted.

26   *winding down*

Merriment over at the Tiger camp attracted Mark's attention. En route to the Flaming Arrow, his hands were full of used plastic tableware—throwaways that couldn't be burned. He cut across the center path below the cabin so he could check it out on the way to the disposal bin. He paused at the central junction... *what are they doing?* They were all focused on something... whatever it was, it just happened again, because now they were all applauding and laughing. He watched for a minute. Again they were paying attention to something on the ground. Mark couldn't see enough to—

A short mellow tenor tone reached his ears, and he knew at once. He smiled wide. Another burst of applause. *we used to do that. man alive...* he shook his head and headed up the path to the leadership camp. *damn, I wish I could join in for old times sake.* Maintaining decorum had a cost. "One of them there facts of life, Mark old boy." He chuckled ruefully, reflecting on the irony of the moment. *Julian is in a hurry to grow up, and I'm sorry I have.*

He looked back... the Lynx patrol was scurrying over the footbridge to join the party. *I hope the whole troop doesn't migrate over there.*

In the Flaming Arrow camp Tom and Nick were flattening empty bean cans and Danny was washing out the big pot. Mark had instructed them to square away everything before lights out so nothing would carry over to tomorrow. "Where's Julian?" He tossed the plastic spoons into the trash bin.

"I sent him to the cabin so he could make some notes for the newsletter. He really hates this lantern, for some reason." Nick gave the can opener a dark look. "Can we get a new one of these?" It was so loose he could barely get the blade to stay in the cut.

Mark stepped closer to look. "You're right. I'll put it on my list." *I can do that after the briefing in the morning.*

"Die!" Tom stomped an empty can flat.

Mark didn't comment. *a good way to vent frustration.* He looked at Tom... no sign of that. *he's just playing.* He checked his watch. *ten minutes. I might as well call it a night;* he started to leave.

"Great party, Mark." Tom felt the need to show how he felt.

Mark turned. He nodded his agreement. "It's good to let your hair down now and then, isn't it?" He gave Tom a thumbs up. A thought just occurred to him. He stepped over to the table and pulled up his canvas stool.

The patrol recognized his signature move: a meeting had been called. They put everything down and sat down, alert.

"Just a short one, guys." He put his hand on Nick's arm. "Off the record."

Nick was alert at once; this was new.

Mark paused to frame things properly. "I don't generally talk about scouts when they aren't present. This is an exception. I had a talk last night with Julian, and it set me to thinking. I want you to let me know if he has any problems or troubles that..." he paused. "Sometimes, boys are afraid to ask about things they need to know. There are lots of reasons for this, but usually it's because they are afraid they'll look stupid or silly, or because they are afraid it could be wrong." He looked around to see if he was being understood. Obviously he was. Each of these boys had gone through that process.

"Julian complained last night that everyone treated him like he was a little kid. He was very frustrated, and rightfully so. Now don't feel bad about this, because I am probably more guilty of that than any of you are. I'm trying to be more sensitive about it, too."

There were a few revealing shifts on the bench seats. "He was pretty general about it and didn't name anybody in particular." Mark smiled. "He didn't need to. All you have to do is look at him and you instantly want to protect him. We are all responsible for doing that."

Nods of agreement.

"So what I'm asking you to do is to put yourself in his shoes, if you can. Try to find ways to help him learn things about life—basic things that you have learned yourself in the last two or three years. He needs to know these things. And he knows that he needs to know." He pointed to his scoutmaster patch. "There are some things that I can't tell him, obviously. That's where you can help. Continue to protect him, but don't keep him locked away in some kind of padded room. Help him where you can." He waited for a question. He was just as glad one wasn't asked.

He stood up. "Don't overdo it of course." He gave a semi serious glare around to each face at the table. He raised his arm in a salute and waited for a like response. "This conversation never happened." He waited for them to nod.

"Thanks, men. See you for breakfast." He jogged toward the cabin. *I sure wish I was a fly under the table. they'll be buzzing about that for a while.*

Every boy at the table assumed they were super guilty, and felt awful. Each vowed to himself to pay attention to this. They glanced at each other, but no one spoke. Later on, maybe. Not now. Not at all, now. KP duties resumed with great vigor.

—ɯ—

Julian was **trying** to work on that sketch of Max he had promised to do for Nick's article... but his mind wandered all over the place tonight. The songfest was still echoing in his head. *what a great time. I ate too much, too. Mark was so cool... he looked very sexy at the campfire later on, when the sunset came along. after the marshmallows he let me help burn all the dirty plates and cups. he wouldn't let me burn the plastic stuff though... said the fumes were poison.*

A gentle cross breeze passed through—the windows were open to help cool the cabin down. A lot of laughter and cheering came from the patrol camps tonight... *must be telling jokes and stuff. I sort of wish I was back with the Wolves, in a way. we had some good times... 'course, now that I had that secret experiment with Sid, maybe it's just as well. wouldn't want to make a habit of that.*

hum! Julian just realized something. Staying in the cabin was really special. *lucky, really. if Flaming Arrow had a second crew tent like the other patrols, I'd be in that—with Danny, probably. that would be okay, I guess... no bathroom, though.*

And no Mark, remember.

yeah, that's right. He looked at the doodle he'd made and gave a short laugh. *the gag I pulled on Justin at the campfire... I can't get that hot scene out of my mind, for one thing.*

The water polo was a huge disappointment. They're so far away out there... *the only ones who can enjoy it are the ones playing. I thought I'd get to watch Mark and Tom and all those other hot guys... you have to be a dolphin or something to do that. the snorkel would be worthless. I tried swimming out there, but they all moved around so much I couldn't see a thing. they put the playing area right next to where Paul and Doug did their two-man "contest." they have to find a new spot if they ever do that again.*

That was two bent down ones he'd seen now. *what causes that, anyway? they seem to work okay, though. they're big, too, like Tom. hmm... if they weren't bent they'd be nearly the same size. too bad they don't hold a contest for that: see who's the biggest. they could have another contest to see who could shoot the farthest. that guy today was the favorite to win that one. what a great idea! a special kind of Olympics. there would be bun contests, and all kinds of cock contests. size contests, naturally. balls. lowest hanging? hard contests, like speed. who got hard the fastest. who could come the fastest. who could stay hard the longest. oh yeah! what about a do-the-dog contest?* He giggled. *how could anybody stay a spectator? that must be why they never hold any contests like that.*

Shape up, Julian. Think about other stuff for a change.

Julian nodded... *the inside guy is right. Danny and I did a little swimming, but he didn't want to stay very long; he didn't want that sunburn to come back. I made some progress with diving, at least; I'm up to thirty-eight seconds now. that's almost double where I started. a guy out there this afternoon went all the way to the platform swimming on his back. it looked like he would bump into someone, but he didn't. learning to do that at the pool next winter might be an idea.*

Another cheer in the distance. He stood up and looked out... *maybe I can see what's going on. nothing looks special. hmm... I miss being with those guys, sometimes.*

Mark came around the corner and saw Julian standing tiptoe, peering out the east window. *trying to figure out why the celebration. mercy.* Julian's backside was bent over the table... it registered suddenly: *Nick is most certainly correct in his assessment of those.* He remembered last night's inquiry about choice buns. *don't even think about it, Mark.*

He had a pang of conscience. *Julian is missing out, and it's my fault. no way to fix it tonight.* He walked in and closed the door.

"Sorry. Too late for you to cover that for the newsletter. It will be over soon anyway... lights out pretty soon." He shrugged.

"What are they doing?"

Mark tried to keep a straight face. "Torching farts."

Julian was dumfounded. He had never heard of such a thing; and if he had, the last person he would expect to tell him was the scoutmaster.

Mark grabbed the folding chair and dragged it over to the table. *this won't be counted as a conference.* "Sit, sit," he gestured. If only he could snap a picture of Julian's expression. "We only have a minute or two."

Julian turned the chair around and sat.

"We used to do that all the time when I was a scout," Mark said off handedly.

Julian laughed nervously.

"Did you have fun tonight?" Mark did, that was for sure.

He nodded eagerly, but Julian wanted to know more about when Mark was a scout. "Torch?

"Sure. They're flammable, you know. Just like the propane stove. Farts are methane, another kind of gas. Natural gas, you could say."

Julian laughed. *I don't believe this.* He grinned wide.

Mark put his finger to his lips. "Promise not to tell?"

Julian nodded and held onto the chair as if it were about to slip out from under him.

"We used to get into a circle at campouts and take turns lighting them. It's not hard to do; the great thing about it is the flame takes away all the smell. All that's left is the burnt match odor."

Julian laughed. "I never knew that!" *I'd like to try it out.* "What does it look like?" Julian imagined a jet flaming out.

"They can be different colors. They only last a little while, a few seconds."

"Wow! Like the stove? Blue jets?"

"No, no jets. It's usually a cloud about yay big." Mark held his hands about nine inches apart. "The color depends on what you've been eating. I've seen yellow ones, orange... a few sort of whitish blue or pale yellow green."

Julian tried to picture it, but it was hard to imagine someone doing this. "Does it burn?" He just realized it was a *flame.*

"It sure can. You have to be careful of that. You have to leave your pants on, that's for sure." Mark was delighted for an excuse to go extra curricular. "If it has force when it comes out, it's kind of a puff and it floats away as it burns out. But if there isn't any velocity, it hovers right around the area in a flat blob—and it gets **hot**!"

Julian pictured a circle of guys all bent over emitting colored clouds. Wait... "How do they light them?" *must take two people or something.*

"Easy. You just lie down on your back, bend up your legs and reach around with a match."

Whoa... the picture in his imagination morphed into a circle of upside down turtles.

"I'm almost tempted to demonstrate, but I can't."

Julian's eyes popped wide open.

"No matches." He smiled. "I don't have one ready, anyway."

I don't believe this!

"That reminds me. One thing we never discussed about being roommates is what to do when you have to fart." Mark raised his eyebrows a few times. "Eventually that will happen; we did have beans for supper, after all."

Julian had no proposals here. He awaited instructions.

"No point in making a crime out of it. Everyone has to do it at some point—blame it on Mother Nature, okay?"

Julian nodded.

"Just give a warning. If you're close to the door, point your butt out, fan the air, that kind of thing." Mark looked at Julian's very puzzled face. "Not much time left. You have anything saved up to talk about?"

Julian shook his head. Whatever there might have been had been erased by this bizarre, this **wonderful** conversation.

"Good." Mark tapped Julian's knee lightly. "Just say so if you do, any time." Mark pointed to the clock. "We only have a couple of minutes. Let's call it a day."

Julian nodded gratefully. He watched Mark stand and pull the folding chair back to the fireplace. He sat for a minute… he had to catch up. Mark went so fast in these talks it was hard to keep pace in his head. *Mark's surprises are so… so surprising. two nights ago it was Lumpy Louise… tonight he talks for almost five minutes about farts! I am a long way from figuring him out.* He wouldn't trade places with anyone in the world, though.

He looked over at the clothes rack. Mark was hanging up his shirt already. Julian felt a very sudden and deep rush again, like the one at the campfire. It took a second to move. He turned the chair back to the table and stepped in to the bathroom to brush his teeth. That was the usual order of events. *Mark always takes his shower after I'm done.*

He had worked up a good foamy suds and was close to rinsing out his mouth when Mark appeared behind him.

"Don't mind me, just playing through." He pulled the shower curtain to the left and turned on the water.

Julian caught a peripheral glimpse at the left—a piece of clothing landed softly on the toilet seat. He would have turned to look, but the view in the mirror had him spellbound. Mark was just stepping into the shower. When the curtain was pulled he stared at himself in the mirror. *did you see that? did you see that?!!*

Of course I did, dum-dum. He took a couple of quick breaths and rinsed out his mouth.

He reached back and pulled his towel off the rack. The view through the shower curtain wasn't much better up close, but Julian wasn't complaining. He took as long to finish as he dared, then left to take off his shirt.

Julian was almost asleep. He'd done his daily sorting out in his mind; he figured it took about half an hour tonight. Pressure below his belly button brought him back to full consciousness. It didn't happen often, but he recognized the symptom at once: he needed to fart. What to do? *Mark said to give a warning, but he's asleep. we're not supposed to talk after lights out, anyway. what if it wakes Mark up? I never know if they will be loud or not.* His mother about threw a fit if he ever cut a fart, so he was not practiced in the art at all. She and Grandma were very strict about that when we lived in Joliet. Grandpa Oscar was always in Dutch because of that.

He relaxed gradually, and let it release. What a relief… he could barely hear it. *phee-ew!* He pulled the bag tight. *I hope I don't have a lot of those. what happens if I pull my hand out to fan the air? I'll just let that smell out. hmm.* His lack of experience was a problem… *maybe they fade into the bag, somehow?* He lifted the edge tentatively… *almost gone. oh. that's not so bad. good.* He fanned the bag gently. *there. now I can go to sleep.*

About a minute later, just as Julian was nearing the fall asleep threshold again, a deep, very deep sound erupted under the quilt across the room—

> > ***bruuu-uuUUMP!*** < <

Julian awoke instantly. He had never heard such a fart in his life. Mark cuts them in his sleep! Julian started to giggle. It was so **funny**! He couldn't stop. He stuffed his pillow into his mouth. It did no good. He could barely breathe.

After an hour—well, a few seconds that seemed like an hour—he had almost controlled it. But he remembered that incredible sound again and he had another giggle attack. He carefully pulled back the sleeping bag and got up. He grabbed his pillow and tiptoed to the door. He went down the trail a few yards and sat down, pillow stuffed to his face, and let it all loose. He fell on his back and laughed, he rolled back and forth and laughed some more.

He had to get this out of his system, or he'd never be able to look at Mark again without bursting out in laughter. A lot of tension needed release, and this opportunity to catch up was perfect.

Julian was able to relax at last. After a few more chuckles, he felt the cold air attack his bare arms and legs. The goose bumps were persuasive; he returned to the cabin. He took a deep breath and opened the door slowly. He peeked in—no problem. Mark was sound asleep. Julian was back in the sleeping bag in no time, rubbing his arms and legs.

It was no trouble to fall asleep this time.

If there were any other atmospheric events in the night, neither Julian nor Mark took notice.

Coming Next:

The Shooting Gallery:

Julian's Private Scrapbook, Book 3

Days six, seven and eight at Camp Walker

Midway through the two week camp, new enterprises begin and flourish, while stories already begun develop complexity and detail. The comical aspects of being in camp get more attention.

Julian and **Mark's** relationship develops an aesthetic dimension. Julian feels empowered and undertakes a unique challenge: outfitting Nick and Tom's clandestine bedroom. He becomes their self-appointed secret guardian.

Tom and **Nick** flourish. This frees Tom to find ways to resolve and repair problems he caused in his former cheek fetish days. Nick impressed Geoff last week by his intelligence and simple integrity. They become friends, giving Geoff a chance to share his personal secrets with someone he respects. Geoff moves on to seek new challenges: first on his list is Leonard, the Waterfront Director.

We meet several new characters both in and out of Troop Nine. Sid's snorkel comes in handy again. Julian and Sid have to tell their friends about the discovery of the underwater stopwatch contest. This leads to a surprise opportunity for Sid.

Danny has graduated from Geoff's training program and revisits his plan to prevail in Julian's affection.

A new enterprise called the Shooting Gallery gets underway as the second week begins. Danny's surprise promotion and Geoff's daring new quest signal that major events are already developing. Robin and Jack's intense romance leads them to risk everything. Other conflicting interests develop—will they grow to threaten anyone's security? Julian's Private Scrapbook Book 3 is filled with action, fun, and suspense.

a word from Eldot about the style...

Here's a heads up about an unusual device employed in the revised version of Julian's story. The goal is to maximize the reader's ability to get inside the characters while retaining the advantage of being an observer outside.

Standard narrative practice is to place the reader either inside or out, not both: inside means using the **first person,** seeing only what the character sees—usually a single character. Outside means using the third person point of view, seeing the character and the world of the story from outside, akin to watching a film.

The original version of *The Poker Club* employed an experimental style that intermingled first and third person usage; the goal was to enable the reader to get an inside-the-character perspective while retaining the advantages of seeing the character from other perspectives. The device was not a complete success—it achieved the goal, but at a cost—it was awkward in places and to some readers, somewhat annoying.

The revision has dealt with that problem directly by employing visual clues. All first person point of view elements are in *italics*. No other use of italics is permitted. If italics would usually be employed to express emphasis or stress, **boldface** is used instead.

Here's a sample using two of these, quoted from chapter 1:

> *air is kinda chilly...* he rubbed his arms and scurried over to the door. *maybe Mark is out there.* He poked his head out and looked back and forth: *there he is, jogging up the trail!* Wearing a headband, Mark's sleeves were pushed up to the elbows. His feet made a soft plopping sound. *man, he looks so cool.* A sudden breeze... *brrr!* he had turned into a solid goose bump! He shut the door and raced back to the cot.
>
> He wrapped himself in the cover blanket and climbed onto the cot. He sat Indian style and rubbed his arms. It felt funny to sit on the cot this way. He scootched to get comfy and turned his head toward the door. *I want to watch him*

come in... that headband is new. The goose bumps were nearly gone.

Mark planned to shower before awakening Julian. He opened the door carefully... he peeked in, expecting to see the top of Julian's head poking out of the sleeping bag. Instead, he saw a grinning face. What a surprise! Julian's hair was comical; obviously he hadn't been awake for long. The golden rumples were evidence that he probably enjoyed a sound night's sleep. *enviable.* Mark closed the door and walked to the dresser. "Good morning. You're awake bright and early."

look at the sweat run down his temples! Julian had never seen Mark like this. Too marvelous for words. "I never knew you went running. How far did you go?"

"I'm not sure; probably three or four miles. Did I wake you up?"

"Nope." Seeing Mark like this was a revelation. Julian knew Mark only in his scoutmaster uniform or his business suit. *does he run at home every morning?*

>> scree—eep! <<

The fresh underwear drawer complained as usual. "Look at your chest! You sweated a lot! And your armpits!" He had never seen a sweaty man before. He wanted to touch the wet fabric. *I sweat sometimes, but never like that.*

The third person-first person mix is easy to see; the goal is to enhance the reader's engagement with characters.

This technique has been utilized in varying degrees. In many places it is not used at all, in others it is extensive. Generally, the goal has been to get the reader into the character's perception while keeping the ability to see things the character doesn't. So when you run across this phenomenon, you'll know what's going on—I hope it makes the experience of Julian's Private Scrapbook even more fun.

Preface to The Poker Club

[Author's note: this is a segment from the first publication of The Poker Club. It was an expanded version of the original Barr's Meadow preface. It is still entirely germane to the book, but it has been moved here for reader convenience. Two prefaces tend to result in neither being read. Naturally, both are highly recommended.]

The most magical time in a boy's life is when he discovers who he is sexually. It can be scary, threatening, and it can be fun and exciting; it can be a mix of these things. At the end of the process, he is forever changed physically and psychologically. This story looks at that process in a way that is unusual, and perhaps unique. It is not a typical coming of age story, though that is central to the work.

The series makes an unusual underlying assumption. It departs from "accepted" mores of contemporary American society in a central way: it posits a society that is accepting and non-judgmental. Right and wrong still exist—but the puritan ethic and moral code are dispensed with, *as the norm.* Moralizers of the puritan sort remain—they are an archetype, after all. They may be problematic, but they are the aberration in this society. Sexual issues are no longer taboo. They are still complex, private, mysterious, and very special—but they are out from under the mindless repression we know so well.

Therefore, an individual is not faced with the "coming out" drama that preoccupies so much of our society; rather, he is faced with the process of "coming into." That, as the reader will see, is still a full time challenge.

The time selected to play in is the early 1960's, before the technical gadget revolution. The relative naïveté and general optimism of those years is a comfortable fit for the subject, and not so remote in time that it is unfamiliar—nor would the world Camp Walker be preposterously utopian.

The story is meant to entertain, not preach or argue the underlying social issues. Nonetheless, the subject is sufficiently complex to make demands.

Standard modern novel criteria cannot accommodate the matter satisfactorily and fully—space sufficient to remain honest to the material is not available. The solution has been to craft the story into a form that can satisfy both the contemporary rules of length, and the expectations of the subject: it is presented in a series of novels. They progress chronologically and grow in complexity. Each is a complete segment, but the combination as a whole is greater than the parts, allowing the subject to be fully addressed. So this is a hybrid of sorts in structure, somewhere between a Dickens doorstop tome and a modern adventure series.

Readers of these books will be subjected to humor, titillation, and naughty behavior. Any two-week stay at a boy scout camp would have to have that as a minimum. You should expect to have a good time and feel elevated as a human being. This is, above all, a celebration of who we are. You will have to do your own lesson drawing and moralizing, however. And be warned: if you are a puritan at heart, you will not be pleased.

Synopsis of Book 1: Barr's Meadow

This is a summary of the prologue and first two days at Camp Walker, its major characters and events. The order is largely as it was presented, though some summarizing and analysis is provided. The purpose is to provide a concise review for readers seeking background information about the characters and events in Book 2.

Germination

It is early June, 1960. In a small town in central North Carolina, **Julian** Forrest has just turned thirteen years old. He and his mother, single parent Francine Forrest, are formerly of Joliet, Illinois. Julian recently finished his first year of Junior High School. Adolescence has taken him by storm, and he is in a hurry to grow up. His main focus has been Cub Scouts, and he has completed all the levels offered by the organization. His dream now is to become a Boy Scout.

Their neighbor, **Mark** Schaefer, is a manager in a locally owned department store. His wife of three years is a nurse who is studying to become a physician. Mark is scoutmaster of the Boy Scout Troop sponsored by the same church that sponsors Julian's Cub Scout Pack. He invites Julian to join Troop 9. This is a dream come true for Julian, who has long had a fixation on Mark.

Sunday, First Day

Julian has been in the Boy Scout troop for nearly two years. He was recently promoted from Second to First Class, just in time for the annual summer camp. His Troop 9 scrapbook has made him known in the troop. **Mark** has given him leadership opportunities, and he has handled them well.

The first day of summer camp begins with a long bus trip west. The drive provides a glimpse of what is to come in the next two weeks. The Troop hikes to the camp and the scouts get set up in their tents at Barr's Meadow, the prize campsite. The first day is given to orientation and registration activity.

Several other scouts in the troop are introduced. Many of them will be important in the events of the next two weeks. **Sid** Thomas and **Jeremy** Baker are Julian's closest friends, and they are in his patrol. They were Cub Scouts together. **Tom** Dawson, **Danny** Laskey and **Nick** Harrison are members of the Flaming Arrow, the exclusive troop leadership patrol.

The primary event takes place at the end of the day: the start of **Julian's** mentorship with **Mark**. Mark makes the decision to invite him to stay in the cabin, primarily as a shelter from extracurricular activity. Mark is astounded by the extent of Julian's naïveté. His is relieved to discover that his fears about Julian's predatory inclination were overblown. Julian is smart enough to proceed with his plan very cautiously.

Mark had planned for some time to promote Julian as an assistant to the troop scribe. He moves the timeline up, and Julian is transferred to the leadership patrol the first night. Mark lays down strict guidelines about the use of the cabin. Julian thinks Mark has inadvertently moved him closer to his goal. That remains to be seen. Julian is practiced at dissembling about his true feelings, and he has no ego need to boast or brag. His closest friends do not suspect and will never know his secret ambition.

Monday, Second Day

It is the first full day of regular camp activity. **Julian's** routine as a member of the leadership patrol is established. He gets to know each member of The Flaming Arrow. **Tom** Dawson, the Junior Assistant Scoutmaster, is accustomed to being the kingpin. He spots Julian first thing and sets out to add him to his very long list of sexual initiates. **Nick** Harrison, the Troop Scribe, has been assigned to mentor Julian as a troop journalist.

He is savvy about Tom and engineers escape plans without either Julian or Tom's becoming aware. **Danny** Laskey, the Senior Patrol Leader, is also new to the patrol; he is assigned to team with Julian in camp operations. He has a crush on Julian and lures him into a private space where he hopes to establish himself as Julian's steady boyfriend. His clumsiness and inexperience make it possible for Julian to turn the event into an exploratory game.

At days end **Julian** witnesses **Mark** shaving, satisfying a long held wish.

Leonard Stafford, the staff member in charge at the lake, is introduced. The lake is a major center of what happens at the camp—much of that is because of Leonard's efficient but benign rule.

Merit Badge study is a major part of scout camp, and Julian attends his first class meetings. **Justin** Blake, a younger scout that Julian has been mentoring, is with him in Forestry, and Cory Summers, the scout with a water phobia, is Julian's Archery partner.

The highlight for Julian's day is helping Nick qualify for his Lifesaving Merit Badge. His pretend drowning fools everyone. He becomes friends with Nick, who makes a passing comment about Julian's derrière that preoccupies Julian for days. He has been oblivious to backsides until now, and sets out to study the phenomenon of Choice Buns.

The first Troop Nine campfire is held. The process of selecting a Troop Skit is begun. **Max** Webster's is the first to be presented. It is a fable that involves the entire troop. They are divided into small choral groups that punctuate the narrated story line similar in style to the ancient Greek chorus.

The major event of the day comes after lights out: the relationship between **Nick** and **Tom** is explored. Nick surprises Tom and himself with a sexual maneuver of his own. Neither had guessed that a familiar after hour activity could be so consequential. Nick succeeds in shattering Tom's shallow self indulgent frame of mind—sexual gratification as he has understood it is transformed.

Site Descriptions

Camp Walker

Camp Walker is in the Blue Ridge Mountains near the Nantahala National Forest in western North Carolina and the Chattahoochee National Forest in northern Georgia. The extensive acreage has areas for a variety of activity, large and small. There are seventeen troop campsites available, each having five to eight individual patrol mini camps. Trails to the sites radiate out from the central headquarters buildings. A separate permanent village serves the counselors and staff. Each camp session averages between five and eight hundred scouts. Nearly a hundred miles of internal trails connect the camps and provide for training and hiking activity. South of the HQ are areas for large multi-troop assemblies, recreational fields, and over a mile of lakeshore. When not in use by the Scouts, parts of the facility are leased to outside groups. Prior to Affirmative Action in 1970, the Camp observed the late nineteenth and early twentieth century custom of nude swimming at segregated sites. Women were not allowed in camp.

Each troop has a reserved campsite for the two week session. The unusually dry climate condition has forced Camp Walker to replace all cooking fires with propane stoves. Closely monitored troop ceremonial campfires are allowed, but all fire starting skill building and fire suppression course activities have been suspended. [See map, page 48]

Barr's Meadow

Barr's Meadow camp features a small one-room cabin with an indoor bathroom. Four campsites with a cabin were available at Camp Walker, but this one was the best. It had its own well, electric pump, and water heater. The site was a favorite during the winter and outside groups paid a premium to use it. The small fireplace on the west wall was for wintertime use only.

An ancient Cherokee system of paths and carefully fashioned water access points were maintained to keep the meadow as natural as possible. Campers were expected to use the trails and paths at all times. The troop campfire assembly area was a hundred yards up the trail on the northern edge of the meadow. The latrine was down slope of the campsite string, near the entrance trail. The six stalls and urinal trough were maintained by Camp Walker, not the client campers. No individual camp trash facilities were permitted. Refuse had to be packed out weekly to a central collection area at HQ by each camp. Patrol Leaders generally assigned this duty to scouts needing to erase demerit points. A shower platform for general use near the latrine had two separate shower spaces, supplied with cold water from an overhead tank. Scouts worked the built in hand pump to fill the tank. No laundry facilities were available in the camps. Each troop had a two hour block reserved in the HQ laundry room mid way during the camp.

South of the cabin, patrol campsites consisted of three tents grouped around a picnic table and cooking area. Footpaths connected the individual campsites to each other, the latrine, and to the main trail. Thirty to forty feet of meadow separated the camps from each other. All scouts were assigned to a two or three man wall tent. Each camper was supplied a folding canvas cot and a footlocker for clothes and personal belongings. No camps were closer than twenty feet from the spring fed creek. The meadow was open except for a few yellow birch trees and some scrub pine. A small marshy zone above the latrine had dried up years ago. All other campsites at Walker were in forest locations. [See map, page xii, 117]

Glossary for terms in Julian's Private Scrapbook, Part Two

Adirondack: A three sided structure with a shed roof; originally a lean-to shelter, they range from collapsible tent-like units to permanent structures made with whole logs. The name comes from the mountains in upper New York State; it is an Anglicized version of the Mohawk *ratirontaks*, (the tree eaters) a derogatory slang name they used for neighboring Algonquins.

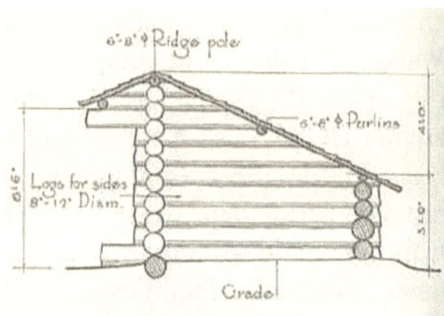

Adonis: a mortal in Greek Mythology famous for his extraordinary physical beauty. His story is varied and complex. Aphrodite fell in love with the beautiful youth because she had been wounded by Eros's arrow. Aphrodite sheltered Adonis and entrusted him to Persephone; she was also taken by Adonis' beauty and refused to give him back. The dispute was settled by Zeus: Adonis was to spend one-third of every year with each goddess and the last third wherever he chose. He chose to spend two-thirds of the year with Aphrodite. Adonis died in Aphrodite's arms after being wounded by a boar.

Army Chair: During World War II, American Seating produced 5 million chairs for the U.S. Military. The chair was designed by Erwin F. Kurth, a professor of Forestry. It was one of several products designed by a special wartime team to reduce the military's demand for steel that could be used for weapons. The back and seat were identical curved plywood panels; the supports were hardwood. The innovative design allowed for compact storage and

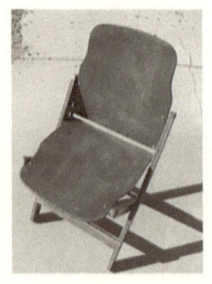

attaching into multiple seat configurations. Several manufacturers made the chair. Sarge was able to get a couple of dozen of these for Camp Walker at a Fort Bragg surplus sale.

Bear: Second year of Cub Scouts. Julian's mother completed that year as a Den Mother in place of Margery Baker, expecting her second child.

Big Ben: The Westclox Company made the Big Ben and Little Ben wind up alarm clocks. First sold in 1909, they evolved over the years until 2001. The clocks featured glow in the dark numerals on the face until the late 1960s, when radium-based paint was discontinued. The clock in Barr's Meadow was a Style 6, manufactured between 1956-1964.

Blue Ridge Mountains: the eastern portion of the Appalachian Mountain Range that runs from Georgia in the south, and ends in Pennsylvania. The highest point is Mt. Mitchell, North Carolina [6,684 feet].

Bow Painter: The mooring line at the front of a boat. The rowboats at Camp Walker are moored to the boat dock bow first, ready for use during camp sessions.

Buddy System: Primarily a safety structure that requires all scouts to remain with another scout at all times when outdoors in the wild. It has broadened to the entire scout program as an expedient in organizing and monitoring progress. At Camp Walker, special Buddy Badges were given to each scout. It showed their swimming proficiency and was required to be presented at the gate prior to lake access.

Chattahoochee National Forest takes its name from the river; its headwater is in the north Georgia Mountains. The name originated with the Cherokee and Creek Indians native to the area. It borders the Nantahala National Forest in North Carolina.

Cherokee Double Wall: The most intricate Cherokee baskets are made from river cane, which can be woven in both single and double layer designs. Cherokee basket makers also use materials such as white oak and honeysuckle to execute their distinctive basketry traditions. The process of making a basket, from finding good materials to weaving a complex geometric design, takes skill, concentration and a great deal of time.

Cheshire Cat: A character in *Alice in Wonderland*. The animated film version featured a wide closed tooth open lipped smile.

Code Green: During the previous summer camp Nick and Tom devised this special term to signal that after hours they would sneak off to have some privacy for their lovemaking; they were evading the Troop Bugler, who was in the same three-man tent. Code Red meant a no go for now

East Midlands: The eastern central section of England. Geoff's father, Alistair Staples, was from Lincolnshire. He left the BBC to become an independent television and radio consultant shortly after the Korean War.

Expert: The third and highest level of achievement at the rifle range. Marksman is the first level, Sharpshooter is the second.

Explorer: In 1949, the BSA consolidated the senior programs, with the exception of Sea Scouts, into Explorer Scouts. At that time, a boy could be an Explorer in the troop or in a stand-alone unit called the Explorer post. The Explorer advancement program included the Bronze Award, the Gold Award, and the Silver Award. The last Silver Awards were earned in 1966 as Exploring began to turn more toward career emphasis. Venturing was officially created to replace Explorers in 1998.

Gold, Silver, Bronze Palm: Palm branch badges are awarded to Eagle Scouts who continue to earn Merit Badges.

Green Stool: Julian made a stool his first year in Cub Scouts. He used it routinely to compensate for being short.

Gunsmoke: Popular CBS radio and television series. Its setting was Dodge City, Kansas in frontier times, when Kansas was in the Wild West. At the time of this story, the  radio version had been off the air for a year and the TV episodes had been extended to fifty minutes. Amanda Blake played Kitty, and James Arness was Marshal Dillon.

Incredible Hulk: In Marvel comic books. Created by Stan Lee and Jack Kirby, the character first appeared in *The Incredible Hulk* #1, May 1962, one month before the time of this summer camp. Tom is a huge comic book fan.

Jack Spratt: refers to a nursery rhyme character who could eat no fat, and whose wife who could eat no lean. Together, they licked the platter clean.

Joliet, Illinois: a community near Chicago. Julian's childhood home. His mother leaves because she wants to raise her son in a smaller community, well away from urban influences.

Life: The rank between Star and Eagle.

Max's Skit: in Part 1, Max Webster presented his proposed skit for the troop to perform at the closing assembly. It was a spoken choral parable about courage.

Nantahala National Forest: Located in the mountains and valleys of western North Carolina. The terrain varies in elevation from 5,800 feet to 1,200 feet (along the Hiwassee River below the Appalachian Dam). It is the home of many western NC waterfalls. It borders the Chattahoochee Forest in Northern Georgia.

P-38: A folding pressed metal can opener issued with the military K-rations, they were inexpensive and widely available in war surplus stores; a later, larger version was named P-51. The names were taken from WW II fighter aircraft.

Sarge's rig: The Indian Scout motorcycle was built from 1920 to 1949. It rivaled the Chief as Indian's most important model. Chiefs, Scouts, and

Junior Scouts were all used in small numbers for various purposes by the United States Army in World War II, and extensively by overseas Commonwealth military forces under the Lend/Lease Program. Sarge's rig was a 1942 Indian Scout 500, the 741, made for the US Army. Sadly, company mismanagement

saw the brand decline and all but disappear. Grassroots support for the bike continued, but the Indian Manufacturing Company folded in 1953. Sarge made modifications so that he could attach a sidecar and small trailer. It enabled motorized access to remote sites that could not be accessed by full sized cars or trucks.

Star: The next advancement in rank after First Class.

Studebaker: Automaker that stopped production in 1966. The 1947 coupé

introduced innovative styling features including the flatback "trunk" instead of the tapered look of the time, and a wrap-around rear window. The new trunk design prompted a running joke that one could not tell if the car was coming or going.

Troop Shake: The left-handed Scout handshake is made with the hand nearest the heart and is offered as a token of friendship. The handshake is made firmly, without interlocking fingers. Troop 9 used it as an enhanced personal oath, substituting for a salute. The "Solemn Version" included interlocking fingers and two lateral twists followed by two vertical shakes.

Winchester: Originally located in New Haven, Connecticut, the Winchester Repeating Arms Company's Model 52 was a bolt-action .22-caliber target rifle introduced in 1920. Known as the "King of the .22s," for many years it was the premier smallbore match rifle in the United States, if not the world. A very desirable sporter model of this action was also made from 1934-59. Camp Walker bought 12 new for the 1962 camp.

Wolf Patrol: Julian's first home in Troop Nine. He was placed there with his friends Jeremy and Sid.

Zebra Patrol: Newly added to allow the troop to grow in size. One of the West twins was made patrol leader because of his outstanding leadership ability. His brother is patrol leader of the Lynx.

Song Credits

The songs referenced at the Troop Nine songfest were selected because they are representative of the time period and likely would have been popular choices. They are described briefly here, alphabetically.

The Ballad of Davy Crockett is a song with music by George Bruns and lyrics by Thomas W. Blackburn. The song was introduced on the television Davy Crockett, first telecast on December 15, 1954, on ABC's Disneyland. Fess Parker played the role of Davy Crockett and continued in four other episodes made by Walt Disney Studios. The first recording of the song was made by Fess Parker.

Day-O (The Banana Boat Song) is a traditional Jamaican mento folk song, the best-known version of which was sung by Harry Belafonte. The song is widely known as an example of calypso music. It is a song from the point of view of dock workers working the night shift loading bananas onto ships. Daylight has come, the shift is over and they want their work to be counted up so that they can go home. In 1955, singer/songwriters Irving Burgie and William Attaway wrote a version of the lyrics for the Colgate Comedy Hour in which the song was performed by Harry Belafonte. This is the version that is by far the best known to listeners today, as it reached number five on the Billboard charts in 1957 and later became Belafonte's signature song.

He's Got the Whole World in His Hands
is a spiritual, written by Obie Philpot,
a Cherokee Indian. He wrote the song
while serving in WWII. The song made
the popular song charts in a 1958 version
by English singer Laurie London with the
Geoff Love Orchestra, which went all the
way to #1 of the Most Played by Jockeys

song list in the USA and went to number three on the R&B charts. The
record reached #2 on Billboard's Best Sellers In Stores survey and #1 in
Cashbox's Top 60. Mahalia Jackson's version made the Billboard top 100
singles chart, topping at number 67. To date, it is the only gospel song to
hit #1 on a U.S. pop singles chart.

Hound Dog is a twelve-bar blues selection
written by Jerry Leiber and Mike Stoller
and originally recorded by Willie Mae "Big
Mama" Thornton in 1952. Other early versions
illustrate the differences among blues, country,
and rock and roll in the mid 1950s. The 1956
remake by Elvis Presley is the best-known
version; it is his version that is #19 on Rolling
Stone's list of The 500 Greatest Songs of All
Time.

Poor Little Fool is a pop/rock song written
by Sharon Sheeley. It was based on her
disappointment following a short-lived
relationship with a member of a popular singing
duo. The best-known version of the song was
recorded by Ricky Nelson on April 17, 1958, and
released on Imperial Records 5528. It holds the
distinction of being the first number-one song
on Billboard magazine's then newly-created
Hot 100 chart, replacing the magazine's Jockeys and Top 100 charts.
It spent two weeks at the number-one spot. The record also reached
the top ten on the Billboard Country and Rhythm and Blues charts.

Sixteen Tons: a song about the life of a coal miner, first recorded in 1946 by American country singer Merle Travis. A 1955 version sung by Tennessee Ernie Ford in 1955 became a standby on his television program that ended in 1961.

The Yellow Rose of Texas is a traditional folk song. The original love song has become associated with the legend of how a slave named Emily Morgan helped win the battle of San Jacinto, the decisive battle in the Texas Revolution. The Center for American History at the University of Texas has an unpublished early handwritten version of the song, perhaps dating from the time of the Battle of San Jacinto in 1836. The author is unknown; the earliest published version, by Firth, Pond and Company of New York and dated September 2, 1858, identifies the composer and arranger as "J.K."; its lyrics are "almost identical" to those in the handwritten manuscript, though it states it had been arranged and composed for the vaudeville performer Charles H. Brown.

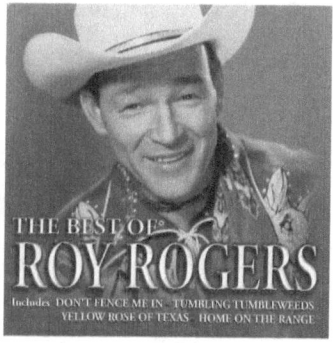

Index of Names in The Poker Club

Name   **Brief description**

Alex Trent: Star scout, member of the Lynx patrol. Son of a Major in the Marine Corps, highly principled and ambitious. Shows Julian how to use the camp wash station.

Andy Ashbaugh: Life scout in the Tiger Patrol.

Arnie Shaw: Patrol Leader of the Badgers, Life Scout (Miss Kitty).

Ben Bradley: Recreational Director, Camp Walker

Ben Jasper: Tenderfoot scout in the Panther patrol.

Billy Bradford: Tenderfoot scout in the Wolf Patrol.

Brad Fisher: Star scout in the Tiger Patrol. Afterburner specialist.

Brian Rogers: Junior Assistant Scoutmaster of Troop 127, Atlanta. Eagle Scout, All-State wrestling team member for two years. (labeled a Beefcake by Nick).

Bruce Ruggles: Second Class scout in the Badger Patrol (Sheriff Dilly) Seriously overweight. Volunteered to help in the Lifesaving final exam.

Calvin Radcliffe: First Class scout in the Panther Patrol. Robin's Buddy in the Rowing class.

Casey Snyder: Star scout in the Wolf Patrol. A friend of Robin's; they play blackjack on the trip to camp.

Chef Pièrre: Full time chef at Camp Walker.

Chris Smith: Second Class scout in the Tiger Patrol.

Chris & Ted: A duo from another troop that Julian and Justin see in the forest.

Chuck Nelson: Life scout in the Badger Patrol (Doc Apple).

Chuck Thompson: Junior Assistant Scoutmaster of Troop

Cory Summers: Second Class scout in the Zebra Patrol. Julian's Archery partner. He has been stuck at Second Class because of his inability to master a water phobia.

Counselor Mason: Junior Counselor assigned to assist in the program areas of Sharp Shooting and Archery. His attitude needs improving.

Dale Baker: Life scout, Tiger Patrol Leader.

Danny Laskey: Star scout, newly appointed Senior Patrol Leader of Troop Nine, he has passed several able scouts because Scoutmaster Mark sees him as the best leader potential to become Assistant Scoutmaster. He has had a crush on Julian for a little more than a year. Though he lives across the fence, he and Julian have only had a nodding acquaintance prior to this camp. He is assigned to supervise Julian in the daily breakfast and camp inspections, and makes his first attempt to seduce Julian. Afterwards, he gets sunburned at the lake.

Don Bennett: Tenderfoot scout in the Panther patrol.

Don Felton: First Class scout in the Badger Patrol (Fester).

Doug Tucker: One of the "stopwatch duo." A First Class scout in the Panther patrol; he was introduced to sexual activity by Tom two years ago one day after school. He is self-indulgent and not interested in serving Tom's needs.

Erik: Mark's first love, killed in an airplane crash when Mark was a college Junior. Until this year, he has been Mark's only romantic partner.

Frank Ferris: (Frankie) Troop Nine Bugler. Not at camp this year; family finances have required him to work full time during the summer. He has been a sexual playmate of Danny's for fun, not romance.

Freddy Scott: Tenderfoot scout in the Badger Patrol (Billy the Kid Jones).

Gary West: Patrol Leader of the Lynx. Life Scout, twin of Jim.

Geoff Staples: Junior Assistant Scoutmaster of Troop 419, Atlanta. Life Scout, recently from Burbank California.

Greg: Junior Counselor assigned to kitchen duty.

Jack Haley: Junior Assistant Scoutmaster of Troop 152, Atlanta. Eagle Scout, recruited by Geoff to join Brian's private poker game.

Jay Porter: Life Scout, assistant patrol leader of the Tigers. An excellent swimmer, earned his Lifesaving Merit Badge on the first day of camp.

Jeremy Baker: Julian's friend, First Class scout in the Wolf Patrol; was a Cub Scout with Julian.

Jim West: Zebra Patrol leader, Life Scout. Twin of Gary.

John Jorgensen: Serving his fifteenth year as Director of Camp Walker.

Julian Forrest: First Class scout, main protagonist. An only child, unaware that he has inherited an extraordinary artistic talent from his father, a Greenwich Village sculptor whom he has never known. Serious and single minded, determined from an early age to spend his life with Mark, a close neighbor. The first night at Camp, Mark invites him to stay in the cabin. His talent for acting comes to the fore the next day when he takes part in the lifesaving class.

Justin Blake: First Class scout in the Zebra Patrol. Julian's protégé and Forestry Buddy.

Kurt Davis: Star scout in the Zebra Patrol.

Leonard Stafford: Waterfront Director at Camp Walker. Has an uncanny ability to remember names and faces.

Mark Schaefer: Scoutmaster of Troop Nine. He is a retail purchasing agent and manager. When he was a senior in college, he was asked to replace his former scoutmaster who died suddenly from a heart attack. His five year marriage is one of convenience; he devotes all his free time to scouting.

Matt Smith: Swimming instructor, Camp Walker.

Max Webster: Life scout, Assistant patrol leader of the Lynx. Talented musician. Author of the Johnny fable, proposed as the Troop Nine skit to be performed at the end of camp.

Nathan Jensen: Panther Patrol Leader, Life scout.

Nick Harrison: Secondary protagonist, a Life scout. Troop Scribe, member of the Flaming Arrow Patrol. A talented writer who has had a crush on Tom for three years. Appointed to mentor Julian as a troop journalist. He heads off Tom's plans for Julian and on the second night makes a surprise move of his own for Tom's attention. It is far more successful than he had planned.

Norman Miller: Star scout, assigned to help Julian on the first day at camp. Assistant Patrol Leader of the Wolf Patrol.

Paul Harris: First Class scout in the Lynx Patrol. One of the stopwatch duo.

Phil Jensen: Camp Walker rowing instructor.

Robin Simmons: Life scout in the Lynx Patrol. He is a buddy of Casey's and an experienced outdoorsman.

Ron Carville: Senior Counselor assigned to Rifle Range.

Ryan Kruger: Star scout in the Panther Patrol; assigned to be Jack's Basketry Buddy.

Sarge Oliver: Camp Ranger/Quartermaster.

Scott Olson: Scoutmaster of Troop 419, Atlanta. Teaches Second Class Rank to Tenderfoot scouts.

Scoutmaster Fuller: Troop 8, teaches Basketry.

Scoutmaster Simmons: Troop 152, Atlanta. Teaches Indian Legends.

Scoutmaster Soames: Troop 6, teaches First Aid. Annoyed by Mark's continued success.

Scoutmaster Strauss: Troop 13, teaches Marksmanship.

Scoutmaster Taylor: Scoutmaster of Troop 2; teaches Backpacking and Climbing Merit Badges.

Shawn McGee: Tenderfoot scout in the Tiger Patrol.

Sid Thomas: First Class scout in the Wolf Patrol. Julian's friend from school and Cub Scouts. He is known for his prankster sense of humor and his extremely skinny physique. His mother bought him a new turquoise blue air mattress for camp.

Stuart Walker: Wolf Patrol Leader, Life scout.

Tad Benson: Second Class scout in the Zebra Patrol.

Tom Dawson: Junior Assistant Scoutmaster of Troop Nine and Eagle Scout. Outstanding leadership ability, but has long had a fetish for fresh adolescent backsides. A secondary protagonist in the series. He relies heavily on the analytic ability of his protégé, Nick Harrison. He helps Julian at the first free swim at the lake as a ploy. But his plan to seduce Julian gets derailed by Nick. His sexual world gets turned upside down when he allows Nick to show him a new way to make love.

Tommy Carlysle: Star scout in the Badger Patrol. (One Eyed Joe)

Tony Johnson: First Class scout in the Tiger Patrol. He is awarded demerits frequently for a variety of minor infractions. He is the troop's most talented actor and clown.

Troops 9 Mark Schaefer, Scoutmaster

1 Panthers

1 Nathan Jensen	[16] L
2 Charlie Larson	[16] L
3 Ryan Kruger	[16] S
4 Calvin Radcliffe	[15] 1st
5 Doug Tucker	[16] 1st
6 Ben Jasper	[14] 2nd
7 Don Bennet	[13] T

2 Tigers

1 Dale Baker	[16] L
2 Jay Porter	[16] L
3 Andy Ashbaugh	[16] L
4 Brad Fisher	[16] L
5 Chris Smith	[16] L
6 TonyJohnson	[16] L
7 Shawn McGee	[16] L

3 Lynx

1 Gary West	[16] L
2 Max Webster	[15] L
3 Alex Trent	[15] S
4 Robin Simmons	[16] L
5 Paul Harris	[16] 1st
6 Jason Jones	[14] 2nd
7 Sandy Smith	[13] T

4 Wolves

1 Stuart Walker	[16] L
2 Normal Miller	[15] S
3 Casey Snyder	[15] S
4 Sid Thomas	[14] 1st
5 Jeremy Baker	[14] 1st
6 {Julian Forrest}	
7 Billy Bradford	[13] T

5 Badgers

1 Arnie Shaw	[16] L
2 Chuck Nelson	[15] L
3 Tommy Carlysle	[15] S
4 Don Felton	[15] 1st
5 Bruce Ruggles	[14] 2nd
6 Freddy Scott	[13] T
7 Josh Green	[13] T

6 Zebras

1 Jim West	[16] L
2 Kurt Davis	[15] S
3 Cory Summers	[15] 2nd
4 Justin Blake	[13] 1st
5 Tad Benson	[14] 2nd
6 Clint Walker	[14] 2nd
7 Open	

Flaming Arrow

1 Tom Dawson	[17] E
2 Nick Harrison	[16] L
3 Danny Laskey	[15] S
4 Frank Ferris, bugler	[16] L
5 Julian Forrest	[14] 1

Ranks

E= Eagle	(1)
L= Life	(14)
S= Star	(8)
1st= First Class	(9)
2nd= Second Class	(7)
T= Tenderfoot	(6)

Position

1-6 Patrol

1-7 Individual

chronological age in brackets [ ]

Camp Walker Staff [June 1962]

Camp Director: **John Jorgensen**

Camp Ranger/Quartermaster: **"Sarge" Oliver**
   Senior Counselors for camp deliveries and maintenance [3]
   Junior Counselors for camp deliveries and maintenance [3]
Associate Ranger, Purchasing, Trading Post, Laundry: **Gerald Madsen**
   Senior Counselors for Trading Post sales [2]
   Junior Counselors for Camp Laundry [2]
Food Director: **Pierre Arsenault**, Chef
   Senior Counselor assistant [1]
   Junior Counselor assistants [5]
Medical Officer: **Harold Symonds**
   Counselor Assistants assigned when needed

Waterfront Director: **Leonard Stafford**
Senior Counselor Lifeguards [5] Billy, Joey, Ted, Ken, Lanny
             Adult Staff Instructors:
   Swimming 1: **Roy Franklin**, Advanced and Intermediate
   Swimming 2: **Matt Smith**, Beginning and Intermediate
   Rowing: **Phil Jensen**; *Senior Counselor* Beebe
   Canoeing: **Sam Brady**; *Senior Counselor* Walls

Program Director: **Fred Russell**
   Special Assistant: * Tom Dawson, JA, Troop 9
   Senior Counselor Assistants: [12]
   Junior Counselor Assistants: [18] Mason
             Adult Advancement Instructors [2]*
   Harold Carter, Troop 2 (1st Class),
   Scott Olson, Troop 419 (2nd Class)
   Adult Merit Badge Instructors: [12]*
   Scott Henderson, Troop 7 (Forestry)
   Ed Taylor, Troop 29 (Backpacking/Climbing)
   Mike Fuller, Troop 8 (Basketry/Leatherwork)
   Archie Samuels, Troop 12 (Archery)
   Frank Thompson, Troop 17 (Pioneering)

Ted Soames, Troop 6 (First Aid)
Rick Strauss, Troop 13 (Marksmanship)
Frank Simmons, Troop 152 (Indian Legends)
Ron Benson, Troop 14 (Reptile Study)
Carl DeBeery, Troop 76 (Fishing)
Sedley Unger, Troop 4 (Wood Carving/Woodworking) Donald
Brimm, Troop 227 (Bird Study)

Recreational Director: **Benjamin Bradley**
Special Adult Recreational Assistant: * Mark Schaefer, Troop 9
Senior Counselor Assistants [6]
Junior Counselor Assistants [6]
Rope Yard: Adult Supervisor Volunteer* (rotating assignment)
Rifle Range: Adult Supervisor Volunteer* (rotating assignment)
Archery: Adult Supervisor Volunteer* (rotating assignment)
Water Polo: Volunteer Coaches* Schaefer, Franklin, Smith,
Russell

* Drawn from Attending Scoutmasters and Scouts
• **Full Time Camp Employee in boldface**
• *Seasonal employee in italics*

a word about the author

Eldot is a simple cipher: the author's first initial spelled phonetically followed by a period [L. = Eldot] Why? When this novel was first published, the subject matter was more sensitive and controversial than it is today. Lest relatives, friends or former colleagues be inconvenienced or victimized, the nom de plume was adopted as a shield. Secondly, the author didn't want media opportunism to distort what the book was seeking to achieve. Media treatment of the subject was the major motivation to write Julian's side of the story in the first place.

All the Julian books received positive critical reviews. The potential for controversy still exists, but the extremist groups have lost their clout—society has evolved rapidly: social media and the cell phone have changed the landscape; the Julian novels are made more topical than ever. The subject matter is relevant and openly discussed; a movie on the same theme is a contender for the 2018 Best Picture of the year. For this reason and to satisfy readers' response, the five books have been revised, updated, and re-issued as the five volume Julian's Private Scrapbook set.

Thus it's appropriate to let the reader get a peek behind the curtain. Eldot has lived in the Pacific Northwest for most of his life. In order to avoid the Viet Nam war, he took an occupational deferment to teach high school Drama and English. The interminable nature of the war and the draft lottery kept him in that occupation so long that the refuge morphed into a successful career. Why change a good thing? He became a local and state leader in his profession. After thirty terrific years as an educator, he retired. Now he's taken up writing. The novels are not autobiographical.

Leland Alan Hall

Publications:

1960:   Emperor Commodus Prompt Book: Use of Masks in Drama
[Honors Thesis, a translation from the Greek, housed at University of Oregon Library]

1979-81:   Editorials Oregon Education

2011:   *Little J and Roger* [eBook only]

2012:   *Barr's Meadow*
The Poker Club
The Shooting Gallery
Thunder and Lightning

2013:   *The Champions*
Inside Eldot's World: a literacy gazetteer [eBook only]

2015:   *You're in High School Now: Julian's Sophomore Year, Part 1*

2016:   *'56 Scrapbook* [PDF and spiral bound]

2018-19:   *Julian's Private Scrapbook, books 1 thru 5*

2020:   *He's kinda tall: Julian's Sophomore Year, Part 2*

2022   *'56 Booken* [PDF and spiral bound]

2024:   The Julian Novels ATP Special Edition

2025:   *Untitled:* Julian's Sophomore Year. Part 3

Author Website Link: http://www.diphra.com
ATP website: eldotbooks.com
Facebook: https://www.facebook.com/AuthorEldot/
Twitter: https://twitter.com/AuthorEldot/
Tumblr: https://authoreldot.tumblr.com/

Reviews

Barr's Meadow: (Julian's Private Scrapbook: Part One)
Eldot
Xlibris, 248 pages, (paperback) $15.99, 978-1-4691-4512-9
(Reviewed: December 2013)

Pleasant, nostalgic and ingenuous, *Barr's Meadow* is set at a Boy Scout camp in the early '60s, the fictional story of a gay young man named Julian.

Julian, nearly 13, is handsome, enthusiastic and affable, as well as a skilled artist. Julian has a crush on Scoutmaster Mark. Mark — who, while married, has been open to same-gender sex in the past — has resolved to confront this with sensitivity and fraternal affection, realizing that Julian's trusting nature could make him the victim of more predatory scouts.

Author Eldot (who writes under one name) explores the daily activities of scout camp and the politics of sex between teenage boys. The author focuses mostly on the gay characters and Julian's sexual thoughts, but this is not really gay erotica (although the back cover warns: "Not for sale to persons under 18"). With the exception of two somewhat explicit (though not heightened) passages, it reflects on same-gender, male sexuality while generally avoiding the salacious.

Eldot gets inside the heads of the characters, including Julian and Mark, as in: "Mark stepped around to the other side of the bed and watched Julian hustle. He bounced on his toes unconsciously. He had faced the unknown here and it had gone very well. I was right about this."

Barr's Meadow is comparable to other teenage boy coming-of-age narratives, such as *The Last Picture Show*, minus the cynicism, sophistication or relative depth. This doesn't mean that it's poorly crafted; only that Eldot's prose is simple, direct and seeks to examine the lives and thoughts of guys who are only beginning to view the world with introspection. Eldot walks the precarious line between making the boys evolved and depicting them as saints. He allows them moments of tenderness and nurturing without suggesting their virility has been tainted.

Barr's Meadow, the first in a series, never breaks through to the transcendent realms of literary brilliance, but it is intelligent, moving, well-grounded and memorable.

KIRKUS
REVIEWS

TITLE INFORMATION

BARR'S MEADOW
Eldot
Diphra Enterprises LLC (283 pp.) ISBN: 978-0-9966325-5-3

BOOK REVIEW

A debut novel tells the story of a young gay Scout's sexual awakening at camp. Twelve-year-old Julian Forrest has been raised by his single mother, never knowing his father. He loves drawing and being a Cub Scout. He has even made a Scouting journal full of drawings of his activities. He has recently become aware of his sexual desire, which is wound up in his habit of watching a neighbor, the adult Mark Schaefer, come home from work every day. When Mark comes over to the house to invite Julian to join his Scouting troop, the youngster can barely contain his excitement—or hide his erection.

Two years later, Julian gets to attend the annual two-week Scouting summer camp at Walker Lake. By this point, Mark is aware of Julian's crush, though he is unsure how to proceed: "What bothered Mark—a little, not a lot—was that Julian had become a presence in his thoughts…*at this point it's only a presence…but it's something new…*it felt pleasant, it made him feel light." The first two days at Walker Lake will prove transformative for many people, including Nick Harrison and Tom Dawson, members of the troop's leadership patrol. In the all-male environment of a Scouting camp, Julian quickly discovers some of the rules of his new masculinity—and a few things about his burgeoning sexuality as well.

Set in the 1960s, this series opener deftly depicts feelings of childhood nostalgia, as evidenced in Eldot's wistful prose: "At last the sausage patties and pancakes were ready and waiting in the oven. Julian helped Danny put out the OJ and milk. *oh! a bubbling sound— the coffee!* He rushed over to the stove to watch." But the author dwells heavily on the sexual thoughts of several characters, including the teenage Julian. While these aren't necessarily erotic, there is an undeniable romanticism to them. This will likely make many readers decidedly uncomfortable, particularly those scenes that deal with the attraction between minors and adults. Eldot may argue that he's depicting an experience common to young gay men, but if this book isn't crossing a line, it's walking right up to it.

An uneven coming-of-age tale.

The Shooting Gallery: Julian's Private Scrapbook Part Three
Eldot
Xlibris, 287 pages, (paperback) $15.99, 978-1-4771-4986-7
(Reviewed: April 2014)

The Shooting Gallery is the third in Eldot's five-part series: "Julian's Private Scrapbook."We find ourselves in a Boy Scout Camp, where our pubescent hero, Julian Forrest,comes of age in June 1962.

Julian is a prodigy when it comes to drawing, a talent that garners many accolades. As we might expect, there are other skills to be mastered at camp: swimming, canoeing, archery, cooking — and, in this case, sex. In *Barr's Meadow* (Part 1) readers came to appreciate Julian's beauty, exuberance, affability and guilelessness. There, Eldot laid out the rituals and routines of scout camp: inspection and clean-up, naked swimming and campfire sing-alongs. In the midst of this cheery beehive, Julian had his first sexual experience with another scout; another encounter involved two older, more experienced boys.

In *The Shooting Gallery*, the author again presents the everyday activities we might expect, but now, sexual behavior is more frequent. While this kind of intimacy is often explored in fiction, it's much rarer to find it imbued with positive, canny eroticism, as it is here. In *The Shooting Gallery*, the tone is somewhat Utopian; the characters are not influenced by the usual shame or taboos society places on sex between males. Boy Scout Camp becomes a refuge where characters freely (though conscientiously) experiment with same-gender eroticism.

Eldot not only examines male-only sexual episodes, he anchors them in verisimilitude. Unlike more fantasy-driven erotica that sets up outlandish, compulsive scenarios, the sex here arises organically from the plot. The author goes inside the heads of the characters, so that we understand their bashfulness, their longing or curiosity. There is a nonchalant, playful tone that removes the stigma of queer intimacy that easily might have tormented teenaged American men in 1962.

All in all, *The Shooting Gallery* is a satisfying, intelligent story, notable for its warmth and credibility. It's perfect for those who appreciate homoerotic content without the usual overblown raunch so common to the genre.

Also available in hardcover and ebook.

Thunder and Lightning: Julian's Private Scrapbook, Part 4
Eldot
Xlibris, 327 pages, (paperback) $15.99, 978-1-4797-5684-1
(Reviewed: May 2014)

This unusual novel, the fourth in a five-part series, takes place at a scout camp during the summer of 1962 and follows several groups of boys as they form friendships, learn new skills, and fall in love. Much of the novel depicts their various sexual explorations, and the author clearly alerts readers to such content. "This series is meant for mature readers," he writes on the back cover. "…This book should be stored in a place not accessible by persons under 18."

In between the sex, several plotlines progress from the earlier books. Tom, an older boy who had been with many others before committing himself to Nick, makes amends for his past treatment of Kurt, an earlier partner. Nick advises Kurt on how to overcome his fear that his past with Tom will sabotage his relationship with his current partner Sid. Julian continues to improve his artistic skills, drawing beautiful portraits of the lifeguard Leonard and his scoutmaster Mark, while taking on further responsibilities in the campground. In a new development, Geoff, another older boy, becomes attracted to Mark and devises a plan for seducing the unwitting scoutmaster. Meanwhile, Mark begins to confront his past trauma.

While the extensive sex scenes may make some readers uncomfortable, they are handled well, showing the tenderness between the boys. Their relationships are fascinating to watch, as many are now committed couples, yet their emotional bonds are strong enough to allow them to learn new positions and techniques in sessions with more knowledgeable boys. Geoff's pursuit of Mark is handled humorously, leading to a situation where both attempt to conceal their erections. The author helpfully includes summaries of the previous novels, a glossary of terms and characters and more at book's end.

Thunder and Lightning is a charming read in spite of the controversial subject matter. As it shows further growth in the series' characters and their relationships, it sets the stage for the concluding tale.

Also available in hardcover and ebook.

The Champions: Julian's Private Scrapbook, Part Five
Eldot
Xlibris, 375 pages (paperback) $15.99, 978-1-4797-8041-9
(Reviewed: June 2014)

The conclusion to a sexually infused five-novel series, The Champions takes place during the last day of a scout camp during the summer of 1962 and follows several groups of boys as they deepen their relationships, build on new skills, and ponder life after camp. Much of the novel depicts their various intimate explorations, from a final ejaculation contest known as "the Shooting Gallery" to the couples pleasuring each other on the bus ride home. In between, several plots building during the previous books reach their end.

Geoff, one of the oldest scouts, makes his move — even with his injured foot — to seduce the scoutmaster, Mark, in the middle of the night. Julian, while working on his remarkable drawings, befriends Sarge, the camp's quartermaster, and draws out the gruff retired Army man's soft side, even calling him "Uncle Max." Tom, continuing his process of maturing, learns how to get out of uncomfortable situations without the help of his lover Nick, and even becomes a confidante to other scouts worried about their relationships.

Mark comes across as one of the strongest figures in this novel, encouraging all the scouts under his care to become the best that they can be. He makes plans for Julian to receive art lessons after camp, further developing his talent. He shows his tremendous strength, both physical and moral, during his late-night encounter with Geoff. It's no surprise that his troop wins all the prizes at the last day's competitions, or that Julian has a crush on the scoutmaster.

Charming and humorous, with sex scenes that are erotic without being over the top, the novel successfully ends the series, while leaving open the possibility of further adventures. The controversial subject matter may make some readers uncomfortable, but for those interested in a sexual adventure told from a gay perspective, this is a wonderful look at boys transitioning between childhood and adulthood.

Also available in hardcover and ebook.

You're in High School Now: Julian's Sophomore Year, Part 1
Eldot
One Spirit Press, 610 pages, (paperback) $15.99 978-1-893075-77-1
(Reviewed: June 2015)

This charming novel continues the story of Julian, from author Eldot's series Julian's Private Scrapbook. Set in the early 1960s, it follows Julian's coming of age as a gay man through the first half of his first year in high school, as he makes new friends, learns about girls, and navigates this strange but exciting new world.

The title refers to the refrain his mother and her friend continually use when explaining to Julian why he must pay attention to his clothes now and other new "rules." Julian's only real concern is his mother's interest that he take out a girl. Since he is only romantically interested in his scoutmaster Mark, that presents an obstacle. Fortunately, he attracts the attention of Rita, one of the school's prettiest girls, who invites him to the Sadie Hawkins dance. Julian's complete ignorance about Rita's intentions during the dance and the car ride afterwards (as well as his description to his mother later) provides some of the novel's funniest scenes."

Julian is certainly experienced when it comes to sex, however. He continues the explorations he discovered at scout camp the previous summer, both as an initiate in a secret society of like-minded boys, as well as with Randall, recently moved from Washington. Randall, a victim of bullying at his previous school, is instantly drawn to Julian when he sees him, and they form an immediate, deep friendship. Julian introduces Randall to his scouting troop and takes an interest in his photography, and Randall is deeply impressed by Julian's drawing skills. The two bring out the best in each other.

While not every reader will appreciate the sex scenes, they are sensitively drawn and important to the story. The only complaint this reader has is waiting for Part 2, where it seems the situation will become complicated. Well-written, with engaging, likable characters, this book skillfully presents the challenges and pleasures boys who love men face in growing up.

Also available in hardcover and ebook.

You're in *high school* now:

Julian's Sophomore Year: Part 1

You're in *high school* now

a romantic comedy
by Eldot

Julian's Sophomore Year, Part 1

Q Press, 626 pages (paperback), 978-1-893075-77-1

Reviewed: **October, 2015**

KIRKUS REVIEW

The Life and times of an adventurous, gay high school sophomore.

In the latest time installment featuring Julian, the affable lead in the Julian's Private Scrapbook YA Series, author Eldot *(The Champions: Julian's Private Scrapboook,* 2013, etc.) re-creates the autumn of 1962 as Julian embarks upon another school year full of books and boys at Jackson High School. Amid a backdrop of artistic inclinations and first-day jitters, Julian's romantic feelings for Mark, his scoutmaster at Camp Walker over the past summer, continue to simmer, with their explanatory fonding lingering in his memory. But his concerned mother, Francine, encourages him to show an interest in girls. When Rita, an attractive, mischievous schoolmate, asks Julian, aka "the blond masterpiece," to the Sadie Hawkins dance, the obvious awkward clashing of orientations ensues.

Humor is one of Eldot's strong suits; he has an impressive capacity for penning farcical, innocently disastrous moments. He also builds a good supporting cast, like Mark, who is in a heterosexual marriage of convenience after his longtime partner died seven years prior; and Randall, a gay virgin and recent arrival to Jackson High. Intimate shenanigans occur at a secret society campout for randy boys, but the author takes care to handle these moments with restraint. Structurally, however, Eldot fumbles a bit. He shifts perspective awkwardly and adds too many diclaimers, style notes, and end matter that are meant to illuminate Julian but result in informational overload. Still, Eldot successfully taps into the experiences of gay youth with a believable blend of engaging characterization, humor, pathos, back story, and teenage angst.

Fun, frolicsome series with good humor and a message of unity and equality; new readers may want to start at the beginning

KIRKUS

You're in *high school* now

Julian's Sophomore Year, Part 1

Reviewed by Amanda Silva, July 23, 2015

This YA romantic comedy reflects traditional coming-of-age themes, further complicated by issues of sexuality and identity.

You're in *high school* now

a romantic comedy
by Eldot

Julian's Sophomore Year, Part 1
Second Edition

Eldot's romantic comedy *You're in High School Now* follows Julian, a young gay man in who is getting to know himself while creating his place in the world. This particular world is high school in 1962, a microcosm fraught with prizes and pitfalls, where bullies abound and fitting in is a constant quest. This narrative reflects traditional coming-of-age themes, further complicated by issues of sexuality and identity. These are sensitive topics for many readers, regardless of age, but Eldot writes with an urgency to connect with those young adult readers for whom these issues might be especially difficult. This story is an extension of Eldot's earlier series, the Julian's Private Scrapbook novels, but can be read in isolation. Readers should be aware it contains sexual content and adult themes layered throughout.

Julian is a sympathetic character, thoughtful and comical in his observations about himself and those around him. His internal struggles and interactions with his peers will likely connect with young readers, regardless of gender or sexual orientation. Self-acceptance rings as a universal desire and pursuit throughout these pages.

Although the writing is clear, the structure is not. While it is admirable for an author to experiment with a new writing style, the clarity of the work can sometimes be compromised. Eldot eventually explains—but not until the end of the book—that the narrative intentionally combines first- and third-person points of view as a means of freeing both writer and reader from "cumbersome conventions" concerning paragraph structure and punctuation. Eldot is a teacher with more than thirty years of experience; his frustration, or perhaps boredom, with convention is understandable. However, the resulting lack of clarity ultimately detracts from his work.

And this is important work. At the very outset, Eldot writes: "The grand social purpose that motivated the *Julian's Private Scrapbook* series lurks in the background, unsolved as always: social change is never as rapid as one would like. There are still bullies … So it's worth the effort to add a positive chapter or two."

Eldot's message is, indeed, as important as ever. When it comes to sharing that message through mainstream media, however, revisions in defense of convention and organization would bring these already bright and positive chapters to greater light.

FOREWORD REVIEWS

He's kinda tall

a romantic comedy
by Eldot

Julian's Sophomore Year, Part 2

KIRKUS

Another memorable snapshot of LGBTQ+ high school life in a bygone era.

HE'S KINDA TALL

BY ELDOT · RELEASE DATE: N/A

The continuing saga of a resilient gay high schooler's adolescent adventures.

Prolific author Eldot picks up where You're in High School Now (2015) left off, with young North Carolina high school sophomore Julian Forrest facing new feelings and challenges in late 1962. The author again succeeds in establishing the era in which his protagonist's youth plays out amid themes of inclusivity, friendship, burgeoning sexuality, and the precarious state of race relations during the school desegregation movement of the mid-20th century. Eldot imparts many life lessons over the course of the narrative; the first is that focused dedication to one's schoolwork will not only garner one good grades, but also beneficial recognition from instructors when one least expects it. Julian's consistently pleasant demeanor, personal flair, and conscientious, hard work make his teachers think of him as a model student. His rare, enviable qualities draw the attention of several teachers who believe he would make an ideal helper for an incoming Black student named Kassa "Kasey" Wood. The son of a prominent Boston scientist, Kasey is a polite, friendly, and impressively talented young pianist who comes to appreciate the time that Julian devotes to helping him adjust to a new town, a new school, and new classmates; in a compelling sequence, Julian even insists on racial equality at a segregated "whites-only" diner. The relationship between these two characters would be sufficient to carry the entire novel, but Eldot has grander visions in mind, carried out by a parade of peripheral teenage characters who take their turns marching through the novel.

Their storylines—some fleeting, some with greater staying power—definitely add some panache to the tale and enliven what becomes a rather overlong tome, as it extends to nearly 600 pages in length. Readers will likely want Julian, a budding artist, and pianist extraordinaire Kasey to remain at center stage, and they often do. However, they're upstaged much too often by other scenes concerned with randy camping adventures, fart jokes, or extended family melodrama. The omniscient third-person narration is often dryly humorous, but the book also explores Julian and Kasey's friendship through the eyes of folks who know very little about them. This narrative twist affords readers a look at what it's like to be observed and blindly judged by casual strangers. As with the other books in this series, the author doesn't ever shy away from the nuances of sexual attraction, which plays a particularly substantial role in Julian's young life. The teens' flirtations and overt physical carnality are portrayed as unashamed and innocently exploratory; they show the characters to be primarily concerned with mutual, guiltless pleasure, but also fully aware of the necessity of social discretion in that time and place. Although the narrative does feel extravagantly expository at times, its overall sense of social consciousness is remarkable. A concluding, expansive glossary, filled with historical references to the 1960s, will be helpful for newcomers to the setting.

Another overly busy but nonetheless memorable snapshot of LGBTQ+ high school life in a bygone era.

Summer Camp!!!

Spring is here—get ready for a fun romp at Camp Walker.

Eldot presents his debut novel about coming of age. Comedy, Adventure, Action and Surprises— it's not to be missed.

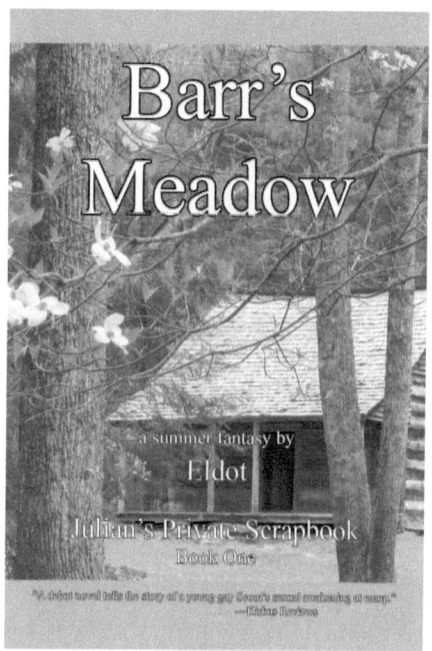

It's the early 1960's

Over 650 scouts are at the two week camp, and many of them have plans. This is one look at days past that goes beyond nostalgia. This is the camp you wish you'd gone to. Here's your chance at last.

This is the story of Julian's very first summer camp. His goal is to land the dream of his life, Mark. The endeavor begins in Barr's Meadow—he soon discovers that it will be a lot harder than he imagined.

Julian's Private Scrapbook is a series of five novels that explores many ways that boys discover themselves and others. Sensitive, thorough, and uncensored; you're sure to recognize more than one of these boys. Some are new at these things... others are highly skilled. Few return home unchanged.

available in e-Book format at:
diphra.com

also at Amazon, Barnes & Noble, and most bookstores

For Mature readers

Published by Kravitz & Sons LLC